FURTANNIA:
THE HISTORY OF THE FURRY
FANDOM IN THE UNITED KINGDOM

by Tim Stoddard

UNCLE BEAR
PUBLISHING™

Please visit us at www.unclebearpublishing.com

Copyright

Furtannia: The History of the Furry Fandom in the United Kingdom

Front cover photo: Daniel Bennett
Back cover illustration: KafesCoffeeCat
Chapter art: Margaret Bodle
Cover and page design: Kevin Hile

ISBNs
Paperback: 979-8-9858304-0-8
Kindle: 979-8-9858304-9-1
EPub: 979-8-9858304-1-5

Library of Congress Control Number: 2023936150

Printed in the United Kingdom and The United States of America.

Tim Stoddard

FURTANNIA

The History of the
Furry Fandom
in the United Kingdom

ABOUT THE AUTHOR

Tim Stoddard, who online goes by the name Gamepopper and is known to his friends as Popper, has been in the furry fandom since 2008. He is recognisable by his Lynx vigilante fursona known by the alias "D," who wears a mask and cape and carries a rapier sword wherever he goes. Not only has he gone to many furmeets and conventions throughout the United Kingdom and Europe over the years, but he has also been involved in furmeets and conventions as a volunteer and staff organiser.

Beginning in 2017, he took an interest in the fandom's history, with a particular focus on his local communities. Since then, he has given history lectures on the furry fandom and furry-themed media at conventions such as ConFuzzled and Scotiacon, as well as written for furry publications such as Dogpatch Press and Flayrah. As a commitment to his research, he has contacted many furries to record their recollections and travelled to archives to view media about the furry fandom as it was intended, aiming to provide the full story of the furry fandom in the United Kingdom.

DEDICATION

This book is dedicated to Ian G. S. Curtis (1948–2021) and Evelyn D. Stoddard (1925–2021).

TABLE OF CONTENTS

FOREWORD
UK FURRY AS I SAW IT
By Simon Barber

Anthropomorphics. They're hardly new in England—think The Wind in the Willows, Rupert the Bear, a host of other mostly children's book characters. I liked them from the start—and I liked getting involved with them the best I could. Back in 1980, I wrote my first anthropomorphic tale, never expecting anyone else to read it—an alternate second half to The Wind in the Willows. Looking back, it was no improvement. (The Sven Hassel cameo and the martial arts scenes only seemed like a good idea.)

Specific fandoms of each series existed for a long time. In the late 1980s I was a member of "Followers of Rupert Bear", which still exists; I attended several meetings. But for anthropomorphics in general—in my case, I started when I made contacts in the USA. Spotting the early Albedo and Usagi Yojimbo comics was a revelation; the letters pages gave me contact addresses and more links to follow, which I did, eagerly. Yes, back then folks were printing their real street addresses for the world (at least, like-minded fans reading such comics) to see. In 1990 I joined my first printed fanzine, the short-lived (5 issues) Furry Press Network, contributing art and tales for the Seattle-area editor to collate, copy, and distribute to the membership. They, in turn, led me to wider connections such as the still-thriving Rowrbrazzle APA that I joined at issue 42 (it's passed 150 quarterly issues now!) and The Canadian 'zine FurThestNorth Crew, too.

But the early British scene? I already was a member of Rowrbrazzle when I returned to the UK from living in Germany in 1992. One of its Australian members, Steve Kerry, had just arrived in England and passed on the four contacts he had. The first was Jan Paxton (who preferred his "fan name" of Porsupah) in South Wales, and another was Ian Curtis. All of this was (for me) pre-internet by a couple of years; we wrote letters, traded photocopies on the lines of "this is what I draw and write; these artists and authors are what I like." Summer 1992 saw what I think was the first UK furry meeting—maybe a dozen fans at Porsupah's family home for a weekend; there were maybe three of those from 1992 to '93. Porsupah was the first British fan I met who had a fursuit—in the USA, he'd bought a professionally made Red Panda of head-turning realism. The camaraderie was excellent; we were a small and specialist group of fans, and we knew it.

There I met Ian Curtis—a defence journalist by trade, and perhaps the most knowledgeable man I ever knew. From what he told me, "Furries" as such had been a scattered population through the 1980s, generally part of the larger science fiction fandom. Some joined via the new and booming anime fandom—and so, by one way and another, we met up.

Ian was the host of UK furrydom, his standard three-bedroom, semi-detached home hosting three or four "Furcons" a year from 1993 through to 2019—ironically, one was booked long in advance for the week the country went into lockdown with COVID-19. The growth of the internet helped spread the word; the "housecons" by the year 2000 were attracting maybe 20 people—some from as far away as Belgium, Sweden, and Germany. Visiting artists and writers would drop by in passing—and for many years the sales team of Martin "The Ferengi" Dudman and John Tatman turned up to sell us their wares, including hard-to-find anthropomorphic and manga comics and DVDs. It was a time of discoveries; people would watch new and obscure films and discuss them deep into the night.

And so it was for 30 years—although in the last decade the crowds dwindled, mostly going online rather than making the trip. But we'd settled down to a core of half a dozen who met regularly—and would be still meeting up in Yateley, south of Reading, had Ian not passed away in the Spring of 2021. We'd met up at the London 2014 World Science Fiction Convention, where panels such as "Furries—Not What You Think They Are" had attracted a wide audience.

I'm impressed to read Furtannia—full of things I remember and 90% of things I never knew! Looks like I've got some contacts to make with the current scene. Looking forward to that.

Thanks, Tim!

The future—well, we're still here, and we like what we like. Long may it last!

ACKNOWLEDGMENTS

This book has been a passion project of mine for over three years, I put a lot of work into source finding, travelling, researching, and writing to put this all together. However, that doesn't mean this book was solely the result of one person alone. This book wouldn't be possible without the generosity of furries willing to offer their time or provide resources to help with research.

First would be Mark Merlino, the first furry I contacted when conducting my research and along with his partner Rod O'Riley organised the first furry event on British soil, as well as maintain the ConFurence Archive as a home to early furry history. Next would be Fred Patten, whom I regret never contacting before he passed away in 2018, whose published works were the most readily available collated resource of early British furry history at the time.

Then it would be Mayfurr, a New Zealand fur who attended the Yateley Housecons in the early nineties and passed me onto Simon Barber, another attendee who also remains an active writer and contributor to fanzines, and Ian Curtis, the founder and host of the Yateley Housecons and effectively one of the founding fathers of the British furry fandom. Curtis also graciously invited me to his home for one such housecon in October 2019, where I also got to meet and speak to Ian Stradling and Rob Deighton, both of whom still active in the fandom.

Stradling also had his hand in the Dainties fanzine, but it's worth recognising the fanzines published by Foxy that profiled artists and writers to the wider American furry scene. The two also organised UK-FurCon (alongside Foxy's brother Prask and Aspirin) that inspired two German furries to run Eurofurence. Martin Dudman, meanwhile, not only distributed American fanzines across Europe but also published his own newsletter and comic book under United Publications.

Then there are the furmeets, to which I wouldn't know where to start if I didn't happen to encounter VulpeculaFox by chance at a Birmingham Furmeet. Thanks to him, I wouldn't have been able to speak to Ia'Kat, co-founder of the LondonFurs which continues to run tri-weekly to this day. A former attendee of which Marcony provided great insight to the costuming of the early days, as did UltraViolet on furry art.

SouthPaw and Rocky Raccoon were early organisers of meets for the NorthernFurs, SlyCat had organised for HantsFurs, and (alongside VulpeculaFox) Budge the Dragon helped provide insight on the Mid-Furs.

RapidoFrog also contributed some information on the LondonFurs, but also the boat party that eventually became RBW. For ConFuzzled, thanks would go to LevLion and WolfieFox, who continue to organize the convention as head of stage and video team respectively since its inception. JasperFoxx founded and organized Britain's first furry rave, Frantic Eufuria, before moving onto running Furcation, which he's still the chairman of.

In the case of resources, there are quite a few. Dogpatch Press and Flayrah have been great sources and news for discussions, the latter holding the archive to the FurteanTimes which documented British furry news in the late noughties. WikiFur, although not a resource that would be deemed reliable without scrutiny, provided plenty of the tertiary information for me to research further.

Same goes to the Fursuit Archive, founded by Timduru and currently maintained by Orthank, which holds not only photos but videos of media broadcasts featuring furries.

When it comes to researching furry representation in the furry media, it wasn't enough to read articles or view recorded segments of reports, I needed to read the whole magazine or watch the entire show to fully understand the context and theme around the media that was depicting the fandom to the public. With that, I give thanks goes to both the British Library and the British Film Institute, both institutions provided well-preserved examples of furry representation in the mainstream media, even if it meant travelling to London to view it in person.

As for writing the book, it wouldn't be what it is without three individuals: Joe Strike, author of Furry Nation, which despite my comments in the introduction remains a fine example of furry historical reading and an influence on my own historical research. David Sula, who provided extensive constructive feedback that helped shaped the book to what it is. Grubbs Grizzly, who you wouldn't be reading this right now if it weren't for him.

Lastly of course, I want to thank all my friends and family, for their love and support as a member of the furry fandom. I wouldn't be where I am today without you all.

INTRODUCTION

The furry fandom is a subculture for fans of all popular media involving animals that have features commonly associated with humans. These features include the ability to talk, use tools, and walk upright. The technical term for such creatures is "anthropomorphic animals."

There is no one way to get involved in a fandom like the furry fandom, nor is there a way I can provide readers with a list of instructions on how to join. This history aims to explain the origins of the furry fandom and how it got to where it is now. Whether or not you have heard of the furry fandom before or you have been a member of the fandom for several years, this book is for anyone interested in the background of the fandom in the United Kingdom.

What makes this fandom exceptionally challenging to describe is that its interests are incredibly broad. There are no boundaries limiting what kind of media is and is not allowed in the furry fandom. Furries have discovered and joined the fandom through novels, comic books, films, television shows, anime, video games, and even original media created by other furries such as artwork, fiction, music, videos, and costumes.

This makes fandoms like the Potterheads or Trekkies straightforward by contrast. While both the Harry Potter books and *Star Trek* TV series have had many spinoffs and adaptations, it is easy for the average person to recognise a fan of one of these franchises.

Even fandoms of a genre such as science fiction or anime are specific enough in their interests to make them easy to identify by the average person, despite the diversity of offerings these genres have.

Like any other fandom, there are three basic requirements for being a part of the furry fandom:

1. You enjoy the media that surrounds it, whether this involves an individual celebrity, a hobby, a storytelling genre, or a specific franchise.
2. You identify yourself as being active in the fandom community, which usually means attending or sometimes

A group of people dressed in fursuits (furry costumes) in Manchester 2018. (Photo: Greskil Vulfhart.)

organizing events with your fellow furry fans or otherwise socializing with them in various ways such as in online communities. It is important to distinguish people who do this versus those who merely like, for example, the Disney animated feature *Zootopia* (or *Zootropolis* if you're British) or the video game Animal Crossing but who don't discuss their interests with a wider community.

3.   You are welcoming, tolerant, and inclusionary of others of all genders, races, and sexual orientations. The fandom is and always has been accepting to everyone of different backgrounds, and its only intolerance is of individuals who are bigoted or abusive towards others.

It was at the age of fifteen that I myself discovered the furry fandom. I was a rather shy and socially awkward teenager who enjoyed professional wrestling, anime, and video games, fortunate enough to have a small group of friends who shared at least one or more of those same interests. I was also a frequent internet user who checked on online web forums, videos, and image galleries to find anything new, write comments in discussions, and occasionally post stuff of my own.

One of the video game fandoms I got involved with was *Sonic the Hedgehog*. Along with enjoying the video games and animated series, I had a keen habit of searching for fanart on art portals. After following a few artists for a while, one of them brought up an art-sharing website they used called FurAffinity.

It did not take long for me to realize that this was a website that artists used to share certain kinds of artwork, all of it featuring animals that were somewhat human. After further investigation, I found fanart and fanfiction for not just Sonic the Hedgehog but also other franchises that I enjoyed, including *Pokémon* and *Digimon*. Eventually, I created an account on FurAffinity, effectively taking my first step into the furry fandom.

At seventeen, I had moved up to sixth form and made friends with a new student named Allan. He enjoyed video games and electronic music as much as I did, so we got along from the start. During one lunchtime, we were talking about things we wanted to do and places we wanted to go to. "I want to go to Anthrocon," Allan casually commented.

> For those outside of the United Kingdom, Sixth Form is a type of school for sixteen- and seventeen-year-olds studying to enroll into university.

Immediately, I recognized what he meant. Anthrocon is a furry convention in Pittsburgh, Pennsylvania, USA. At the time, it was the largest furry convention in the world, and it is still one of the most heavily attended.

While I was somewhat aware of furries living in the United Kingdom, I assumed they lived in major cities, or at least far away from the town Leamington Spa, England. And yet, Allan lived in Kenilworth, a smaller town that was close by.

I just had to ask to be sure, "Are you a furry?" He answered with no hesitation, "Yeah, are you one, too?" Admittedly, I was taken aback, but I did manage to answer shakily, "Yeah, I'm aware of them." The exchange encouraged me to investigate the fandom because now there was someone to whom I could talk in person about it, and I am sure it helped him as well because it was after that talk that I found out something about him that I did not know before: he could draw.

Allan would carry an A4 sketchbook in his bag—almost full and heavily worn—and draw anthropomorphic characters in between lessons, and he shared some online under his moniker, Feros the Wolf.

He was also really interested in animals—wolves, especially. In contrast, I was really into wild cats from a young age, thanks to the Disney film *The Lion King*. Although my favourite animal was the cheetah for their speed, Allan suggested I might lynxes, feeling that I shared a similar personality to them, including how they were supposedly known for their loyalty.

This eventually encouraged me to try drawing furry art. Another influence was watching an anime film called *The Cat Returns* in which a teenager is taken to a kingdom of cats against her will, and a suave feline goes to help bring her home.

The combination of lynxes and that suave cat gave me the inspiration for a character of my own. Using a scene from the film as a reference, I drew an anthropomorphic lynx who wore a silver mask, a red cape and hat, and carried a concealed blade. It would take a few more drawings done by myself and others before I realized that I had created not just a character but an avatar, or what the furry fandom would call a *fursona*.

A few years later, I followed a Manchester furry artist who did regular livestreams, and one day they posted on their journal that they had a table at the dealers' den at ConFuzzled, a furry convention happening in their home city. I remarked on this to Allan the next day during a lunchbreak. "What's ConFuzzled?" he asked curiously.

I had mistakenly assumed that he already knew about it, so I answered, "It's a furry convention happening in Manchester." There was a brief pause about this news that he had never heard about in his life. "There's a furry convention in Manchester?!" he exclaimed with widened eyes, "Tim, we have to go!"

He then made his next instructions noticeably clear to me: "Go and register when you get home. We'll set up a room share and then sort out travel. We're going to this convention." Next thing I knew, I was back home and registering for my first furry convention and planning an excursion to Manchester.

Fortunately for me, I had planned long-distance trips to conventions before with my friends for years, so as far as my parents were concerned, this was not unusual behaviour. Being eighteen by the time

Birmingham Furmeet (November 2011) with me on top-left corner. (Photo: Alexey Zapuskalov)

of the convention, I was eligible to go, and my sister was also a student living in Manchester at the time, so she could help with part of the journey. Aside from the fact that I had to skip classes on Friday to go, Allan and I were heading to our first convention, and our first furry gathering.

Even though we did not know anyone else at the convention, we had a great time checking out some of the talks, going to the dance hall, and playing games. The highlight would have to be the Sunday when we struck up a conversation with two furries, which eventually lead to us checking out an event called "Frankensuits" in which people make costumes from scrap materials in the shortest amount of time. We found the costumes so hilarious we cried with laughter throughout their construction.

The last event we saw was a parade of people in costumes going around the inside and outside of the hotel. We had to leave soon after because it was a Sunday and we had to get back for school the next day. Allan enjoyed the convention so much that he wanted to return next year and have a costume of his own, and while I enjoyed the convention as well, I was not sure about going again.

My fursuit. Birmingham Furmeet (December 2019; photo: AnukuTemple)

The funny thing, though, is how things changed in a year. We finished sixth form, and I moved away from all my friends to go to university. Despite struggling to make new friends, I ended up finding a social circle around campus, thanks to the furry fandom, as another student invited me to a furry meetup in Birmingham. Those meetups helped me overcome most of my struggles with socialising, and I enjoyed more time out with other people instead of spending days alone behind a computer screen.

From that point onward, I was completely on board with the furry fandom. The following year, I picked up my first fursuit at the next Con-Fuzzled and brought my character to life for the first time.

For ten years, I took a fursuit to every furmeet and convention I went to in the United Kingdom, Europe, and even Canada. I would also host a game developer meetup at ConFuzzled, as well as work as an organiser at the very same Birmingham meetup group where I made friends at university and helped organise another furry convention in the north of England.

That is the story of how I got into the furry fandom and is probably a similar story to how some other people joined, although another interesting story concerns how I got into researching the fandom's history. There are videos online from panels in the United States from those who shared stories of their experiences, yet it was not until the publication of *Furry Nation* by journalist and long-time American furry Joe Strike that I took an interest in furry history.

During a road trip to a furry meetup, one of my friends noticed that I was reading the book to pass the time. They took one look at the cover and noticed the book's full title, *Furry Nation: The True Story of America's Most Misunderstood Subculture*, and asked "What about British furries?"

The truth is that, despite my fondness for the book, its information is very American-centric, seldom mentioning any international presence in the fandom. Hence, that question lingered on for the rest of the day because they did have a point. The furry fandom is a misunderstood subculture, but it is not an American subculture: it is an international one.

The furry fandom began in the United States of America, there is no disputing that. The first conventions, fursuiters, and artists originated over there, and to this day the USA is home to the largest gatherings of furries. However, it is also true that the fandom has had international members since not long after those first gatherings took place. Understanding how the fandom grew internationally and how these local communities differ from each other is important, including how this pertains to my home country.

Fred Patten

That is when I began to do research and found what little was properly documented. Fred Patten (1940–2018), a prolific fandom historian, had written about the British fandom in two of his works on the furry fandom: *An Illustrated Chronology of Furry Fandom, 1966–1996*, published in *Yarf* magazine in 1997, and the book *Furry Fandom Conventions 1989–2015*, published in 2017. The furry fandom's information database, *WikiFur*, had baseline information on various moments in the UK furs' past scattered around, some of it citing Patten's work directly, but extraordinarily little is available in the way of primary sources and personal accounts.

One day, submissions for events were open for ConFuzzled 2019. When I read the news, I thought to myself that someone should really do a talk on the history of the furry fandom in the United Kingdom, someone with the experience and knowledge who could talk at length about the fandom over the past thirty years. I wondered where those people were and why they have not done it yet. Then I realized that I had been doing my own research for around a year, so perhaps those people were waiting for someone like me to give it a shot.

As a result, I had submitted "History of Furries in the United Kingdom" as a one-hour talk, and a few months later it was on the event schedule. My expectations were low for the interest and attendance, considering I was previously known only for doing video-game-related events, and I was much younger than those who traditionally do furry history talks. Yet at the time the talk was scheduled to begin, I was standing in front of a room filled with people to the point that several people had to sit up against the walls and gather up at the rear of the room because there were no seats left.

After I talked and answered questions for nearly an hour and received a round of applause, the recorded attendance was over a hundred people, not counting those who left after trying to listen in from the doorway, unable to get inside the crowded conference room. There were several people who showed their appreciation for what I had put together, one of whom said that someone should really write all this information down.

Since I still had my notes, and I had continued to update my research all the way up to the day of that talk, I figured I could give it a shot. This book that you are reading now is the result of years of researching message boards, forums, mailing lists, and printed publications, as well as talking to several furries. The result is an in-depth guide and history to the furry fandom of the United Kingdom.

THE BRITISH CONSPIRACY

The furry fandom is a young community when compared to fan-based communities such as Sherlock Holmes and the science fiction genre, yet people's fascination with anthropomorphism and anthropomorphic art has existed since the dawn of human civilisation.

One of the oldest drawings known to history is a cave painting in Sulawesi, Indonesia, depicting a group of half-animal/half-human beings hunting a large pig or buffalo. The art is believed to be around forty to fifty thousand years old.[1] While researchers debate whether the appearance of these figures reflects a prehistoric hunting strategy or if it is early evidence for an ancient people's belief in paranormal beings, it does support the idea that people may have been worshipping anthro gods and deities for millennia.

Made around the same time as the Sulawesi cave drawings, a prehistoric sculpture carved out of an ivory tusk known as the *Löwenmensch figurine* depicted a human with the head of a lion. It was discovered in 1939, found in a cave in Germany, along with tools and jewellery, not far from another cave with similar, yet smaller animal figurines. The figurines are all suggestive of early religious practices.[2]

Several early civilisations throughout the world depicted hybrid beings, worshipping them for their roles that were represented by their animal characteristics, like the vultures of ancient Anatolia who were carriers of souls to the afterlife.[3] Even the ancient Egyptians depicted their gods as humans with the heads of animals to differentiate them and their roles as gods.

The ancient Greeks used animals in casual storytelling, not for spirituality or religious reasons but for teaching morals with fiction. Most famous of these was Aesop, a slave who lived from between 620 to 564 B.C.E., although his stories would not be written down until centuries after he passed. Aesop's fables used a variety of talking animals to educate adults about religious, political, and social themes; it wasn't until the seventeenth century that the fables were targeted to children.

The fables were the source of many stereotypes often associated with specific animals, such as cunning foxes, quiet mice, and regal lions. These stereotypes were so ingrained by the time of the common era that they were accepted as representative of various animals' true nature, as the Greek teacher Philostratus (c. 170–c. 248 C.E.) explained:

> And there is another charm about [Aesop], namely, that he puts animals in a pleasing light and makes them interesting to mankind. For after being brought up from childhood with these stories, and after being as it were nursed by them from babyhood, we acquire certain opinions of the several animals and think of some of them as royal animals, of others as silly, of others as witty, and others as innocent.[4]

The fables were translated and spread throughout Europe, influencing the folk and fairy tales of those cultures and perpetuating the stereotypes given to animals in fiction, such as the evil wolf in *Three Little Pigs* or the cool cat in *Puss in Boots*.

Fast forward to the nineteenth century, and we see a rise in cartoons and caricature, a ripe opportunity for early pioneers of anthropomorphic art. French caricaturist J. J. Grandville (1803–1847) would publish *Les Métamorphoses du Jour* in 1829, featuring a collection of animals in human clothing going about their lives.[5]

Of course, early instances of anthropomorphic stories and artwork would find their way into Britain. Political cartoonist John Tenniel (1820–1914) would use animals on occasion to depict world politics before being approached by a British author going by the pen name Lewis Carroll (Charles Lutwidge Dodgson, 1832–1898) to illustrate anthropomorphic rabbits, caterpillars, mice, dodos, gryphons, and felines amongst other oddities in the nonsensical world of *Alice in Wonderland* in 1865.[6]

Newspapers and magazines would begin publishing comic strips at the tail end of the nineteenth century, and animal characters were featured amongst the very first—"funny animals" to be specific, a term used to describe comics about talking animals in comedic situations.

Funny animals debuted in the United Kingdom with *Jungle Jinks* by Arthur White (b. 1881) for *Playbox Magazine* in 1898. It was about school antics in a world where children and teachers were anthropomorphic animals. Mabel Francis Taylor (1866–1947) took over the series a few years later[7], and she made it popular enough to spin off into its own magazine.

Jungle Jinks continued until Taylor's death in 1947, making it the longest running British comic strip of the time. Its success influenced the creation of more funny animal comics in the United Kingdom, including Julius Stafford Baker's *Tiger Tim* and Mary Tourtel's *Rupert the Bear*, both of which would overtake *Jungle Jinks* and become their own household names.

Meanwhile, an illustrator and writer named Beatrix Potter (1866–1943) wanted to cheer up the ill son of a governess with a letter, so she wrote a story about Peter Piper, her childhood pet rabbit, causing trouble in the garden of a Mr. McGregor.[8] Peter, his mother, and his three sisters, Flopsy, Mopsy, and Cottontail, would all be the typical size for rabbits, but they were anthropomorphic in both behaviour and appearance and lived in a burrow with small and human-like furniture inside. Potter would later borrow the letters to expand and refine the story she created into a children's book. *The Tales of Peter Rabbit* would be published privately in 1901 and then commercially in 1902.

Beatrix Potter continued to draw and create tales about anthropomorphic animals after this debut, either inspired by her pets or by animals found around her home in the Lake District. Her original characters included Squirrel Nutkin, Mrs. Tiggy Winkle, Miss Moppet, and Tom Kitten. Her characters were amongst the first to be licensed for merchandise, and were adapted to film, TV, and even the ballet.

Another now-famous British author, a retired banker name Kenneth Grahame (1859–1932), also took to writing a story about anthropomorphic animals to cheer up his own ill son, and it was published as *The Wind in the Willows* in 1908.[9] Unlike Peter Rabbit, these anthropomorphic characters would be fully clothed and proportional to human size.

Photo by L. Pirou.
THE FRENCH POODLE,
As played at Drury Lane, in "The Babes in the Wood."

Charles Lauri as "The French Poodle," The Sketch Magazine, 15 March 1893, England. Museum no. 131655. © Victoria and Albert Museum, London

The fanciful and wealthy Mr. Toad, who lived in an upscale mansion, had an compulsive interest in motor cars. His living arrangement was an exception, as the other animal characters lived in more natural habitats, from the underground burrows for Mole and Badger to the wild woods for the Weasels. They did own human furniture and decorations, however, and lived alongside humans as if they were ordinary members of human society.

It wouldn't just children's illustrated books that saw the likes of anthropomorphic animals during this time. The world of theatre had its share, too, with the introduction of actors whose specialty was to dress up like animals. These animal impersonators (also known as "skins"[10] as they would literally wear the skin of another creature) were talented professionals who performed what was called "pantomime," a gesture-based form of expression often based on children's tales and typically produced during the Christmas season.

One of the most famous of these actors was Charles Lauri Jr. (1860–1903), was interviewed in the London *Sketch* magazine whilst promoting a Drury Lane production of *The Babes in the Wood* in 1893. Lauri and others like him would study real animals and make their own costumes in an effort to mimic animals as authentically as possible.

Lauri once said:

> I need hardly say that I am an entire believer in studying from life. When getting my poodle part, I had one always with me at home and it was from him that I learnt nearly all my tricks....
>
> It was no easy matter to get a proper skin or costume made; you see what is wanted when impersonating an animal is really a wig for the body and it was difficult to make anyone understand that, so I not only designed but practically made my first skins."[11]

While skins were common in the world of British pantomime, they were also found in other kinds of theatrical productions. For example, Arthur Hill (1875–1932) played the Lion in a Broadway production of *The Wonderful Wizard of Oz* in 1902[12] and George Ali (1866–1947) was Nana the dog in a silent film adaptation of *Peter Pan* in 1924.

The turn of the twentieth century also saw an invention that brought these cartoon animals to life: motion pictures. A few of the funny animals from comic strips would be adapted to film reels such as George Herriman's *Krazy Kat*, alongside new creations like *Felix the Cat* by Pat Sullivan and Otto Messemar. The gift of motion allowed these characters to show off their personalities and perform wacky antics in front of audiences, entertaining them in shorts before the feature movie.

Most of these characters and animated shorts were productions from American animation houses such as Walt Disney Studios (Mickey Mouse), Warner Brothers (Looney Tunes), Fleischer Studios (home of Betty Boop and Popeye the Sailor), and Paul Terry (Mighty Mouse, Heckle and Jeckle, *et al*). However, the United Kingdom had a few productions of its own.

Bonzo the Dog, an incredibly popular cartoon dog created by cartoonist George Studdy (1878–1948) that ran in *Sketch* magazine, made his theatrical debut in late 1924 in an animated short that premiered alongside the film *Zeebrug* (the first film seen by a reigning monarch in a public

THERE'S A FUNNY TALE GOING AROUND HERE

A postcard showing the popular Bonzo the Dog character by George Studdy.

cinema).[13] The following year, 24 more shorts would be produced, with Bonzo causing trouble as he traveled the world.

People nowadays might assume these shorts were just for children, but they were usually shown before a main feature for general audiences, so the contents were designed to appeal to young and old alike. For instance, in one scene in *Bonzo in Gay Paree* the dog chatted up a barmaid to get drunk off red wine.

America was still far ahead in film and TV animation, however, especially after Walt Disney released *Snow White and the Seven Dwarfs* in 1934, paving the way for animated feature film in Hollywood. But there were moments where Britain would excel, too.

John Halas (1912–1995) and Joy Batchelor (1914–1991), a Hungarian and British animation couple whose London studio produced Britain's first feature-length animated film in 1945, gained international acclaim when they adapted English author George Orwell's (1903–1950) novel *Animal Farm* in 1954. The story of barn animals overthrowing their human owner before suffering oppression at the hooves of smart and greedy pigs in a tale allegorical to the rise of Joseph Stalin and the Soviet Union, the film depicted the same cruel treatment and brutal deaths of the animals present in the book. The result lent British animation a reputation for offering animated films that was much darker in tone than its American counterparts.

This reputation would continue to hold in future British animated feature films such as *Watership Down* in 1978. Adapted by Martin Rosen from the Richard Adams (1920–2016) book of the same name, the story is about rabbits searching for a peaceful new home after humans destroyed their warren. It, too, was dark and violent. The film featured rabbits bloody and bruised after being scratched, bitten, caught in traps, and killed by other animals. Amusingly, both this film and *Animal Farm* are rated by the British Board of Film Classification (BBFC) for Universal audiences, meaning that despite how dark and graphic the scenes were, they were deemed suitable for children.

All of this goes to show how even before the furry fandom existed, people have always had a fascination for telling stories of anthropomorphic animal characters through books, cartoons, comics, and films. It was inevitable that some of these storytellers, artists, readers, or viewers would realise that there could be a community out there that centred around the same appreciation for animals with human characteristics. It was just a question of when and how it would arrive.

BEGINNING OF THE FURRY FANDOM

The furry fandom itself has its beginnings in California, USA, in the late-Seventies and early Eighties. Its membership was small and insular, and its members came from different places.

Some came from backgrounds in comic books, specifically the indie and underground scenes that preferred comics with violence, sex, and political commentary that was prohibited by industry regulations of the time. They would frequently attend comic book conventions such as San Diego Comic-Con, often taking an interest in comic books such as *Teenage Mutant Ninja Turtles*, *Cerebus the Aardvark*, and *Usagi Yojimbo*. The most mainstream comic they would have enjoyed would have been Marvel Comics' *Howard the Duck*.

A large majority of these were likely to be artists—both amateur or professional—and a number of them got together to start a periodical called *Vootie*, which ran from 1976 to 1983. It was an Amateur Press Association (APA) fanzine by Reed Waller (1949–) and Ken Fletcher intended to publish a variety of funny animal stories and cartoons as "a showplace for irresponsible silliness." The founders felt that comics at the time were "entirely too serious."[14] *Vootie*'s membership was restricted to people who could draw to a high standard, so all the members who could submit and receive issues were artists.

These high standards led to some of the fandom's earliest influential content, such as the comics series *Omaha the Cat Dancer* by Waller —and American writer Kate Worley (1958–2004), but also to its decline and cancellation as membership waned. Fortunately, a new funny animal fanzine called *Rowrbrazzle* took over in 1984, allowing artists and writers of any level to contribute and keeping the community alive.

Some contributors came from animation backgrounds, whether they were industry professionals or fans. This was largely thanks to animation from Japan receiving limited airings in the United States, gaining a niche and curious audience. The Cartoon/Fantasy Organisation (C/FO) was a Los Angeles club founded in 1977 to screen cartoons and animation, predominantly tapes of Japanese animation that were either recorded from test airings in Hawaii or traded with Japanese fans of American TV shows.[15]

The C/FO would not only expand to have branches across the country,[16] but they would also diversify their screenings with American cartoons as well. A popular property was *Animalympics*, an animated feature originally commissioned for the 1980 Moscow Olympics, featuring anthropomorphic animals competing in various Summer and Winter Olympic events. Originally intended to air in two parts, it was broadcast on TV and released on VHS tape as a single feature film after the United States boycotted the games.

Lastly, some fans would come from science fiction conventions. Whilst they were obviously focused on science fiction, they were generally accepting towards more niche and unrelated nerd communities and interests. For instance, *Watership Down* had an official preview at the 1978 World Science Fiction Convention (known as WorldCon 36 or IguanaCon II for short) in Arizona,[17] so it wasn't unheard of for interests unrelated to science fiction to have a space at those conventions, including the main stage.

For these West Coast U.S. furries, the primary events were California-based sci-fi conventions such as LosCon, Westercon, and WorldCon. They would often meet up at a hotel party organised by one of the attendees to watch animation and share artwork of anthropomorphic animal characters.

One of the hosts of these hotel parties was Mark Merlino (1952–), who not only had a connection between all three of these genres (sci-fi, comic book, and animation), but he also had a hand in running these groups. He was a science fiction fan going back to working as a projectionist at *Star Trek* conventions in the Seventies, an artist who made contributions to *Vootie*, and an animation film fan who was assistant president of the International Animated Film Society's Hollywood chapter.[18]

Along with fellow science fiction fan and fandom historian Fred Patten, he was a co-founder of the C/FO and drew the club's mascot, a Skiltaire named Fanta. At meetings, he handled most of the tapes and screenings of the Los Angeles branch, even obtaining a rare 1980 broadcast of the *Animalympics Winter Games* to create an extended cut of the film to fans.

With his partner, Rod O'Riley (1964–), he hosted funny animal parties, starting in 1985 at their Orange County, California, home that they called the "Prancing Skiltaire" as well as hotel rooms at local science fiction conventions. Guests received fliers with art that Merlino drew himself. These funny animal hotel parties were successful, often getting twenty or more people sitting in a small room to watch animation and swap sketch books to draw in.

Skiltaire is a fantasy species invented by Mark Merlino around 1971. It can be best described as alien pine marten creatures, recognisable for the antennae.

By 1986, the community had a new name, and the name of the hotel party at Westercon 39 changed with it. It was called a "Furry Party." The term "funny animal" was dying out in favour of the more generic label of "cartoon," and fans who were writing serious stories featuring animal characters found little sense in describing their work as "funny animal" content. Whilst there were other terms thrown about such as "anthro" and "fuzzy," as the most popular characters being drawn all had fur on them, furry was the term that stuck.

It is worth noting that while historians generally agree that the newly formed fandom transitioned from "funny animal" to "furry" sometime in the mid-eighties, the origin of the name "furry" is a mystery. Mark Merlino credits it to Lee Franks, a non-furry tabletop gamer who was a resident at the Prancing Skiltaire, and went by the BBS moniker of Dr. Pepper.[15] An alternative theory, brought up by Joe Strike in his book *Furry Nation*, was that it was coined in a fanzine back in 1983, although his sources couldn't agree on which individual used it first,[16] leaving the credibility uncertain.

What was certain though, was that following the furry party at Westercon, the fandom had settled on a name for itself. House parties, fanzines, newsletters, and bulletin board systems all self-identified as being part of the "furry fandom." Merlino would continue to host furry parties following from Westercon, and his next big one would introduce the fandom to the United Kingdom.

THE FIRST UK FURRY PARTY

The date was 29 August 1987, and thousands of science fiction fans from around the globe gathered at the beach city of Brighton for the 45th WorldCon. For British science fiction fans, it was a momentous occasion. Not only was it the thirtieth anniversary of LonCon, the very first WorldCon to set foot outside of North America, but it was also the fiftieth anniversary of the first science fiction convention in history, which took place in January 1937 at the Theosophical Hall in Leeds.

The official short name was Conspiracy '87, which in hindsight, ended up being a rather fitting name. Those who attended tell of stories that would make furry conventions seem civilized by comparison—from a hotel manager who prohibited fans from entering that led to police encounters from attendees sneaking in[18] to a conspiracy where the Church of Scientology rigged the Hugo Awards so their late-prophet L. Ron Hubbard could win the Best Novel prize at the convention's award ceremony, only to fail spectacularly.

There was a meetup in the United States between New York and Philadelphia fans in 1936, but fandom historians dispute its standing as a convention.[17]

While all that was going on, readers of the convention's daily newsletter would have spotted a peculiar event in the announcements section for that day:

> FURRY Party, 9 PM Saturday night for fans of Anthropomorphic Art, Comics, Lit. and Animation. Downlands Hotel, 19 Charlotte St., Room 6.[19]

In what would be the first official furry party in the UK, Mark Merlino travelled to the convention with his partner, Rod O'Riley, as well as friends Andre Johnson and Ken Sample, and they were planning to run a furry party just like the ones they ran in the states. If the announcement in the daily newsletter was not going to gain interest, their own fliers featuring an anthropomorphic vixen in a sultry pose and an American sense of humour probably would.[20]

As both newsletter and flyer stated, the party did not take place at either the Hilton Metropole or the Brighton Convention Centre. Instead, it was held down the road on Charlotte Street, Kemptown, at a B&B that was called the Downlands Hotel, which is known today as the Paskins Town House. A crudely drawn map was also featured at the bottom of the flier to help give directions.

It seemed that getting anyone into the room was not as

Furry Party Flyer for Conspiracy '87. (Artwork by Mark Merlino.)

straightforward as letting people walk in. "We set up a sign on a string that went down to a banister on the street. Guests pulled the string, and we'd go down and let them in," Mark Merlino recalled.[21] "We had some furry art to show, as well as animation."

Twenty people would end up meeting inside Room 6 of the small hotel, a good size for a small meetup. However, as Merlino related, it felt very different from how he would run them in the United States: "The 1987 party was a bit strange," he reflected, "because furry was relatively new and we had a few curious types who showed up that we had to try to explain furry to. I was also still involved in the C/FO at the time, and I had a tape of *Royal Space Force (The Wings of Honneamise)*, which had just been released, and some anime fans were very eager to see it on my tiny 7" screen, with me explaining it, since it was not subtitled."

Communication between American and British science fiction fans had been stable since the Thirties through fanzines, but by this time the furry fandom was still a young offshoot from California.

As far as the British fandom was concerned, it was incredibly rare for any of them to have prior knowledge of the furry fandom, or even the funny animal fandom. Although not known for certain, older British fans at the time could have mistaken it for the "silly animal fandom," an inside joke involving certain science fiction societies having animals as totems, or the Ratfandom, a radical movement within the British sci-fi fandom that was prominent in the Seventies.[22]

Fortunately, with the help of plenty of material that the Americans brought from the states, including original furry art, independent comic books and fanzines, and Merlino's cut of *Animalympics*, those who went enjoyed a unique experience.[24] It was possible that there were some newly invested furry fans who discovered a community they didn't know existed previously.

The UK house party didn't create the same impact as it did in the States, and no more furry fandom events took place at conventions for the rest of the decade. Nevertheless, the furry party at Conspiracy '87 did create some awareness of the fandom, so it was only a matter of time before the United Kingdom would have its own furry fandom.

THE FIRST BRITISH FURRIES

While the British science fiction and anime communities did not warm up to the furry scene as much as they did in the United States in the 1980s, they would soon see more infiltration from the West.

One of those influencers would be Steve Gallacci (1955–), an American artist who began as a graphics specialist in 1974 for the U.S. Air Force before becoming a self-published comic book illustrator in 1978. In 1980, he made a name for himself in the funny animal fans community thanks to a painting of an anthropomorphic feline combat pilot who was the titular character of a science fiction military comic he had been publishing called *Erma Felna: EDF*.

The community interest around *Erma Felna* encouraged Gallacci to share more of his work in his hotel room at conventions. These were not much different from Merlino's furry parties. After noticing the success of *Vootie* and *Rowrbrazzle* in telling silly-yet-adult stories involving anthropomorphic animals, Gallacci saw a market opportunity for serious and mature stories and began publishing his own comic anthology series in 1983, calling it *Albedo Anthropomorphics*.

Albedo would not only publish Gallacci's issues of *Erma Fena: EDF* but also provide a platform for other comic book artists to produce serious comics featuring anthropomorphic characters, such as Stan Sekai's *Usagi Yojimbo*. Thanks to Britain's own small press comic book scene with its abundance of mail-order services and comic book shops, small and large nationwide, British comic book readers got their hands on *Albedo Anthropomorphics* and became furry fans.

Simon Barber

One such reader was Simon Barber, an upcoming writer from Yorkshire who had already developed an interest in anthropomorphic characters as early as 1985 and who worked on his own musketeer-themed comic titled *Occitanians* in 1987, completely unaware of the existence of a fandom related to his interest.[26] That was until he found a copy of

Albedo while visiting a comic book shop in Oxford around 1988. The stunning revelation compelled him to write to Steve Gallacci to find out more.

From his new contact, he discovered more about furry independent comics and found a call for artists and writers for a new furry APA in the back pages of an issue of *Usagi Yojimbo* and eagerly applied. This publication would come to be called the *Furry Press Network*.

While Barber was not the only European member of this APA (other members included Valerio Pastore and Ferrero Mariana from Italy), he was one of the more active members, submitting multiple stories, comics, and artworks per issue, most of which were based on his own anthropomorphic science fiction series called *Toho Academy*.

> According to Barber, Sutton disappeared from the fandom because of a mental breakdown. However, fellow FPN member Arthur Yee claims Sutton left the fandom after joining the U.S. Air Force.

Unlike the historical setting of Ocittanians, Toho Academy is described as what would happen when "all the Japanese Monster films, James Bond films, and H. P. Lovecraft tales are real, and folk get along with it uncomplainingly."[27] Throughout the 1990s, Barber would write stories, comics, draw artwork, and even publish a text-based adventure game based on the universe.

Through *FPN* he would get to know Fred Patten, who helped several FPN members join *Rowrbrazzle* in 1992, where Barber still contributes writings and illustrations for. FPN, on the other hand, would be short-lived, ending abruptly after five issues. The cause was disputed amongst those who knew Sutton and the APA.

Ian Curtis

Barber was not the only British furry during this time who discovered the fandom through the independent comics scene. Robert Deighton became a fan of furry comics when he started reading a funny animal superhero comic book (*Cutey Bunny* by Joshua Quagmire) in his local comic book shop in Hull sometime between 1988 and 1989.

In the back of one of its issues he discovered *Albedo* and wrote to Gallacci. In turn, Gallacci passed Deighton on to Pauli Kidd, an Australian furry fan who also worked as a professional game designer at Beam Software before becoming a popular furry writer. Kidd introduced him to another furry fan who was not only from England but who originally came from Hull himself, Ian Curtis, now considered a founder of the furry fandom in the United Kingdom.

Born in November 1946, Curtis had had an interest in anthropomorphic animals in comics and books since childhood, reading the comic strips and annuals of the British comic strip *Rupert the Bear* and *Adventures of Curly Wee* during the 1950s. He was especially a fan of annuals of the character Bonzo the Dog, about whose history he would write, along with its illustrator, George Studdy, for a 1991 issue of the fanzine *Furtherence*.[13]

He would also enjoy reading novels like Jane Thornicroft's *Mink Was No Ordinary Cat* (1948) and Rudyard Kipling's *The Jungle Book* (1894), as well watch the black-and-white animated shorts from Walt Disney Animation during the earliest days of television.

When he became a student at Liverpool University in 1965, Curtis developed a further interest in comics as well as fantasy and wargaming. These interests would continue to grow as he communicated with other young adult fans of niche subcultures during the 1970s and 1980s.

While working as a British correspondent and editor for *Defense & Foreign Affairs* magazine, Curtis would travel on multiple occasions to the United States. It was during these work trips that he would attend science fiction and comic book conventions and discover the furry fandom. He also communicated with furries online, although, as he recalls, the unreliability of the internet in the late-1980s led him to prefer written and in-person communication.

> The job gave me access to a computer with a modem, and I tried repeatedly to access one of the first furry bulletin boards. As I recall, I managed to stay connected for more than a minute just once. In the same period, I got to two Baltimore SF conventions and the Boston Worldcon, each of which was more useful than all the computer access.

1991 INTERNATIONAL COMICS FESTIVAL

In November 1991, it was announced that a small group of prominent furry fans and comic artists were planning to go to the International Comics Festival that takes place annually in the commune of Angoulême, France. The occasion was massive, being mentioned in numerous fanzines and newsletters of the time, such as Rod O'Riley's *In-Fur-Nation*:

> This four-day event attracts more than a hundred thousand comics fans and creators from around the world, and this is a great opportunity for some of our

favorite anthropomorphic and small-press comics to pick up valuable new markets overseas! The folks attending include MU Press folks Ed and Diana Vick, *Red Shetland* co-creator Jim Groat, *Yarf!* editor Jeff Ferris, *Rhudiprrt* writer Dwight Decker, *Erma Felna* creator Steve Gallacci, *Desert Peach* writer/artist Donna Barr, and long-time comic artists Monika Livingston, Roberta Gregory and Colin Upton.[28]

Patten also joined the group, deciding to miss out on an upcoming ConFurence in the process. In his announcement of the event, he mentioned other people who were part of the group travelling to Angoulême, such as another editor of *Yarf* named Kris Kruetzman, and mentioned that the group would plan to tour England as part of their travels:

> After the comics festival in Angoulême … most of this Furry tour group will go to England for another week of touring there, and possibly–if it can be set up–the first get-together of English Furry Fandom. I certainly don't want to miss the chance to participate in this event, even if it does mean missing ConFurence 3.[29]

Ian Curtis was writing to Monika Livingston at the time this tour was being planned, and Monika had asked Ian about the possibility of meeting British furries. It was from these letters that a plan was set: the American furry fans would travel to Yateley, and Curtis would invite British fans over to his home and spend the weekend together for a housecon.

Housecons were nothing new and not exclusive to science fiction and furry fans. One of Ian Curtis' inspirations was from the fans of the wargame *Diplomacy*.

As early as 1963, many *Diplomacy* fans played by mail, sending their moves to a games master, who would then collect and send the outcomes to the players. The correspondences were lengthy and entertaining enough that fanzines were created just to publish ongoing games. Fans would meet up at someone's home to play wargames and share fanzines, with some of these gatherings being big enough to be regarded as small conventions. This led to the name "Housecon."

Various other interests were part of the discussion at these housecons, including other games, comics, books, and other media. This would lead to individuals setting up their own housecons specific to those other interests.

One such interest was the board game *ElfQuest*. During the 1980s, Ian Curtis organized a housecon devoted to this game. Attendees would often spend the weekend enjoying the comics and occasionally roleplaying outside his home. With his experience and knowhow from running the *ElfQuest* housecons, Curtis was more than willing to offer a place for furry fans to stay and provided them with plenty of opportunities to socialise. The first British furry the Americans met was at the festival, as Simon Barber (who was working at a Royal Air Force base in Berlin at the time) travelled to Angoulême to meet them. He purchased some of their comics, introduced them to North African food from a street vendor, and talked about contributing to their fanzines.

Sadly, that seemed to be one of the few positive moments from their time at the festival.

As most of the Americans were comic book artists and writers, they had high hopes to get a lot of sales and interest from European comic book fans. However, they were left largely disappointed when they discovered the mostly French crowd preferred buying hardbacked comics over the paper-thin comics that the Americans and British were used to.[30] Once the festival was over and the Americans made their way to England by ferry, their troubles weren't over. Edd Vick held back no punches on what he thought of the Angoulême Comics Festival and the journey afterwards in his report in *Rowlbrazzle*:

> That was when it seems worthwhile to have wasted thousands of dollars on a con where nobody even looked at our material; to have gotten to Dover too late to change any money and wound up staying the night at a ratty B&B that would accept my charge card; to have schlepped over a hundred pounds of baggage all over Europe up and down stairs and across train tracks and into and out of subways and… you get the idea.[32]

While most spent some time sightseeing in in London, Dwight Decker, Jim Groat, and Fred Patten made a slight detour and visited Milt Withers, a Scottish furry fan who they knew as the only European subscriber to the furry magazine *Rhudiprrt*. His parents ran a hostel near Loch Ness, which they stayed for a night, and endured heavy fog around the Loch the following day.[31] As Decker opted to stay an additional day in Scotland, Groat and Patten travelled down to London to meet up with the other furries, so they could go to Yateley to see what Ian Curtis had to offer.

THE YATELEY HOUSECON

On the 1st and 2nd of February, of the dozen Americans who were touring England, Kris Kreutzman, Jeff Harris, Dwight Decker, Edd Vick, Jim Groat, Monika Livingstone, and Fred Patten decided to make the additional excursion to Yateley. Of the British fans, Ian Curtis was present with Robert Deighton, Warwick (Tim Baverstock) from Manchester, Porsupah (Jan Paxton) from Wales, and Fenthe (Dan Mitchell) along with his friend Paul Costello. The British furry fans got an opportunity to hang out with the American furry fans in what would be the first British organized furry event. Unofficially, it was called the UK MicroConFurence.[32] The event proved be a grand opportunity for British furries. They got to talk with everyone while watching British animation like Aardman's *Creature Comforts,* admire furry artwork by those who brought it or drew that very weekend, and purchase comics and fanzines that were impossible to find in the country.

Fenthe was purportedly the only British fan who could draw, as such the American furries were also happy to teach the "artistically inclined" whose efforts appeared in a collaborative comic report in *Rowrbrazzle* 33 (April 1992).[33] The entire weekend concluded at a pub in London, where a small furry party was had with more discussions and furry art to be shared. While it was a small affair—and, based on the reports at the time, people had to deal with extremely cold weather—it was generally regarded as a worthwhile experience for the British furries.

"Even though it was an extremely small affair, I felt privileged to be able to meet, and get to know closely, our U.S. visitors," Robert Deighton reflected in *In-Fur-Nation.* "We were able to buy lots of stuff like comics, zines, etc. which were usually impossible to find here; the artistically inclined even got involved in an 'artists masterclass' (and a

Panel done by British furries at housecon in issue 33 of Rowrbrazzle.

The 1992 Yateley Housecon as depicted by Kris Kreutzman in Issue 35 of Rowrbrazzle.

'juggling masterclass' with Mr. Kreutzman!)... I don't know if we'll ever have anything like that again (unless anthropomorphics really take off here like they have in the U.S.), and I know I'll never afford to go to a ConFurence proper, but it was an event I'll never forget."[34]

There are not many accounts from the Americans of the housecon itself since the prime event from their journey was the comics festival in Angoulême. However, Edd Vick gave a few sentences in his report that imply his visit with the English furries was the calmest part of his adventure:

> I visited the English furry crowd, all seven of them.
> (When I got back, someone asked me what English
> fanboys looked like; I said that they were just like
> American ones except they're thin. Jobs weren't in
> great supply there, or usually as lucrative.)[35]

Kris Kreutzman would describe his experience in the visual form of a comic strip report, complimenting Ian Curtis but making fun of the state of his home, not to mention the amount of furries in Britain at the time.[36]

We can assume that the seventh English furry would-be Simon Barber, who did not join the Americans in England after the International Comics Festival.

As for Robert Deighton, his hopes would obviously come to fruition. Porsupah organized his own housecon at his home in Tonyrefail, South Wales, on the 5th through the 7th June 1993. Ten furries attended. The following year, the housecon returned to Yateley, whereupon it was decided to make it a regular affair, with the two prior events retroactively linked to this series. Although the original proposed name was the Furry Housecon, most people would call it the Yateley Housecon because of its location.

(From left to right) Kev Beeley, Ian Stradling, Simon Barber, and Ian Curtis, outside the Yateley house in 1997.

The housecons would run on a quarterly basis, usually to coincide with the larger furry conventions in the States such as ConFurence and ConFurence EAST. As Mayfurr (Terry Knight) described it, they were rather relaxed affairs[37]: "[The housecon] was informal with no particular schedule, [we] were typically drawing and sharing furry artwork, as well as watching furry animation and anime films in the evening, along with trips into Yateley for supplies."

While a few attendees spent the night at nearby hotels, several of them brought sleeping bags and stayed at Ian Curtis' house. This was manageable back in 1992, when a little more than half of the thirteen

Artwork by Kev Beeley, depicting one of the bedrooms at a Yateley Housecon.

attendees spent the night, but as the housecons grew more popular, and more people found it affordable to sleep anywhere within the house, poor Curtis found himself managing a free hostel. Simon Barber described it this way:

> You have to visualise this is all taking place in a standard Fifties three-bedroomed house, and at its height, perhaps twenty to twenty-five people turn up. Not all stay overnight. But there's been folk piled in six to a room, sleeping on floors, in corridors, on chairs, in the bathtub—you get the idea. Crowded house.

Most attendees came from around the United Kingdom, although there were a few international furries who had attended during this time, such as the previously mentioned Mayfurr from New Zealand, as well as furries from Germany and Denmark.

INTERSECTION '95

In 1995, a small group of American furs returned to the United Kingdom as the World Science Fiction convention Intersection '95 took place at the Scottish Exhibition and Conference Centre in Glasgow. Mark Merlino and Rod O'Riley returned to run a furry party for both British and American furries in attendance, and while the party's flyer and the convention's newsletter *Voice of Mysterons* had listed the party as taking place at the Forte Crest Hotel,[38] Mark Merlino described the party as somewhat of an upgrade to their last affair in the United Kingdom:

> We actually got a meeting room in the convention complex. Once again, we had some art to show, and video (both times I had my 8mm camcorder, playing tapes I recorded to show on a 7" portable color TV, since it was NTSC). I believe attendance was about twenty again.[24]

Fred Patten travelled with Jim Groat to attend, and he described it somewhat differently. He also believed attendance was around twenty people, but he noted that it was much smaller than other hotel parties going on nearby, apparently in the hundreds.

He did also describe that those who did attend "seemed seriously interested in learning about anthropomorphics", which was partially helped by the attendance of Simon Barber, Ian Curtis, and even Scottish

HOOT MON

AYE, TIS BE A FINE FURRY PARTY

FORTE
CREST
HOTEL
ROOM
120
FRIDAY
SATURDAY
9 PM
VIDEOS
ARTISTS
ARTWORK
COMICS
WEIRDNESS
LOCH NESS
ELLIOT NESS

Poster for the Furry party at Intersection '95 (artwork by Jim Groat).

furry fan and artist Nik Jardine sharing sketchbooks and fanzines with the others.[39]

It went much better than the "Meet Furry Fandom" session that the convention allowed Mark Merlino to host, where a measly five people showed up.

The convention ran on the 24th to 28th August, and the Yateley Housecon was a week later. Both British and American furry fans hung out at Ian Curtis' home, and Simon Barber took the Americans on a tour of London and Oxford.

The furry fandom was finally gaining ground and international recognition in the United Kingdom; however, there was another British group that was taking shape during the 1990, making itself known in the virtual world.

THE INTERNET AND UK FURCON

While newsletters and fanzines were how the furry fandom thrived outside of conventions in the 1980s and early 1990s, a new piece of technology called the internet allowed the furry fans to connect and talk to each other over greater distances, despite being rather primitive and limited at the time.

The Prancing Skiltaire had a Bulletin Board System (BBS) set up in 1982 by Andre Johnson known as the Tiger's Den, which allowed users to send messages to each other within storyboards. While there had been several furry fandom BBSs over the years, these systems were limited by how many people could connect and send messages at a time. Merlino and O'Riley have joked about how Tiger's Den had around four hundred users connected through one phoneline, so anyone who sent a message would not get a response for at least a week.

Because of the limitations of BBSs, the international growth of the furry fandom can be attributed more to Usenet, a similar discussion board system first introduced in 1980. Unlike BBSs, Usenet distributed information across multiple servers, allowing discussions to be easily sent and received without queuing.

For its first few years, Usenet was only useful for professionals and academics, thanks to its restrictive requirement that newsgroups had to fit into one of eight specific categories. This changed in 1987 with the inclusion of the alt.* category, which Usenet provided with almost complete flexibility. Alt.* enabled many niche communities and fandoms to create newsgroups and take advantage of the service.

Fans of Gallacci's comics decided to create their own newsgroup in October 1990 called alt.fan.albedo "for discussion of funny animal comic books, such as *Albedo, Critters,* and *Quack!*"[40] However, fans quickly moved to a newly created newsgroup called alt.fan.furry to participate in more general discussions about the fandom. This avenue provided a place to discuss furry art and media as well as to talk about upcoming events and fanzines.

Usenet boards like alt.fan.furry were not the only ways people could communicate through the internet back in the 1980s. Students had the opportunity to play multiplayer adventure games thanks to the MUD (short for Multi-User Dungeon).

The MUD was created by two Brits: Roy Trubshaw while he was a programmer at the University of Essex in 1978, and fellow student Richard Bartle, who further developed it in 1980. It was a text-based adventure game inspired by Dungeons & Dragons[41] Users could create characters that explored a virtual world where they engaged in quests and fought monsters. MUDs allowed them to do this in online teams without the necessity of playing in the same room.

Granted, you needed to be connected to a university network to play, but it was a hit among fellow students and faculty members and, later, members of the public who had access to ARPANET, one of the earliest online networks.

After a student from the University of Aberystwyth named Brian Cox got to play the Essex MUD, he worked with a team of students to produce their own, AberMUD, which spread to multiple other universities and eventually the world.

MUDs would spawn an entire community of avid players and game developers, with many variations based on gameplay styles, functions, and visuals. One such variation was TinyMUCK, which was first introduced in the summer of 1990. It was an expansion on its predecessor, TinyMUD, to allow more complex world and social interactions, and little to no monsters with the sole purpose of attacking.

FURRYMUCK

As one American furry and avid American MUD player named Drew Maxwell explained back in 1998, there were a few MUCKs that were somewhat furry-related on account of online Disney fans. As a student at North Carolina University and a member of its small computer club, Drew found an opportunity to build his own MUCK with fellow students BlueMage (Neil M) and Gypsy (Melissa Whitfield):

> Our first attempt was to try and build a model of Disneyworld (you can imagine how daunting a task this was): DisneyMUCK, as it was tentatively called. Unfortunately, since we could not actually build everything, [it] was later scrapped. When they decided that they were going to give up the project, they still had a MUCK server sitting around. I said, "Could I start that over again?"[42]

Drew would also describe how the furry fandom, while having the right ideas and concepts for what they wanted the community to be about, had slow forms of communication, which meant roleplaying and discussions were "crippled." He also had the opposite view of the MUD community, where they had fast-paced online systems, but most lacked a strong community. As he was becoming a furry fan at around the same time he was playing with MUDs, it was no surprise that, when given the opportunity to restart the MUCK project at that computer club, he would bring them together as FurryMUCK, which went public in mid-October 1990.

Within months, a team of administrators (called wizards) was formed to build a lively world where furries could hang out. The starting point was called Furry Avenue, which would lead to the main town, where streets are named after popular people in the fandom, such as Sable Street, after Sy Sable, a name Mark Merlino went by. Several social locations would soon appear from taverns and clubs to the bandstand and more. In less than a year, the MUCK would be too large for the University of North Carolina to host, moving servers twice in the space of two years.[43]

As MUDs have their origin and activity in the United Kingdom, it is no surprise that British furries would end up discovering FurryMUCK and making friends there. While there is no exact record of who or when the first British furry joined FurryMUCK, Ian Stradling (Sylvermane,

Other variations of MUD include MUSH, which allow any player to extend the virtual world they play in through a scripting language, and MOO, where any player can write object-orientated code to extend the world and change in-game behaviour.

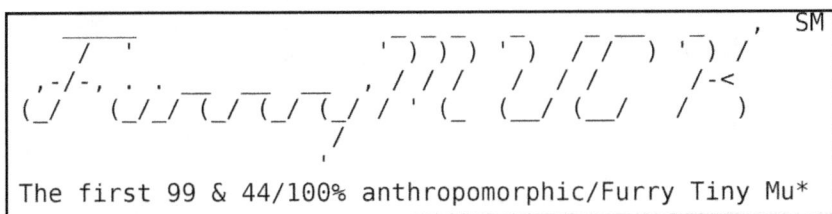

The first 99 & 44/100% anthropomorphic/Furry Tiny Mu*

FurryMUCK SM Banner

organizer of UKFurCon 2) believes he created his character on the site in late 1992.

Stradling was already involved in the furry fandom through collecting art and communicating through Usenet as early as 1990. He got invited to the Yateley Housecons, but he was particularly active in the early British furry fandom through the online and anime fandoms.

"Communication then was mostly through FurryMuck, with the European furry group online in European daytime and the North American furries usually not starting to appear until early afternoon," Stradling explained.[44] While this part of the community was extremely active through the MUCKs, they did congregate at other fan conventions, whether they were longtime and firmly established fans or just as young as the furry fandom was. "A lot of us were also involved with wider Science Fiction or Japanese Anime/Manga fandoms, so I often met at Anime cons in particular."

Another furry from this era who was also a fan of anime was Foxy (Tiffany Fox), an artist and writer from East Sussex. "I came across FurryMuck [in] January 1993," she explained. "My brother (who is three years older than me) found furry stuff originally, as they were at university before I went.... I was able to connect to it through their university green screen terminals from home at that point! I've always liked animals and nature, and animal people seemed like a cool thing to be a part of!"[45]

Wanting to socialise outside of the MUCKs, a new housecon was organised. Foxy says that this housecon was given its name of "UKFurCon" as a joke "given it wasn't a convention size at all!" Fred Patten's "Illustrated Chronology of the Furry Fandom" states that the first UKFurCon was organized solely by Aspirin (Adam Moss), although Foxy gives the impression that the organization was a group effort: "We helped organize it, but we were able [to use] Aspirin's student digs at university because it was in the summer and their roomies were all home at that time."

The UK Fur CON ran from 9 to 11 July 1994, but, seemingly unbeknownst to them, this would clash with the Yateley Housecon that was taking place during the same weekend of the 8 to 10 July. Patten wrote that this date conflict led to accusations that the FurryMUCK users hijacking the housecons.[46] It probably didn't help that there were a few people within the fandom who received invitations to both events.

> So far as I can tell there were two UK furry cons
> which happened on the same weekend — neither
> group seems to have been aware of the other. I was
> invited to both of them, about a week beforehand, but
> I was already committed to participating in yet a third
> con (CAPTION94) that weekend.[47]

This situation could be described in jest as one of the earliest instances of furry drama in the British fandom, given the implicitly heavy debates around the two events clashing. Like the online furry drama of the present, the situation was possibly exaggerated. When asked about the incident, Stradling didn't recall the confusion leading to discussions being as vitriolic as it seems: "It was just a case of 'it might have been a good idea to check before you set this date because we have already set this date to something else.'"

Regardless, the discord was calmed and settled, and a resolution was reached between Britain's FurryMUCK and non-internet furry fans. The premiere UKFurCon was considered a success with fifteen people at-

Drawing of attendees at UKFurCon II in Bristol by Unci.

tending, including one American and one German, according to Patten. Patten's number might be a bit generous, though, as Foxy wrote later in 1994 that it "had a massive attendance of ten people … [and] was also great fun."[48]

It was only a week later that someone brought up the idea of doing UKFurCon the next year, and Stradling became its host. UKFurCon II took place at his home in Bristol on 26 to 30 May 1995. Patten's chronology claims this event drew a bigger crowd of around twenty people, including one from Germany. It also credits the housecon as being the British premiere of several cartoons from a prominent animator in the furry fandom: the Ohio native Eric Schwartz.

Foxy and Prask took on organizing and hosting duties for the next two UKFurCons in 14 to 16 June 1996 and 21 to 23 March 1997. Foxy, being a student at Coventry University at the time, ran it from her student house. The pair were a lot more eager to advertise possible activities, including LaserQuest, a cinema, football, and a variety of food options. A trip to Coventry University to access FurryMUCK was also a common activity.

The UKFurCons were well received, considering their stable attendance numbers, but the lack of variety in venues was apparently an issue as Stradling and Foxy routinely opened the forum to offers to host future UKFurCons. Despite a failed attempt earlier in the year, it would run once again in Coventry on 11 to 13 September 1998.[49]

Luckily, a major opportunity arose thanks to the help of the British anime fandom. Shinnenkai was an anime and manga convention that took place at the Radisson Edwardian Hotel near Heathrow Airport in London and was hugely successful in both 1997 and 1998. Shinnenkai's main attractions were its video rooms and masquerade, taking cues from the science fiction fandom, but focused on the growing niche of anime and video games instead of sci-fi and fantasy.[50]

Foxy was able to find connections through her own involvement in the anime fandom and got approval from the convention's committee to organise UKFurCon as a furry programming track within Shinnenkai's schedule. Foxy provided a detailed plan, including giving one of the five video rooms a furry theme. There were also promises of furry animations from both Japan and the West, as well as the possibility of including the furries in the anime masquerade, a masquerade dedicated to furry, quizzes, and furry comics and fanzines in the dealers' den.[51]

Shinnenkai, in turn, openly embraced the furry fans during a few promotions, changing the title of the event to "The Shin and Kai Con PLUS UKFurCon" on the official website and advertising the convention to alt.fan.furry:

UKFurCon is [bringing] help at the lush and opulent
Radisson Edwardian Heathrow over the weekend of

August 28 to 30. It will take place simultaneously with
The Shin and Kai Con to give UK Furs a chance to
enjoy a bigger con with more stuff to do and a great
anime cross over.

There will be dedicated furry events, a furry section
to the masquerade and we're always willing for anyfur
to send us suggestions about what they'd like to see/
have/enjoy at the convention.[51]

But things were not going well behind the scenes, as Foxy remarked
three years later: "Ah yes, the wonders of Shinnenkai, and being given
one week to plan the entire programming schedule, only to be told just
after completing it 'there's no convention now.'"[52]

On 13 September 1999, the convention's chairperson, Judith Lewis,
announced the convention's official cancellation, citing the Raddisson
Edwardian hotel's sudden withdrawal of the conference facilities around
six weeks before the convention was to open, only keeping their promise
to honour any existing hotel reservations. At the time, Stradling theo-
rised that the hotel decided to back out because not enough attendees
were willing to book rooms at the hotel, a theory he still maintains whenever it is brought up:[53]

When you run a convention at a hotel, you either have
to pay for the conference facilities up front or make an
agreement to have your attendees buy a certain block
of rooms. Either way is for hotels to make money.
Not enough people were willing to stay at the Raddi-
son because it was an airport hotel in London, so the
hotel decided to pull the plug.[53]

The late notice plus lost expenses meant the convention couldn't
recover and closed. UKFurcon 1999 went with it.[54] Although Foxy and
others never officially cancelled UKFurCon, no further plans or proposals were made after 1999.[55]

One can wonder how the rest of the British furry fandom would
have turned out if Shinnenkai had proceeded as planned with UKFur-
Con as a permanent furry track; it is possible that the furry fandom
might have had an earlier mainstream presence in the United Kingdom
as a result, as well as a stronger appeal to anime over western furry related media. This sort of speculation may or may not sit too well with furry
fans of today who might feel alienated by anime. Gatherings, meanwhile,
expanded to furmeets and conventions, making housecons less relevant
to traditional, in-person gatherings.

THE DECLINE OF HOUSECONS AND MUCKS

Even if they had survived, the housecons of the 1990s would not have remained as prevalent today because the furry fandom's culture was beginning to change. The world wide web and the ability to share artwork and stories digitally made fanzines less relevant, taking away one of the appeals of housecons. There was also growing interest in organising more outgoing events at parks and pubs, settings a lot more enticing to people planning the gatherings compared to the prospect of a day in a crowded house.

Neither have gone away entirely, however, as Yateley was still running until 2020. The last public advertisement of the housecon was published in March 2001,[56] while more modern ones such as BrumCon and KryllCon still exist for those who are in the know.

The same thing can be said of MUCKs, which, while still very much active as the prime source for online roleplay, would be taken over by the likes of Furcadia, an MMORPG launched in 1996 with an isometric visual landscape that allowed players to explore with customisable anthropomorphic avatars. The advent of SecondLife, a 3D MUCK by Linden Labs, in 2003 also offered an appealing alternative to the MUCK.

While the latter was made for more general audiences, it allowed fully customisable 3D avatars that made fully modelled furry characters possible. It also allowed users to sell virtual creations and set up their own virtual locations such as stores, bars, dance clubs, and homes. A lot of FurryMUCK users and members of the fandom jumped ship to SecondLife, becoming a large enough presence to be credited in *Computer Games* magazine as a major user-base in October 2005.[57]

This does not take away from the impact that these housecons had. While the British fandom was small and far behind America when it came to conventions, they had a place to gather and socialise, and the community would become more personal. No longer were British fans feeling alone with their interest in cartoons and comic books. They could make friends with others in the UK. While they could—and some very much did—travel to America to enjoy being furries, housecons allowed them to enjoy being furries at home.

BrumCon was a Birmingham furry housecon for local furries to hang out the weekend before ConFuzzled, running from 2008 to 2010.

KrllCon was a housecon hosted by Krll Gojira at his home in Wales from 2017 to 2019.

THE UK INFLUENCE ON EUROFURENCE

As mentioned earlier, the UKFurCons usually had at least one attendee from Germany. According to *Gucky and the Fluffbutts*, an article written for Andromeda-SF, the country's fandom has its own detailed history, one that has roots in the early 1990s through films, comics, and books. Germans stumbled upon the American furry fandom by sheer luck by discovering a furry newgroup at a university IT server.[58]

An active German FurryMUCK user, Tes-Tui-H'ar (Gerritt Heitsch), went down to the first UKFurCon to hang out with the British furries, and like the others who attended, he took advantage of the computer labs at Aspirin's university to access the net[59] and send messages back home through FurryMUCK.

Fellow German-born fur Unci (Tobias Köhler), a friend of Tes and an avid MUCK user in his own right, would be one of the recipients of his messages and would later attend UKFurCon II and III. Unci even documented the second UKFurCon with a group drawing of himself, Foxy, Stradling, BlackLion (Mikel Norwitz) and Prask.

In late 1994, Unci would post a proposal on alt.fan.furry for a new gathering that he and Tes were planning. "There was some talk in the park today about a get together of all European furrys. I am maintaining a list of euro-furries … and there are dozens; mostly in Britain, some in Sweden and Germany, some in Finland and some elsewhere."[60]

Hosted at Tes' family vacation home in the North Sea coastal municipality of Kaiser-Wilhelm-Koog (near Hamburg), it went under the name "Eurofurence" and took place from 30 June to 3 July. A total of nineteen furries attended: eleven from Germany, six from the United Kingdom, and one each from Finland and Sweden.[61] The first Eurofurence was considered a success, and so it would return the following year in Sweden, nearly doubling the attendance. It continued afterwards as an annual organised convention under Cheetah (Sven Tegethoff) as chairman.

By its fifth iteration, Eurofurence was organized under the registered organisation Eurofurence e.V. It grew to be not only the European continent's largest furry convention, but also the longest-running ongoing furry convention in the world, with Eurofurence 26 (24 to 28 August 2022) hosting 3,495 attendees from around the world.

While *Gucky and the Fluffbutts* claims Eurofurence was possibly influenced by American furry conventions, there is a stronger argument that it was the British housecons that were a key inspiration in the creation of Eurofurence. This can be based on Tes and Unci's close connections to the British furry fandom through MUCKs, how many oversea attendees were from Britain, their involvement in the FurryMUCK and UKFurCon groups, and comments from Unci himself.

In May 2006, on a discussion page of the furry information resource WikiFur, Unci recalls the time he received those messages on FurryMUCK from Tes back during the first UKFurCon: "I was just surprised when he suddenly mentioned on FurryMUCK that he is with British furries. After the experience, we got to know a few Central European furries and decided to hold EuroFurence."[62]

This was not the first time Unci credited the British housecon with the creation of Eurofurence. Three years earlier, he wrote about his first ten years in the furry fandom on alt.fan.furry, which included meeting Tes online, joining FurryMUCK, and Eurofurence: "In 1995 I worked together with Tes again to hold the first larger furry convention in Europe, EuroFurence, in Kaiser-Wilhelm-Koog (in a house owned by his family). That was partly a reaction to UK FurCon I, a spontaneous meeting of furries in late 1994 that I unfortunately could not attend (I had not heard of it until it was running). Also in 1995 I took part in UK FurCon II in Bristol."[63]

It is cool that one of the oldest and most recognisable furry conventions in the world, one that would pave the way for the furry fandom to grow in Europe, got its start because a bunch of mostly British furries wanted to hang out for a weekend after talking amongst each other on an online role-playing game.

FANZINES AND COMICS

In the present day, sharing photos, images, videos, and stories, is commonplace and almost instantaneous on the internet. It is taken for granted, thanks to social media and content-sharing websites like YouTube, Twitter, Facebook, Reddit, and Instagram, not to mention art sharing websites like DeviantArt, FlickR, Tumblr, and personal websites and blogs. Like everyone else, furries have the luxury of using social media, as well as furry-tailored, art-exchange websites, to post and share artwork.

Back in the late 1980s and early 1990s, however, this kind of file transfer was nigh on impossible for the average consumer. As Ian Curtis explained, "If you had told people that it would be possible to access immense quantities of full colour art on the internet, they would have replied, 'What's an internet?'"

Usenet boards, BBS, and the MUDs and MUCKS, were all text-only forms of online communication, and while digitized images have been functional on the world wide web since 1992, it was only possible for the few companies, universities, and organisations like CERN that had the technical and financial resources to do it.

Not everyone in the fandom had the access or resources to a server to upload or download images. And doing this for audio and video was a complete impossibility as it took over an hour to download a three-minuteaudio file back in 1994.[64]

This was why one of the main attractions of furry parties and housecons was to meet with artists directly and share work by photocopying art. Attendees would recall the early years of the Yateley housecons in which it was a tradition to walk to the corner shop or the post office to make excessive use of their photocopiers so fans could have personal copies of drawings and pages of text produced by some of these artists.

This would also include the artwork and stories written in fanzines, thanks to those few who were members of the APAs. Copying fanzines published in the USA was a happy pasttime for British furs who envied the quality of work produced by their brother and sister furries across the Atlantic. Gradually, British fans were starting to improve their own artistic skills, and it would not take long after the first Yateley housecon before these artists wanted to produce and share art in fanzines of their own design.

Slate (Damien Cugley) was an Australian-born mathematics and computation student, and, later, a department lecturer at Oxford University in the early 1990s. He was also a member of both the Oxford University SF Group (OUSFG) and the University's comic book society. In 1992, he became a founding member of Caption (Britain's longest-running comic book convention dedicated to small press), along with Adrian Cox, Jenni Scott, and Jeremy Dennis. Slate would also work with Dennis to establish a publishing house called Alleged Literature that same year.[65]

Throughout the rest of 1992, Slate and Dennis worked together on editing and publishing SF and comic fanzines until an opportunity arose to work on a personal project, a furry fanzine they called *Furry Furry*.

FURRY FURRY

In a November 1992 Usenet post, Slate explained his creative process and work in progress:

> My first thoughts were partially inspired by finding a colour PostScript printer with an A3 paper tray in our Computing Service — I have colourized scans of my furry pictures & could generate a colourful A4 cover or a poster. It would be cheaper than a colour photocopy and probably look better because the colours would be pure rather than scanned.
>
> So: I have furry pix, a few unfinished furry articles, and a niche "market" of fairly dedicated furry fans. I've drawn (non-furry) strips, so I could make a stab at a furry strip. I don't doubt that there are people on JANET and the Internet who'd like to donate text pieces. I have edited and produced zines before. So I have the technology to make at least a one-off zine. A furry zine would also have the political advantage of *not* looking like a rival to the zine I just left.[66]

This post was made with the intention of finding potential interest amongst the British furry fans to both purchase and contribute to such a publication. Although it took several months to get off the ground, it eventually became a reality. An official press release announced the publication of the first issue of *Furry Furry*, a 32-page, A5, black & white fanzine, on 18 September 1993. It was sold at Caption '93, with copies available to purchase through mail-order.

The fanzine largely focused on comic strips and science fiction stories, as that was what both Slate and Jeremy Dennis were traditionally known for producing. Along with the fanzine editor and the designer of its typeface, Slate also produced the longest strip in the zine, a story of his insert character and his sister-in-law Prrell living on an alien world called "Picnic." Dennis also provided a strip called "Salvaged" about a starship full of canine people chasing a feline spy. John Miller, an SF fanzine regular, also contributed a story with Zooty the cat, illustrations by graphic artist Lee Brimmicombe-Wood and reviews of furry works by Foxy.

The second issue would be published on 7 May 1994. It featured a continuation of "Picnic" called "Visitors Part 1" as well as a new comic strip from John Miller. New contributors to this issue included Craig Conlan, who wrote "Funky Chicks," which is literally about two chicks and their misadventures with sea monkeys. Howard Stangroom (Will Morgan) and Stephen Lowther added a single-page comic titled "The Pet Shop Boys" about a gay bar; Simon Barber penned a short story set in his "The Toho Academy" universe. Unfortunately, this would be the last issue because Slate and Dennis moved away from producing comics to pursue steadier career paths.[67]

While it did not have enough success to go beyond two issues, *Furry Furry* was a quality publication that showed that fanzines could be produced and sold in the United Kingdom. It would not take long before others in the United Kingdom would make their own.

DAINTIES

It was around 1999 that Silvermane would begin a fanzine project and establish his own publication house in Bristol: Crownmede, Ltd. In the summer of 1999, he made a call around the furry art scene on alt.fan.furry and fanzine Web rings for contributions on a lingerie theme for the fanzine under the name *Dainties: Serving Your Clinical Need for Furrys with a Low Clothing Quotient*. Said Silvermane:

> It would be nice to think of *Dainties* as being a mix of
> the Furry Catwalk, like a mail-order lingerie catalogue,
> or furs wearing something special for their mate and
> family home photographs, where the subject isn't
> deliberately posing but is just caught on camera while

relaxing around the house. Already wearing a coat of fur, our furry friends are unlikely to wear more than necessary in the privacy of their own homes.[68]

The intent of the fanzine was made clear in the submission's guidelines, which stipulated that the content would include stories of a "PG-13" rating, but with no explicit nudity, and "casual, candid or cute" poses. Although there were a few that cynically derided the project as just another mature-themed fanzine, the premise did interest plenty of artists for the first issue. It was printed with help from Seattle publisher Jarlidium Press in October 1999 in time for Conifur Northwest.[69] The final issue featured 45 pages of black & white artwork, as well as two colour pages for the front and back covers, from 21 artists. including Mayfurr and Foxy.

Dainties cover by Shelley Pleger

As the first issue was being sold at Conifur Northwest, Silvermane was even then preparing contributions for a second issue.[70] By the following summer, he confirmed that he had gotten feedback from one of the distributors saying there was plenty of demand for a second issue, although contributions were lacking despite an open deadline.

This all changed by October 2000, when Silvermane announced a rapid rise in contributions from 21 artists, with a further four or more stating they had pieces in the works.[71] Although he now intended everything to be done by the end of the month so it could be prepared in time for Further Confusion in February 2001, technical issues forced the project to be delayed, so it was not released until before Anthrocon in June.[72] *The Dainties Second Collection* was 58 pages in length and contained work from 26 artists in total, four of which were in colour.

Dainties Second Collection was the last of the short-lived series; Silvermane saw no need to work on future issues and ended his fanzine project.

LAZY FOX STUDIOS

Furry Furry and *Dainties* were not Foxy's first contributions to fanzines. Even in 1993, the then-18-year-old aspiring artist had submitted numerous drawings to fanzines throughout the year. After a lucky break with *Yarf!* magazine, she quickly set up a publishing house under the name Lazy Fox Studios with her brother, Prask (Sean Charlesworth), all whilst studying at university.[73]

Setting ambitions high, Foxy and Prask started work producing their first fanzine, enlisting the help of SmackJackal (Sean Wally), Ed Zolna, and fellow student Aspirin (Adam Moss) to produce a fanzine with art, stories, poems, reviews, and more, although the student-driven nature of production did not make things easy.

"Publishing was an interesting challenge!" Foxy explained. "Aspirin's university (University of Essex, Colchester) had a print shop that worked with external clients, too, and we put the idea of publishing a fanzine to the print shop there, which they were fine with. Nothing was digital, we were cutting and pasting art onto pages back at the start! I had access to a program called Impressions, on the RiscPC, which was like a Word clone, and I was able to do some layout for pages with that; I'd then print everything out hard copy and hand them 64 pages of material ready to go."

AnthropoMORPHINE #1 *Cover by Foxy*

The fanzine would be given the name *AnthropoMORPHINE*, and its first issue was published in December 1993 as a 38-page, black-and-white fanzine in time for sale at ConFurence V, which was at its new venue, the Airporter Garden Hotel in Irvine, California. Luck was on the new fanzine's side: the convention had a surprisingly high turnout with over six hundred attendees. The resulting high sale volumes were enough incentive to publish reprints and new issues.

Lazy Fox Studios produced new issues of *AnthropoMORPHINE* using the same production method. The second issue grew to 54 pages, and subsequent issues published at a full 64 pages. Issues were thereafter published twice a year (winter and summer) and sold through Ed Zolna's distribution company, Mailbox Books, and at ConFurence with an initial 50 print run.

This ultimately cemented it as the first successful fanzine to come out of the United Kingdom, attracting plenty of big-name artists from the USA to contribute, including XianJaguar, Terrie Smith, Michelle Knight, Flinthoof, and Tygger, as well as some regulars from the Yateley housecon scene like Mayfurr and Simon Barber.

They also produced special fanzines, including a vulpine-themed trilogy called *Foxes Are Neat,* between 1994 and 1997, as well as a special 36-paged one-off in 1997 called *Furrabian Nights,* using this same non-digital approach. In fact, the only fanzines in which production diverted were the two issues of the mature, equine-themed *Hot to Trot* in 1995, which Foxy edited and which was then published by American publisher UniGraphx, and *Fire & Fur,* an APA that was based around a Western-themed comic series produced by Foxy in *AnthropoMORPHINE* called "The Wildside," which had a lower budget as Foxy explained:

> *Fire & Fur* was printed at whatever printers I could find at the time; it was an APAzine, which is to say, it wasn't made publicly available, copies went to the membership, and we discussed each other's art. I printed at the lowest cost I could while still keeping it a decent quality!

Meanwhile, in 1998, Foxy attended Leicester University and got connected to the anime fans at a society known as the Leicester Anime & Manga club (or LANMA for short). Now experienced with art and fanzines, she published the club's official fanzine titled *Animosity* under a new label, Studio Kitsune.

Studio Kitsune continued publishing manga fanzines, and in 2001, Foxy joined up with several other British manga artists to form Sweatdrop Studios. None of this had an impact on Lazy Fox's production of furry fanzines, but unfortunately business ashore would.

According to Fred Patten in his Dogpatch Press article "History of Furry Publishing," Ed Zolna retired from fanzines by selling Mailbox Books and its assets, most going to Limelight Publishing Company in the Summer of 1997.[74] Limelight was primarily interested in selling to the anime fandom, which meant many fanzines had lost their primary distributor to the American market.

While Lazy Fox Studios was not deeply impacted, they found their furry fanzine production less and less viable, and so they made their tenth issue in March 1999 with the intent that it would be not only their biggest (being 80 pages and covering both front and back in full colour for the first time). According to a statement printed in the issue, however, it was potentially the last:

> Lazy Fox Studios have seen fan support for our 'zines steadily decreasing (in fact, to about 1/10th of the *Foxes Are Neat* #1 days). A lot of time, hard work and effort goes into putting a fanzine together, and it's such a shame that more folks out there can't appreciate that.[75]

Fortunately, Mailbox Books returned to its furry publishing roots when the company was resold to Sean Rabbitt in April 1999. Sean, and later his partner, Andrew, still run the business to this day as a distributor and publisher, although a copyright dispute with the educational book publisher The Mailbox would force them to rename it Rabbit Valley Comics in October 2001.

As a result, Lazy Fox Studios returned to publishing *AnthropoMORPHINE* in 2000, releasing Issue 11 in time for Anthrocon as its new convention of choice. Publications would no longer be as frequent, though, and Issue 12 did not come out until the summer of 2001. Four more years passed before Issue 13 came out for Anthrocon 2005. It was distributed by Rabbit Valley Comics and Ed Zolna, who returned from retirement to set up a new distributor called Second Ed in 2003.

AnthropoMORPHINE #14 *by XianJaguar*

Issue 14 came out in May 2010, featuring a full front and back cover in colour for a second time. This would also be the final furry publication by Foxy in the United Kingdom, as she moved to Connecticut to work and live full-time with her partner in 2014. Lazy Fox Studios and Studio Kitsune continued releasing comics and fanzines, including a fox-themed comic titled *Voop* in 2017, as well as an anime slice-of-life comic and an adult-themed colouring book in 2020.

UNITED PUBLICATIONS

No chapter about the small world of British furry fanzines and comics would be complete without talking about one more big name in furry publishing: Martin Dudman. Dudman joined the fandom in the early 1990s through a local roleplaying club, enjoying games that featured furry characters like Traveller, Justifiers, and Other Suns, as well as following furry characters from Commodore computer games and the animation of Eric Schwartz.

He saw a rising demand from other British furry fans at the Yateley Housecon and alt.fan.furry for furry publications in America. As such, he set up an import mail-order business from his home under the name of United Publications in 1993, and his partner John Tatman joined him soon afterwards.

The new business was able to negotiate with a few publishers to sell comics and artwork directly within the United Kingdom as well as around Europe. Some early works included the American fanzine *American Journal of Anthropomorphics*,[76] as well as comics such as *Albedo* and *Furrlough*.

Within less than a year, however, United Publications begn creating original work. Wanting to promote itself and highlight talented artists, the companhy produced a 28-page newsletter. Edited by Dudman, the first issue of *Fur Scene: The Anthropomorphic Newsletter* was made available for purchase on 11 November 1994.[77]

The quarterly newsletter contained artwork, stories, news of conventions, fanzines, comics, and other happenings, as well as reviews. Although some issues had slight delays, the release schedule remained consistent, and by 1996, fans could pay for an annual subscription.[78] Several people from the fandom contributed to the fanzine over the years, including the regular active contributors like Simon Barber and artist Terrie Smith, as well as Ian Curtis, who wrote a multipart essay on the history of furry books.

Fur Scene #1. *Artwork by Terrie Smith.*

Meanwhile, the business itself expanded further. The official website launched in January 1997, and the company extended its catalogue to include physical artwork prints and cold-cast models of furry characters. It also increased its library beyond furry-related media to manga and anime, including publishers such as Dark Horse and Antarctic Press.[79]

The eleventh issue of *Fur Scene* had a significant five-month delay, partially due to a new project. United Publications partnered with Limelight Publishing in February 1998 to release the first issue of its own comic book series, *Wild Side*.[80] Although the premiere issue featured a manga-style comic written by Pauli Kidd and front cover from manga artist TAB, this was primarily a British furry comic book.

Fur Scene would be discontinued that same month, and with the first *Wild Side* issue being a commercial success, this meant it would continue as a quarterly publication. Each issue featured three-to-five PG-rated stories, at least two of which were ongoing.

Terrie Smith provided art once more, this time for a sci-fi buddy cop series called "Lark & Key," which was written by one of her frequent collaborators and prolific comic creator, Mark Bernard. Wiltshire-based comic book and songwriter Talis Kimberly wrote her own comic with artist David Morris called "Zen Zebras," another sci-fi following the adventures of a touring musical group. Kidd also added numerous stories for the comics, most notably one about the fantasy world of "Third Eye" with artist Freddy Anderson.

After six issues, United Publications announced that *Wild Side* would go on a small hiatus to prepare to make it a larger and higher-quality magazine, starting in July 1999.[81] It returned in June 2000, this time promising itself to be an annual publication. While *Wild Side*, Volume 2, featured a continuation of "Lark & Key," and it was now primarily an adults-only publication, including stories such as "Fangs of Breastula" and "Tank Vixens: Flicks," both written by Kidd.[82] The struggle to find regular con-

Cover of Wild Side *Issue #5 by Shane Fisher.*

tributors meant there were no more issues released from that point onward.

United Publications did not give up on publishing, however. They saw how furry writers were struggling with selling their work to mainstream publishers, one of whom was Pauli Kidd, whom they approached.

Kidd was an experienced author. Her oeuvre at the time included a renaissance-era series called *Mus of Kerbridge*, which was printed in *Rowrbrazzle* before it eventually got compiled and published by TSR Books in 1995. After that, an American furry book publisher called Vision Books published another of Kidd's previously unsold fantasy stories titled *A Whisper of Wings* in October 1999.

Next, Kidd and United Publications reached an agreement to publish another *Rowrbrazzle*-serialised story that was based on "The Arabian Knights," *Fangs of K'aath*, in April 2000. Unlike his previously published books, which were paperbacks with illustrations by Terrie Smith, this was a hardback book with the cover and over 30 interior illustrations done by Monika Livingstone.

From this point onwards, publishing new works would begin to slow down, as Dudman and Tatman focused their business more on importing and selling manga and anime over furry content, including DVDs and CDs, and becoming officially incorporated in 2003. They released two 80-page volumes of stories from Brock Hoagland's award-winning series *Tales of Perrissa* in 2001 and 2004. This was followed in 2006 by two more books, Pauli Kidd's *Fangs of K'aath II: Guardians of Light* and a collection called *Tales of the Fur Side* by Vixxy Fox with art by Dark Natasha.

There is one more artist that United Publications works with to this day: Eric Schwartz. Along with being a recognised furry animator from the 1990s and early 2000s, Schwartz is best known for his *Sabrina Online* webcomic, a slice-of-life story about a young adult anthropomorphic skunk who works as a graphic designer and IT technician for an adult movie studio. The webcomic began in 1996 and was updated monthly until it officially ended in 2016, making it one of the longest-running webcomics not only in the furry fandom but in the history of webcomics.

Schwartz had been selling prints and cast models of his characters with United Publications since the mid-1990s, but beginning in 1998, United Publications began selling printed volumes of *Sabrina Online*, continually releasing them as collections of each year up until January 2012. This was then followed with an April 2012 release of *Sabrina Online: A Decade in Black and White*, a hardback trade of the first ten years of Sabrina, and then in June 2017 with *Sabrina Online: The Tail of Two Decades*, which collected the second ten years of the webcomic.

Eric Schwartz did not stop there. His follow-up, online, Patreon-funded comic, *Sabrina Online: Baby Steps*, was published in 2018, and his most recent publication is a collection of comics titled *Tales from Fur After Dark*, which is named after Schwartz's premium adult art archive.

Ultimately, fanzines and comics lost favour with audiences because of the improvements in computer technology and the world wide web. Thanks to improved internet communication, it became easier to share images and text online. Several furries were able to create their own websites in which they could share their own or commission fanart much quicker than ordering and waiting for a fanzine or traveling to someone's house to photocopy a friend's issue.

Some of these websites would get a good amount of attention from the fandom, such as Aspirin's Fox Box,[83] and others would expand to allow users to upload their own work such as the Velan Central Library, Yerf, and FurNation. Sharing drawings and stories when the internet was still relatively primitive was a key selling point for fanzines.

As a positive, the advent of online websites meant artists could share and deliver much more of their work to their eager fanbases, and it allowed comic artists and writers to thrive by publishing comics and artwork online.

While not the most dominant art form for furries to find themselves in, furry writing remains an active part of the fandom. United Publications furry publications might be superseded by their anime and manga imports, while several publishers still exist and regularly sell their books throughout Europe at the dealer dens of furry conventions.

Plus, thanks to crowdfunding, artists have been able to self-publish books of their own work, so the business of printed publishing remains alive and well.

CHATROOMS, EMAIL, AND THE FIRST FURMEETS

As the internet grew more advanced, so did methods of communication as the world started to adopt an era of online networking that would later be given the name Web 1.0. Internet Relay Chat (IRC), an internet protocol for easy transfer of text-based messages through clients and servers, originated in Finland, but it did not see a surge in use until the mid-1990s.

The first furry IRC network was established on 23 September 1995 and was called YiffNet. The name was taken from the onomatopoeic word "yiff" that is used as a happy greeting in the fictional fox language on FurryMUCK by Revar (aka Foxen or littlefox). Unfortunately, the adult role players on FurryMUCK co-opted "yiff" to replace their erotic slang term "yipp," forever tainting the word.[84] Unable to do anything about it, the YiffNet administrators were forced to keep the name of their network, much to their chagrin.

YiffNet housed the main fandom discussions in its channel #Furry, but it also allowed for the creation of channels specific to websites, subjects, and regions, which led to the creation of the #UK channel for British fans to talk to each other. In November 2001, allegedly after its main operator grew tired of maintaining the network, it unexpectedly shut down and wiped the YiffNet servers.

In response, two Germans and one American furry created a new IRC network under the name FurNet. Many of the original channels were restored, including #UK, and the network remains active to this day, allowing furries to chat with each other instantaneously, although this wasn't the only way communication between furries was more accessible.

Email became more efficient and commonplace by the 2000s, and the ability to send messages to large groups of people on specific subjects in a thread became more popular for discussions in electronic mailing lists. While mailing lists were initially used by academia, they thrived in fandoms.[85] Many regional and country-specific mailing lists appeared.

Some would be hosted by a bunch of the website and email hosting services of the time such as OneList and Yahoo, but thanks to the technically gifted members of the fandom, there were several furry-organised web-hosting services such as Catbox, Purrsia, Tigress, and Critter, the latter of which hosted the earliest United Kingdom–specific furry fandom mailing list on record, UKfur, created by Farthing W. Fox in June 1996.[86]

LIFESTYLERS

Furry lifestylers are a subset of furries who, unlike furry fans, have an interest in anthropomorphism based on identity and spirituality. This includes a belief that they are part animal.

Mailing lists also allowed for making groups for subsets within the furry fandom, as was the case for furry lifestylers. Although there was never a strict separation between furry fans and furry lifestylers, negative backlash on lifestyle-related posts on alt.fan.furry lead to the creation of alt.lifestyle.furry in 1996. At the same time, the British furry lifestylers also created their own dedicated mailing list called UKALF to provide for local discussions amongst lifestyler furries. The UKALF Community had its own gatherings, such as an Oxford meeting of seven furries running from 6 to 9 August 1998[87] and a slightly bigger Portsmouth gathering in February 1999. Some groups sought to engage communities that were in nature therianthropic, a belief that some humans are partly animal, such as Were and Otherkin. These included Eurohowl, which had three iterations, starting in March 1996, along with a one-off BritHowl in 2002, and Therians in May 2000.

MegaDog, Utlah, Dave Hughes, Little Dave, Sci, Polenth, Swampy, Old Lone Wolf, Starfury, and Chris Marmachut at EuroHowl in Exeter 1999

A REPLACEMENT FOR UKFURCON

For furry fans, however, a new gathering felt like it was needed after UKFurCon went into hiatus. The Yateley Housecons were not held frequently enough, and the only other gatherings were overseas.

Ia'Kat (Toby Williams) already had a small group of friends in the fandom whilst living in St. Albans and studying at Hertfordshire University, including Vexen Crabtree. The pair decided to try running a set of regular meets in London's Soho district, starting in March 1998. Unlike the previous housecons, these meets were single-day affairs, initially meeting in Soho Square before eventually settling on a pub as a regular venue. The pub chosen was the Intrepid Fox, located on Wardour Street in the Soho area.

Despite what you might initially think, The Intrepid Fox is actually named after Charles James Fox,[88] a prominent British politician from the 18th century.

Ia'Kat chose the venue less for its fitting name and more for its environment:

"I picked the pub as at the time lots of the furs were into alternative subcultures and it seemed somewhere that would be more accepting." Ia'Kat explained "The pub was never actually hired for the events, we just turned up *en masse* and took it over."

In April 1999, Vexen Crabtree and Ia'Kat decided to set up a mailing list under the name LondonFurs. As Ia'Kat explained in an alt.fan. furry post announcing the new mailing list:

> This is aimed at furs who live in London (London, UK that is) and surrounding counties and is designed to help create a sense of community among London furs through discussing and organising informal meets etc and talking about the local furry scene with no boundaries between furry fandom and life styling.
>
> The aim is also to take posts centred around London off other mailing lists so as not to bore furs in other parts of the UK who can't easily get to the city.[89]

Earliest photo of a LondonFurs meet from 3 July 1999. From left to right: Torne, Hawx, Matt Squirrel, Darkclaw, Ruin (photo by Yarwick).

The mailing list was shared as accepting of both fans and lifestylers, reducing the requirements of entry and leading to the group growing in members "much beyond its initial expectations." While the mailing list was used for the sporadic housecons and get-togethers in the London area, the main purpose of this new group was to establish regular meet-ups, which were scheduled tri-weekly.[90]

The LondonFurs group advertised to both furry fans and lifesty-lers on the main avenues in the online furry space at the time, but given that it is more local and intended to be more accepting, Ia'Kat also ad-vertised directly to Londoners. He made paper flyers and left them in shops, pubs, and clubs that appealed to alternative subcultures, stating that the meets were "for fans of anthropomorphic art, weres, clubbers, lifestylers, costumers, writers etc"[91] throughout London. Unfortunately, the flyers seemingly no longer exist, Ia'Kat no longer has any copies of them, but he does recall them being most effective at attracting people to the meets.

> Some of the folk who turned up came to furry
> through this route without even being aware other furs
> existed! Hence, we had a very varied range of people
> for the first few years, we had clubbers who just liked
> dressing up, sci-fi authors who wrote about animal
> characters, furry artists, and just people who liked
> anything new that seemed a bit weird.[91]

The diversity of attendees meant a whole range of activities from shopping, sharing artwork, watching videos, and messing around on computers to trips to comic stores, toy shops like Hamleys, and night-clubs in the evenings. The meets in these early days would have on average around twenty attendees, but they exceeded forty on occasions. This increase in size meant that the venue had to change several times in the space of two years.

Later we moved to The Devonshire Arms in Camden Town, then a goth pub until there was so many of us, we got on people's nerves a little, as it isn't a big pub. After that I decided we needed our own event space so hired a function room above The Jorene Celeste in Kentish Town, convenient for Thameslink as I lived in St Albans at the time, they also did Thai Curry downstairs, quite a thing in 1999 London in a pub![91]

Speaking of costumers, one of the other activities the LondonFurs did was an organised walk from the pub to either a city square or a park. It was this activity that showcased costumers at their prime. They dressed up as their animal of choice and interacted with the public in an open space, pretending to be said animal for fun. As costumes were the most attention-grabbing aspect of the LondonFurs meet, most surviving photos from those days feature at least one furry in costume.

There were different kinds of costumes furries would use to pretend to be animals. The most popular way nowadays—the "fursuit"—boasted a full- or partial-body mascot-style costume made of faux fur and foam.

Historically, fursuits in the United States existed as far back as 1987, although they were called many names, until 1993 when one American costumer, Robert King, created the FURSUIT mailing list, its name being a play on the words fur and pursuit.[92]

The visual aesthetic of fursuits and the act of performing in fursuits known as "fursuiting" were influenced by sports and theme park mascots. Inspiration came from the character performers at Disneyland, who portrayed the animal characters such as Mickey Mouse, Donald Duck, Goofy, and the cast of Winnie the Pooh.

In fact, one of the men often credited as the inventor of fursuits, Robert Hill (195?–2018), had an early professional career as a character performer at Disneyland.[93] The fursuits he made from 1987 to 1997 used

LondonFurs group on 13 May 2000 at St James Park (photo by Yarwick)

the same process as the Disney company: the head was made from fiberglass out of a clay mould, and faux fur covered everything else.

Although the quality of Hill's fursuits like Annabelle the Bear and Hilda the Bamboid were incredibly professional for the late-1980s, the production

> Anabelle the Bear, a fursuit created by Robert Hill and introduced at the 1987 San Diego Comic-Con, is the earliest known fursuit on record. There are a few claims of fursuits appearing in 1986, but with no documented proof.

process was too high-skilled and expensive for most fans. Instead, the vast majority of fursuits of the time wee made using a process common with sports mascots and influenced by another recognised fursuit pioneer, Shawn Keller. Keller was a professional animator who cosplayed as animal characters at conventions with costumes made using faux fur and carved foam from 1990–2005.

Fursuits grew in popularity in America throughout the 1990s, with event panels, shows, and parades dedicated to them. However, the expense of buying a costume and the lack of skilled fursuit makers made them an uncommon aspect of the fandom compared to illustrators and writers. During the entire decade, the number of fursuiters in any American furry gathering never exceeded 5% of total attendees.

While British furries were keenly aware of fursuits from the odd photo or visit to America, fursuits in the United Kingdom were an incredibly rare luxury items that very few could afford. During the housecon era, it was lucky if even one person to bring a fursuit. For instance, Porsupah owned a red panda fursuit that, according to Ian Stradling, he once wore during a Yateley Housecon to entertain shoppers during a visit to the local supermarket.

> Although his first documented fursuit was Charlie B. Barken from *All Dogs Go to Heaven*, performed at San Diego Comic-Con in 1990, Fred Patten claimed Shawn Keller had made suits during the 1980s alongside Robert Hill.

However, Porsupah got his fursuit at an American convention in 1993.[94] which was a method that was financially out of reach for most British furries. Even buying a generic animal costume was too expensive,[95] as most British furries at the time were either students or unemployed. There were also no skilled fursuit makers, and Britain didn't have access to convention workshops and panels like their American counterparts, so for any furry who wanted to fursuit usually rented a generic animal costume for the day.[96] There were a few that attempted to make their own, but the results have been described as any-where between mediocre and hideous by the furries who witnessed such creations to those early meets.

Because of the difficulty in creating or obtaining fursuits, the more popular kind of costuming for LondonFurs involved bodypaint and prosthetics. Instead of furries looking like giant fluffy cartoon characters that could entertain a football match, they looked like Fish the Cat, a white tiger made from paint, hair dye, latex claws, elf-ears, fangs, contact lenses, and cheap felt and fun fur,[97] something one might see performing in musical theatre.

Although not every furry put in that much effort, plenty had a friend apply bodypaint to them, with a few others adding simple tails and fake teeth for additional affect. In fact, the official LondonFurs website had an entire page dedicated to body painting and costume prosthetics, stating that it "seems to have become popular amongst the LondonFurs community as opposed to fursuits of the mascot variety."[98]

Along with being affordable, it was also much more accessible, thanks to London having several make-up and costume suppliers in the West End. Marcony (Donald Thompson) was one of several costume furries who regularly attended while wearing full body paint and using fangs inspired by Fish the Cat. He was also into the Goth scene and be-lieved that their inclusion contributed to the bodypainting trend:

> The fur scene included a lot of Goths, and it's not just
> our eye liner game that's on point. With others like
> Ruin and Kitten in on the makeup scene, we just plain
> outclassed the available fursuits, and so it was us who
> people took as role models.[99]

Ia'Kat also believed that the trend had to do with the inclusion of lifestylers and spiritualists, creating a community within the furry fandom with a more liberal definition of what being furry is about, particularly when it came to individual characters:

"There was less of a concept of a 'fursona' as it is understood today; it was less about playing a character and more about accentuating the features of the animal we felt we were. For most of us not in a literal 'were' sense, although there were a few of those, too. The idea of having multiple 'fursonas' and even buying and selling them would've seemed very strange!"

Both Ia'Kat and Marcony also agreed that London's clubbing scene had a role in making it the trend in LondonFurs. As Ia'Kat explained, "Some of us liked going clubbing in some of the stranger scenes in Lon-don; at that time there was a lot of dressing up. A gaggle of folk turning up to a Goth club in tiger stripes, ears and tails was just a lot of fun, punk, and dare I say ... sexy." Marcony, on the other hand, saw bodypaint and prosthetics from a slightly more practical point of view, saying "it pays to wear something that you won't melt in, and we could take being party animals to another planet all together."

With the meets being tri-weekly, this meant meets close to certain holidays could be a more special. For instance, they also held a special event in December in time for Christmas. Marcony held a house meet in 1998 at his home in Hatfield, where 15 furries watched videos, ate food, and slept over. This then progressed to a Christmas dinner the following year at the Chiswick Mongolian Barbecue, which Marcony paid for out of pocket to serve 60 furries.

After Marcony backed out, another LondonFur by the name of Clawz took over the following year, booking the Mongolian Barbecue, where the number of participants were said to have been even larger.

Since then, the LondonFurs have decided to make it a tradition to arrange a large, booked event for the final meet of each year. Called the LondonFur Christmas Dinner or Christmas Banquet, it was usually held at a restaurant in Chinatown or the Piccadilly Circus area, such as the New World Chinese in 2002.

LondonFurs and their meetups were not exclusive to Londoners, as the group would eventually boast having over a hundred members and attendees from around the United Kingdom and even mainland Europe.[100] However, not every furry was willing to travel into London on a regular basis, so this created a demand for furmeets outside London.

FURMEETS ACROSS THE COUNTRY

S maller groups started hosting one-off weekend furmeets in places like Southend-on-Sea and Leamington Spa, where ten to twenty furs would watch TV shows, have food and drinks, wander around the local area, and get into animal-like antics. A few London furries—and, in one case, an American furry—were willing to travel to these tiny gatherings.

However, there were individuals who successfully created their own furry groups for furries in their own regions outside of London. The first was SlyCat, a furry from Hampshire. He discovered the furry fandom in 1997 but met other furries in real life at a LondonFur meet on 4 September 1999. He later established the HantsFurs on 1 March 2000.[101]

The HantsFurs organised furmeets on a semi-regular basis, primarily in Southampton and sometimes in Portsmouth. These meets were rather small at around ten to fifteen people. The typical itinerary included

Anthropuppy, TK Tiger, Spots the Dalmation, and SouthPaw, headless standing in the cricket ground at Balmer Lawn Hotel. Image dated 24th June 2001 (photo courtesy Thomas King).

grabbing something to eat and drink at pubs like The Hobbit or The Dungeon and an inevitable visit to nerdy places like Forbidden Planet. Unfortunately, after the deletion of the mailing list in 2012, not much documentation of the early days of the HantsFurs remains today. While there are photos from a HantsFurs photoshoot at the Balmer Lawn Hotel from 24 June 2001,[102] there is no source or recollection for when the first furmeets took place in the region.

Another group called the North West Furs was formed in the same year and ran the first confirmed furmeet outside of London in the city of Chester on 15 April 2000. According to the meet report, the gathering was small at nine people, including Krll, Balooo, Crimson, and Ssthisto. There was no planned venue, but the group did have lunch at a Pizza Hut, followed by bowling and Laser Quest.[103] The North West Furs later ran meets in Chester until the group was changed, and a mailing list was set up by Balooo in August of the same year called NorthernFurs.[104]

The earliest furmeet organised under the new group took place in Manchester on 26 August. On 5 December—by which that time there was another meet in Manchester and one in Liverpool—the founder and moderator of the mailing list, Cabbit (Anthony Stevens), posted a new plan after talking with several furs in the chat:

> So, starting from the last weekend in January, there shall be a meet every month (this is so that if certain people can't attend, they can always go to the next one, not too far away). The meets shall always be held on the last weekend of every month.
>
> The first meet will be in Manchester with the Manchie furs organising things to do, then in February, the meet is going to be in Chester with Balooo organising things to do, then in March, Liverpool, with the scouse-furs sorting things out and then it's back to Manchester.
>
> So, the first meet will be Saturday 27th January, details coming nearer the time on where to meet up (Maybe the Arndale, maybe Victoria Station....)[105]

Although the meets on 27 January and 17 February went well, the plans for Liverpool did not go through, which meant resorting to Chester as a backup location. Not being a fan of Chester as a location, a member by the name FoxCub updated the website with a provisional plan to hold the meet in York instead. With other furries liking the idea, and another moderator named Avon DeRussate offering to scout the city ahead of time, York received the highest votes to be the same location as the March meet.

Avon DeRussette did the scouting once again for the NorthernFurs in April (this time for a furmeet in Leeds, which he would eventually run himself), and when the March poll recognised Sheffield as another popular contender for a meet location, it was then added for May. Manchester finally got to have a furmeet again in June, while Liverpool would not have its meet until August.

Once July rolled around, arguments started brewing over what the next location would be, with some complaining about traveling distances and overall fairness. The discourse culminated in a major update to the NorthernFurs management, which kept Cabbit and Avon as moderators but also included FurbleFox (Michael Francis) and two others as admins of the website. Another effect was the establishment of a strict monthly location rota with the order as followed: Chester, York, Liverpool, Leeds, Manchester, and Sheffield.

As there was already a specially arranged Sheffield furmeet in November, the rotation did not go into full effect until the start of 2002. Each city had two meets running a year, each with a designated set of organisers, While the group had an administrator for the mailing list, meet locations, and the website.[106]

Although there was some resistance to the idea of a rotational meet system, Cabbit remained adamant on the system as it was intended to help the regional community:

> Basically, for those who weren't around when I conceived the list and rota system, it was set up for the benefit of NorthernFurs. Basically, up North, furs are more spread out than they are down South, so the rota was made in order for furs to occasionally save lots of money in travel costs when a meet was [close to or in] their city....
>
> What I'm trying to say is that the rota was set up for a reason, changing it about willy-nilly is unfair to the furs who were just about to save money, as it was their turn.[107]

Once the meet rotations went into full motion, more furries joined and attended the meets. Unlike the LondonFurs, the NorthernFurs comprised a majority of furry fans, while lifestylers and others were welcomed, but there was a significant contrast between the dark and gothic

Photo from a NorthernFurs meet in February 2002. Taken at Liverpool Lime Street Station by Darkhorse Winterwolf.

bars for the furries in London compared to the bright and mainstream pubs the NorthernFurs attended.

Fursuits were, of course, welcome, although this time the mascot variety was the more preferred costumes. A Sheffield Furmeet Report posted on the NorthernFurs mailing list in April 2001 about a moment when Kuvo brought his leopard mascot costume, and he wore it around the pub, giving the landlady a shock as a result.[108]

NorthernFurs thus ended up becoming the largest regional group outside of London, eventually boasting over 190 members registered on their official website, and its mailing list peaked at over 270.

While most locations had reasonable attendance in the double digits, some locations attracted more furries than others. As furmeets were more loosely organised affairs than housecons, attendance records were not kept and are therefore practically nonexistent today. However, various accounts consistently credited Manchester and Sheffield as being the two most popular places for NorthernFurs, the official website claiming that both enjoyed over a hundred attendees during their peak.

London and the north of England found a bridge when Lone Wolf, a Were from Coventry, established the MidFurs mailing list in January 2001 with the expressed intent of proposing and organising furry meets and social events in the area.[109]

Lone Wolf organised the first meet in Birmingham on 10 March that year, and they gathered at the Newt and Cucumber Pub.[110] From then on, fellow members Xanni and semaJ held meets on a semiregular basis. Then, in February 2003, the group decided to plan a regular furmeet schedule after seeing the success of the London and Northern furmeets.

Although Lyken Blue Paws (Chris Palin) proposed to hold the regular furmeets in Birmingham, and Michelle D'Israeli suggested doing meet rotations like the NorthernFurs,[111] the group ultimately decided to vote on locations for each month.

It wouldn't be until Makenshi Fox and Fated Snowfox took over organisational duties that MidFurs would establish their own meet rotational format in 2004, with meets in Birmingham, Leicester, and Nottingham.

Because of they were still smaller than their London and Northern counterparts, there was never a fixed venue for each city, but the most popular ones in the early days were the Pit & Pendulum in Nottingham, The Corn Exchange in Leicester, and the Old Sly Fox in Birmingham. There were also one-off meets in other cities like Derby, Milton Keynes, and Lincoln for special occasions.

> Unlike with LondonFurs, the Old Sly Fox was indeed named after the cunning creature!

The MidFurs also introduced Coffee Meets in Birmingham in 2004. Unlike the weekend Birmingham meets, these were very casual weekday meetings at a café with a short walk around the city and seldom any plans for a big event.

As more British furries took notice of mailing lists in these regional areas, a demand grew for mailing lists targeted towards their own regions as well. SouthFurs, for example, was set up for furries to meet up in the Bristol and Bath areas. Hence, they sometimes referred to themselves as SouthWestFurs to differentiate themselves from the HantsFur group.

Starlight (Christopher Muir), a 17-year-old furry writer from Wallsend, joined the NorthernFurs in March and managed to attend a few meets, although the distance and travel expenses made it difficult. He was also aware of a few other furries that lived in the counties of Tyne, Durham, Middlesbrough, and Cleveland. In October 2001, he created a website and mailing list for furries in the Northeast of England under the creative name of Newcastle upOn Tyne anthroZ, or *NOTz* for short. (According to Starlight, NUTz was not catchy enough.[112])

Outside of England, there was a mailing list group for Welsh Furries, and even Scotland had ScotBeasts and ScotFurs, with a general Scottish themed furry mailing list called ScotchFurs. ScotFurs was set up in December 2000. They had their own meet rota for meets in Glasgow, Aberdeen, and Edinburgh, while ScotBeasts was a Therian & Furry group that ran meets in Glasgow from 2004 to 2006.

By the end of 2006, there were regional furry groups for the entirety of the United Kingdom, from Scotland to Hampshire, Wales to Essex and even Northern Ireland.[113]

Most regional groups also had websites set up and maintained by local members of the community to act as an introductory point for

This map shows how the furry regional groups were organized in the United Kingdom in 2006.

ScotFurs

NoTzFurs

N.I.Furs

NorthernFurs

MidFurs

WelshFurs

CambridgeFurs

LondonFurs

WestcountryFurs   HantsFurs

newcomers, to understand what the furry fandom is, and for general information about planned meets. LondonFurs' early website was set up by Makali (Matt Robinson), allowing members of the group to register with a user account and receive relevant news regarding the meet, as well as providing general information.

UKFUR.NET

In September 2002, Makali decided to set up a new website that was general enough for the whole of the United Kingdom. Simply named UKfur.net (later UKfur.org) it allowed users to create accounts, write articles, promote furmeets, and form groups. Registered members of the LondonFurs website had their profiles transferred over, giving the new website an established community.[114] There were also web services provided for users to host mailing lists and send webmail directly to other members for a £5/month fee.

The UKFur forums allowed a more open access to discussion, since visitors did not have to join or register to read posts, while also allowing more specialised and local discussions by categorising topics into subforums. Even in the first year of the forum, the website had just over a hundred registered users, who could go to subforums for general discussions within the United Kingdom, as well as for LondonFurs, NorthernFurs, ScotFurs, and MidFurs.[115]

As the years went on, the userbase increased, as did the number of topics and subforums. While some regions maintained their own communities like the SouthFurs, others would more often use UKFur as a central hub for discussions and meet organising. Other online spaces were also increasingly accessed, such as LiveJournal for blogs and Furmeets.co.uk, as more dedicated places to find local furmeets.[116]

Some groups abandoned mailing lists entirely due to the convenience of having an accessible, central website for the local furry community. Unfortunately, most of these would be deleted entirely as they were deemed unnecessary. Consequently, a lot of early discussions have been lost to time, and whatever ones remained were left dormant.

Critter.net, the largest host of British furry content including the UKFur Mailing List, was victim to a "catastrophic failure" in 2014, resulting in the complete loss of the server's data and backups.[117] In 2019, Yahoo announced that at the end of the year it would wipe all data from their Yahoo Groups service, which was the most popular mainstream mailing list service for the furry fandom, and remove the service entirely in 2020.

FURMEETS OF TODAY

As the 2000s progressed, furmeets started to change as the tradition of having furmeet locations on rotation fell out of favour.

The NorthernFurs introduced "mini meets" in certain cities by late 2006. Unlike the traditional, larger, bi-annual NorthernFurs meets, these were intended to be smaller, monthly meets for local attendees. These mini-meets proved popular, with Manchester, Sheffield, York, Liverpool, and Leeds eventually deciding to branch-off from NorthernFurs in 2012 and branding themselves as MancFurs, SheffieldFurs, YorkFurs, Scouse-Furs, and LeedsFurs.

But warning signs of the end of NorthernFurs had started to show by 2011. The original NorthernFur meets in Chester had waned in popularity to the point that the January 2011 meet only had three people. Despite attempts to drum up support for the next Chester meet in July 2011, a lack of interest resulted in those meets being cancelled entirely.

Although WikiFur claims that NorthernFurs officially disbanded in early 2013, Web archives show that the NorthernFurs group remained active for the rest of the year, hosting the Great Northern Fur meet in Manchester in May and November of that year. The York meets also continued to run on their traditional main meets at the end of the months of February and August, as opposed to the mini-meets, although they were run by the YorkFurs organisers as opposed to NorthernFurs.

By 2014, all online presence of the NorthernFurs would be removed with exception of the website. The group remained online to provide basic information about the furry fandom as well as the most recent dates for meets in the northern part of the country. All of this was run by the local groups independently of the NorthernFurs brand. The Great Northern Fur Meets changed to the MancFurs Summer and Winter Parties, which took place two weeks after the MancFur meets in June and November each year.

After the NOTz group stopped running furmeets soon after Starlight stepped down in 2003, and activity died down in 2005, Middlesbrough furry Packwolf Lupestripe resurrected them under the TyneFurs name in December 2007, with updates posted on the NorthernFurs website.[118] Lupestripe ran the TyneFurs until he left the Newcastle region in

2011. This resulted in a decline of activity until the NewcastleFurs rebooted the meets in 2012.

MidFurs attendance dwindled and meets became less frequent starting around 2009 after Fated Snowfox stepped down, leading furries in the local areas to consider running their own meets. This led to new monthly furmeets in cities such as Birmingham, Lincoln, and Nottingham. Even the small town of Stafford held their own monthly meets around this time, with its furry community centered on its former Film & Technology campus of Staffordshire University.

This restructuring of the furmeet groups encouraged individual furries to arrange smaller furmeets in new and unexpected places. The HantsFurs area, for example, started having meets in Basingstoke and Bournemouth around this time, and after many years of only running furmeets in Cardiff, WelshFurs in the north started running meets in Llandudno in 2013.

Modern furmeets often share a similar format: they usually meeting on a Saturday; the main venue is a bar or pub, so those in attendance can get food, drinks, socialise, and share art. The main event will usually be a fursuit walk, with an organised route established to take the fursuiters around a part of the city that will allow as much opportunity as possible to interact with the public and get plenty of photos, including a group photo, with as many fursuiters as possible.

That is not to say that all furmeets have the same design. The current Sheffield Furmeets keep the original NorthernFur style meets alive by running on both Saturday and Sunday and have a slightly more detailed schedule that includes a pub quiz and raffle and trips to lively parts of the city such as Graves Park or Extra Life Gaming Lounge.

LincolnFurs go with a more diverse approach to meets, opting to have a different main activity for each month, whether it be a cinema, bowling, picnic, BBQ, festivals, museums, or just a fursuit friendly meet. There are also more niche furmeets, such as BarkadeFurs, which is a day for furries to enjoy a plethora of arcade games from the Heart of Gaming venue in Croydon.

LondonFurs remains the oldest continuously running furmeet in the United Kingdom, and the only furry regional group to remain in original form. While there have been individuals taking it upon themselves to run meets in the outer London area such as Surrey, Hertfordshire, and Kent, the LondonFurs' tri-weekly meet in the London city centre is still the largest and most common meetup group for the entirety of London.

FURMEET ORGANISATION

By 2008, the size of LondonFurs, as well as their placement in the capital city, required a committee to keep it organised. This led to the formation of LondonFurs Management Ltd. in 2012.[119] It is often the norm for furmeets to have a small group of individuals responsible for organizing the meets. They arrange a venue, handle attendees and fursuiters, and moderate the community during the event and online, whether it be social media, the UKFur forums, or in chat groups on the mobile, instant-messaging application Telegram.

There is no single entity in charge of running furmeets nationwide, but the managers of large furmeets do communicate with each other regarding serious incidents or individuals of concern.

On Saturday, 25 July 2009, the LondonFurs celebrated ten years of meets by extending their usual furmeet at The Saint with a party at Jamie's Bar on Fleet Place.[120] Highlights were recorded by organiser committee member Miyabi in an impressive quality for the time.[121] Although there was no official 20th anniversary celebration in 2019, the LondonFurs ran their 300th meet on 3 November 2018. LondonFurs Management Chairman Ani Boxer reflected on his experiences as being both an attendee and an organiser of the group:

> It's amazing that an off the cuff meet up of four
> friends became such a large part of people's lives…
>
> Joining the committee gave me an insight into the
> stress and commitment it took to put these events on.
> I saw the best and worst of these moments including
> committee members leaving due to pressures of want-
> ing nothing but the best for attendees. It's not always
> been easy; there have been plenty of times where it's
> been hard to keep motivated, but I always go back to
> where I was during that first meet, who I have met and
> who's lives I have been a part of since then![122]

Plenty of furries happily shared their memories of the first LondonFur meet they went to on social media in the lead-up to the day, often crediting the meets for introducing them to the fandom, making friends, and helping them on a more personal level. Some of them had been around since near the very beginning.

THE FURRY CONVENTIONS
THAT WEREN'T

At the end of the 1990s, the furry fandom was growing not just in the United Kingdom but across the world. No matter what kind of gathering furries had back home, many would go seek the biggest event of them all, the furry convention.

The first furry convention in history began because of science fiction conventions in California being tired of seeing more and more anime fans at their own spaces, and politely asking them to leave. Mark Merlino and Rod O'Riley responded with their own plans to run a convention that had plenty of space to share furry art, perform in their own fursuits, and hang out just with furries.

Deciding on the name ConFurence, they tested the waters with a prototype convention in 1989, advertising it in several fanzines and magazines, including the British Sci-Fi magazine *Starburst*.[123]

The advertisements attracted furries from around the United States as well as overseas, including a few from Australia and one from the United Kingdom. The success guaranteed that ConFurence would debut in 1989 as the premiere furry convention in the world. The first year was called ConFurence 0 because it was considered a trial run.

For its first four years, ConFurence was the *only* furry convention in the world, and it experienced exponential growth of attendees each year, peaking at roughly 1,250 attendees in 1998. More conventions sprang up across North America beginning in 1994. Although ConFurence started to decline in attendance numbers from 1999 to its eventual closure after 2003, there were now several big events for furries to go to, especially if you were living in North America.

These conventions had small international followings, but if you were unable to travel to North America, your options were limited. What options did exist were in no way comparable to American events in terms of size and scope.

In Vexen Crabtree's 1999 essay, "An Intimate Exploration of the Furry Fandom," he makes this point well known in his opening statement on conventions:

> There are now several other large furry cons in North
> America such as Further Confusion, Albany Anthro-
> con, and Feral—a sort of furry summer camp.
>
> Europe has less in the way of furry conventions, there
> is only one convention of any size known as Euro-
> Furence, which has previously been held in Germany
> and this year in Holland.[90]

A pedantic researcher with the advantage of up-to-date information can point out that Crabtree's statement was technically incorrect. For the European fandom, 1999 did see the beginnings of a smaller convention in Germany called Mephit Mini Con as well a party in Moscow that would eventually become Rusfurence, Russia's largest furry convention. Even Australia had an annual furmeet called Melbourne in December (MiDFur for short) that evolved into Australia's premiere furry convention.

But at the time, Eurofurence was the only full-scale furry convention in Europe, having surpassed a hundred attendees by 1999, making it larger than even a few of the furry conventions in the United States.

EuroFurence's early concept of running its convention in different European nations inspired the formation of other conventions and gatherings in the early to 2000s, such as the French furry convention FranFurence and Česfur in the Czech Republic to go along with the Russian and Australian conventions.

The closest thing the United Kingdom had to furry conventions was the housecons, and later the furmeets. Both the Yateley Housecon and UK Fur CON have been described as conventions on a few occasions, with the September 1995 Yateley Housecon supposedly being dubbed the "British Furry Convention." Stradling described UK Fur CON as "an annual furry convention someplace within Britain" on his list of UK furry cons. Foxy herself, though, has described the UK Fur Con as a joke idea, given it was nowhere near the size of traditional furry conventions like Eurofurence.

Furry conventions are much more organised than housecons and furmeets, with set registrations and schedules of organised events, as well as a dedicated venue. In contrast, housecons had common activities but no set schedule of events. Attendance was through private invitation, and the venue was someone's home. Large furmeets had established venues, but they differed from cons in that they were more frequent and casual. Also, they had no set schedule or events and attendance was open to anyone. LondonFurs have made it clear that they are not a con. As Ia'Kat described them, they are "more of a spontaneous gathering than a 'con' as such, the meets are a good way of meeting [lots] of UK furs at once, but then I would say that as I run them."[124]

The British furry population was safely in the hundreds by 2001 and was increasing thanks to the growth of furmeets and the fandom's online presence. Since not every fur could afford to travel to America or Germany for the con experience, there was a demand for one closer to home. All that was needed was for people to organise one and give it a name.

BRITFUR

The earliest known serious discussion of a potential furry convention within the United Kingdom was on 25 August 2002 in the alt.fan. furry group. A writer and long-time LondonFur known as ANTIcarrot announced he had set up a mailing list called UK_FUR_CON to enlist help in creating a furry convention in the United Kingdom,[125] although in his original post his initial intentions for the mailing list were to discuss the problems that face running a furry convention outside America:

> What I'm looking for is people who know what they're talking about (Susan Deer, Uncle Kage, Cheetah etc.), people who want to help, and anyone else in a similar situation who's trying to kickstart a con from nothing.

> And again, that's it. We've found a number of venues, but I gather that's only half the problem. And I'm hoping for some help with the other 50% so we don't have to go groping around in the dark too much.

Although discussions on the mailing list initially suggests having a furry track attached to an anime convention (like UK Fur CON's furry track concept with Shinnenkai), the mailing list members were already discussing the idea of going it alone à la Eurofurence.

Though many people in the group had a keen interest in having it named Furtannia, a name proposed by FurbleFox, participants at the first meeting voted in favour of going with the name BritFur, which was suggested by Ruin (Katie Funnell). The new furry convention was to take place in February 2005, with Peckforton Castle in Cheshire being the most popular choice of venue.[126]

ANTIcarrot was elected chairman, with Ruin as advertisements director, Marcony as event coordinator, Anthropuppy (Anthony Vauden) as treasurer, and UltraFox as secretary. Other members of the London-Fur community were also part of the organisers crew such as UltraViolet (Cassandra Gunn), BhavFox, and Camrath.[127] In October, the BritFur official website went live and laid out its intentions for accessibility for all of those within the fandom as an overall goal:

FURTANNIA

> Britfur is the first large-scale annual anthropomorphic convention ever held in the UK. Briftur intends to appeal to the widest possible constituency of Artists, Writers, Lifestylers, Spiritualists, Comic collectors, Anime collectors, Fur-suiters, costumers, and all other parts of the Furry Fandom.
>
> The first Britfur is scheduled to take place in the stunningly beautiful Peckforton Castle (a medieval-styled castle built in the mid-nineteenth century) in the last week of February 2005, after which it will become an annual event.
>
> Britfur's secondary aim is to bring down the costs of convention attendance for those living in the United Kingdom. This will be achieved through careful planning, fund raising events, and a financing scheme that will allow people to pay for attendance on a monthly basis, rather than all at once. Thus the real life fantasy of stunning location and lavish accommodation can be made affordable to the widest possible spread of fans.[128]

Over the course of the year, there were several art competitions, including one to see who would design the mascots Windsor the Lion and Piccadilly the Unicorn. This honor was awarded to Caribou (Sara Palmer). There were also artists vying for the privilege to create the convention T-shirt and calendar. Meanwhile, several ideas for events were considered, from workshops and talks to dances, dealer rooms, and game rooms.[129] There were even discussions over inviting the UK Wolves Conservation Trust, although arguments broke out when it was suggested that real-life wolves could be brought in.

Unfortunately, the Peckforton Castle raised its prices and refrained from telling the organisers for months, causing plans to fall through with the venue. The Loch Lomond Youth Hostel near Glasgow was chosen as the new location, with a venue in Brighton as an alternative, but neither seemed favourable.

The public was not informed about this, as Marcony and UltraViolet went silent and prevented anyone from accessing and updating the official website. By February 2004, the convention was officially placed on hold "until some positive interest would be shown,"[130] and by April there was no more online discussions. BritFur died before it got off the ground.

The struggle to find a venue appears to have been the official reason for BritFur's cancellation, as ANTIcarrot once stated in another mailing list in July 2004:

> One of the BIG stumbling blocks (as opposed to all
> the little ones) for Britfur was finding a suitable consite
> that didn't cost £200/person. We found three, but the
> first practically doubled their prices on us, the second
> suddenly told us they would be knocked down before
> then and no one seemed to like the third.
>
> If you're not too fussy about the ticket costs
> being in the £120–£150 range or if you don't mind
> things being noninclusive then there are a lot
> more options. For instance, a £40 convention
> (ex food or accommodation) with some onsite
> accommodation from $180pppn is possible, if
> people don't mind it being in London....
>
> The other big problem is that organising a conven-
> tion IS A LOT OF HARD WORK. For one or two
> years sometimes. It's not a hobby, it's practically a
> full-time job. You just don't get paid for it.[131] the
> second suddenly told us they would be knocked down
> before then and no one seemed to like the third.\n\
> nIf you're not too fussy about the ticket costs being in
> the £120-£150 range or if you don't mind things being
> non inclusive then there are a lot more options. For
> instance a £40 convention (ex food or accommodation

Others who were also involved in the organisation and discussions took issue with the overall organisation, focusing more on what the convention would be about before considering how the group should operate or handle the business side of things, as Lamar (John Barbiero) recalled:

> [The] majority of the discussion tended to focus
> around the things people would like to have at a
> convention, rather than the actual functional parts of
> organizing and funding a convention. Sometime in
> 2003, Anti-Carrot appointed himself chairman of the

convention, and started "organizing." However, this organizing did not involve things like forming a PLC to limit liability or contact other UK conventions to get their budgets to use as examples and estimates.[132]

Marcony himself criticised how open the mailing list when it came to accepting newcomers in the forum. Anyone could suggest ideas and make recommendations, regardless of whether they were part of the staff or not.

> This proved very destructive as it was mostly full of a bunch of furs (some with less sense than others) all trying to make the con happen the way they imagine it. The biggest problem was that everyone had a different view as to where it should be (Many wanting it in their part of the world). and everyone wanting to be in charge and seemingly thinking that being in charge was their right.[133]

ANTIcarrot was also target to a lot of criticism both during the planning period and after the cancellation, from questions of his conduct as well as his experience at leading a team and running the group as an organization. While he admitted to having no experience as a chairman (arguing that no one else in the group did either), ANTIcarrot had said that he had been preparing a convention idea for at least a year before initially announcing the UK_FUR_CON mailing list and had organisational experience working at a family-owned travel & accommodation business.[134]

Funds were also an issue surrounding the convention. The website mentioned selling calendars with the intent of fundraising, discussions in the mailing list included ways of fundraising for the convention and LondonFurs did donate a small amount of money directly to BritFur as part of a charity policy. ANTIcarrot was also accused of taking money from the LondonFurs Christmas Party and putting it into the BritFur funds without knowledge from the attendees.[135]

FURCON UK

On 7 July 2004, a new mailing list was set up called Britfurcon with an admin-specific mailing the following day. The domain name for brit-fur.co.uk was now directed to a new and simple webpage welcoming a

British Furry Convention, although after a vote the name was quickly changed to UK Fur CON due to legal concerns.[136]

After a few months, a Web forum was also set up for further discussions. This time the planning was led by FoxyDragon, with Antharro (David Baxter) acting as webmaster, and was initially planned to take place in January 2005. Administrative talks were active in the first few months, and even ANTIcarrot was willing to offer his advice and support after BritFur's cancellation.

Discussions from November suggest that it would take place at Margam Country Park, an 850-acre estate that's two miles from Port Talbot in South Wales.[137] It is possible that camping was being considered instead of a hotel, as the price of accommodations was a main factor in the cancellation of BritFur.

January came and passed, but there was no news on the convention. It seems that most of the discussions around FurCon UK (and most of its updates and announcements) were posted on the Web forum, but it was never archived, so it is unknown what documentation remains. A post from Ian Selley on 13 February 2005 claims that dates and a venue were still being organised. Only two days later, however, Antharro made an update post to the mailing list that addressed the lack of online updates but also suggested personal reasons for the lack of progress:

> Foxydragon conceived the idea of FurCon (previously BritFurCon) when we were in a relationship last year. We have since broken up. She is a very busy person at the moment, and projects such as this have regrettably fallen to the side, at least for now. I'm not going into any further detail than that. I am still in touch with her, and I will make an effort to contact her and find out just what is going on.[138]

The UK Fur CON website was shut down later in the year, along with the forum, and the mailing lists were abandoned.

BRITFUR 2005

In mid-2004, amidst the FurCon UK and BritFur plans, a parody group was established calling itself the UK FurCon Parody Committee. It was headed by another LondonFur regular and amateur fursuit maker named Tippus Tailus (Dean Swift). The group garnered enough interest to set up an actual convention, using the britfur.co.uk domain to host a new website in early January 2005.[139] The website provides a summary of the convention story thus far to explain its origins:

> The first group had all of the old school members of
> the LondonFurs. The second group had all of the on-
> line personalities. We're not sure about the third group,
> but when we heard about them, we formed a parody
> group. We suggested having a furcon in Manchester,
> UK, at the beginning of May 2005 and people started
> taking us seriously. Why Manchester? It's fairly cen-
> tral, with a glut of accommodation. Why May? It's the
> wettest bank holiday, which is a successful formula for
> both FurtherConfusion and AnthroCon.[140]

What was explained—in elaborate detail—was the timeframe of the
convention. A mailing list post from Tippus, supposedly sent to the UK-
Furs mailing list on 6 October 2004, explained how FurtherConfusion
(in California) and Anthrocon (in Philadelphia) host their conventions
during times when tourism was less popular due to weather in their areas.
It also suggests the May Bank holiday was ideal in the United Kingdom because other bank holidays were taken up by music festivals, and
Manchester was also a prime location thanks to the furmeets run by the
NorthernFurs community.

With early promises of affordable accommodations at the Jurys
Doyle Hotel, a full published schedule was posted that had events
planned for every hour of each day. A guest of honor from America
was also announced later in the month. The go-ahead for the convention
seemed assured, and open registration was predicted to be set for 21
January 2005.

The NorthernFurs were not so confident about the convention's
prospects when Tippus tried not only to promote the convention directly to their mailing list, but propose to replace the Leeds meet with
Manchester in April 2005 to help the convention. A lot of criticisms
from the NorthernFurs mailing list mirror the previous BritFur issues
regarding a lack of organisation and poor conduct from the con chairman. Rallicat, a Birmingham furry who was active in the discussions,
summarised the concerns on his LiveJournal:

> Despite supposed years of planning, this convention
> is being rushed through, and has been badly planned.
> If this con goes ahead and is a failure (as I very much
> suspect it would be), it could seriously damage the
> efforts of other convention groups, who are taking
> their time and putting in real, genuinely good efforts
> to bring an excellent convention to the UK.

Worse still, the valid criticism of those who recognise this as a bad idea, is being smeared as FUD [Fear, Uncertainty, and Doubt].[141]

A poll was opened by NorthernFurs to decide the issue. The result was tallied on 19 January with a resulting vote of 19 to 7, with one abstaining, in favour of keeping the Manchester meet running at its regular time. This was seen largely as a positive decision, but Rallicat felt they needed to warn multiple groups against rushing to organize conventions:

I suspect Tippus may try and push on regardless, and this is bad news for furcons in the UK.

A badly planned convention could damage our long-term prospects of holding something decent, but matters aren't helped by the fact that we have multiple splinter groups trying to arrange conventions.

These groups should, where possible, integrate. There is no reason why integration should not be an achievable goal, providing the people working on it are sensible, level headed people who don't have ego-problems or other such issues.[142]

As expected, Tippus pushed on, quickly moving the date from April to November and including a damning statement at the bottom of the Web page about the convention:

After a poll and extensive discussion on the UK's NorthernFurs Mailing List, it became apparent that the majority would rather be elsewhere. This was extremely frustrating because we only had to make one telephone call to proceed. However, the volume of flaming was lacklustre compared with previous proposals. So, some of us intend to try again.[140]

More controversy surrounded BritFur2005. The similar to other convention names that were scheduled around the same time confused furry fans. Many thought the three cons were the same thing only with name variations, inspiring Antharro had to make a short clarification in his mailing list post.

I must make this next point absolutely clear: FUR-
CON AND BRITFURCON ARE IN NO WAY
RELATED TO BRITFUR2005.

We have no affiliation to them; we are not part of their
organization.[138]

The professionalism of the organisers was also brought into
question for their inconsistency. Some areas were well presented and
somewhat formal, such as the details of registration and the event schedule, while others were bereft of information and even inappropriate. At
one point, the guest of honour backed out of the convention, and the
website decided to reveal the news with this comment: "However, he has
discovered that anime events are better attended (and more lucrative).
Therefore, he is otherwise engaged."

According to Giza (one of the directors of Anthrocon) on a
Wikifur discussion thread for BritFur2005, Uncle Kage was
asked by the con to be the guest of honour, but the con "had
to back out sometime later because of 'financial reasons.'"

While the organisers decided to delay the convention, renaming it
BritFur2006 with the expectation of it taking place in April 2006, most
doubted it would ever take place. One comment on an alt.fan.furry
thread on upcoming conventions for 2006 simply commented, "That
one is dead and will never be."[143]

As early as the January poll, there were those who suspected the
convention was an elaborate prank. Rusty Fox, a furry fan from the Czech
Republic, believed it was a trolling exercise directed at the NorthernFurs
because furries in other groups such as LondonFurs were unaware of
its existence. Another reason for suspicion was Tailus himself, who had
been in the fandom since 2001. His online presence gave the impression
of his being not only a very impressive Web developer but also someone
who was either full of himself or a jokester, depending on whom you
asked.

Others believed it was more likely a legitimate event organised by
people who lacked experience and professionalism. Unlike the other
furry convention attempts, BritFur was incorporated (by Tippus Tailus) on 16 August 2004 as BritFur, Ltd. a private limited. Tina Lescott
served as acting secretary.[144] Although there was very little activity filed
under the company during its two years of operation, it is possible that

there were serious plans to organise a convention, even if the individuals themselves didn't have enough preparation and professionalism to convince others in the fandom of its legitimacy.

Whatever the intentions, the outcome did not fare well for its chairman. While ANTIcarrot, FoxyDragon, and their associates have moved on, continuing an active presence in the furry fandom for many years after this fiasco, Tippus Tailus has not been seen or heard of since 2007.

WHAT ELSE?

The World Science Fiction Convention returned to the SECC in Glasgow 4–8 August 2005 under the name Interaction,[145] the result of a successful and mostly unopposed bid in 2002. For the furry fandom, it was a rather big event that promised a potential furry gathering, and so BritFur and Furcon UK took the timing into consideration to avoid scheduling conflicts. Furries from America such as Rivercoon (David Bliss), Fred Patten, Rod O'Riley, and others made plans to go, talking about it with any British furs who might be eager to attend.[146] Simon Barber, for one, had plans to give the American furries a tour around Yorkshire. Unfortunately, Fred Patten unexpectedly suffered a stroke in March 2005, leaving him physically unable to attend. As a result, Barber's plans were cancelled. The ScotFurs did advertise a furmeet opportunity at WorldCon although there's no evidence of any furry-related event or gathering based on reports and convention documents.

Despite all the hard work from individuals in the fandom, this would be the closest the British furry fandom would get at the time to having a furry convention in their home nation, and it was only as a small unofficial part of another, much larger, fandom.

There was also an option with hosting Eurofurence in the United Kingdom, but attempts at such a proposition were often shutdown for two reasons: one was the cost of accommodations because Eurofurence takes place in the summer, when hotel prices are high; the other reason was that the convention committee comprised mostly of Germans, and therefore suspected to have a bias towards Germany. ANTIcarrot once described the typical response to hosting Eurofurence in the United Kingdom:

> It has been suggested in the past. Their usual response is to have a great big hearty laugh and then say, "No, no, really. Does any other country want to host Eurofurence next year? Serious answers only please."
>
> … [W]e'd have to be able to prove to the EF con staff that we could do [EF] in Britain for around £80 or so.

> At which point they would still likely say no. If they held it in Britain, they'd have no way to gauge just how many European furs would come, since it would be much further away for most of them than [EF] is.

> In the past this has been the standard reasons given by high ranking con staff why they believe it's impractical.[147]

The last time Eurofurence was hosted outside of Germany was in 2003, and the host nation was the Czech Republic. After Eurofurence 10, the convention abandoned any open proposals for new locations and remained in Germany. This effectively eliminated any hope of a British Eurofurence.

For those who had hoped to have a local furry convention, seeing multiple attempts fail was demoralizing. Some furs referred to a British furry convention as a running joke because anyone who organised one made a disaster out of it. This led to many doubting there would ever be a full furry convention in the U.K. Those in the fandom who could afford to travel decided there was no alternative but to attend the conventions in mainland Europe or North America. Everyone else would just have to make do with the furmeets at home.

RED, BLUE & WHITE

Some furmeets held special events on occasions, such as the LondonFurs' Christmas Banquet. In 2003, the LondonFurs lead organiser was RapidoFrog, another old guard furry from the days at the Intrepid Fox. The furmeets were manageable even with the rising numbers in attendance, although, as he recalled, the size did make it more difficult to maintain the old traditions, and he had to come up with a solution. As RapidoFrog recalled:

> The original Xmas meals were just large bookings in pizza places in the West End, nothing fancy but in those days the group numbered around twenty, so it wasn't so bad. Around 2006 the group was getting so big that no one wanted to organise a meal for so many people and there were literally no volunteers for this either. So, I thought about a party night and somewhere different where we could have a laugh in a nice safe contained environment and those with fursuits could party, and then I remember[ed] some Thames party boats I had been on at university so I enquired how much one would be and then set on selling tickets.[148]

The LondonFurs Boat Party, as it would be called, was limited to 85 places. It was scheduled immediately after the Christmas meet on 2 December 2006. The main meet was held at the LondonFurs meet's regular venue, the Theodore Bullfrog, before moving to the Festival Pier, where the party began at exactly seven o'clock on the M.V. *Golden Star*. The ship sailed down the river Thames, passing the Houses of Parliament and going through the Thames Barrier.[149]

There was plenty of music and drinks to be had, although the main highlight was an hour-long performance from 2 Gryphon, an American furry and stand-up comedian known for rants and jokes of a vulgar and controversial nature.[150]

In 2017, after news broke that 2 Gryphon had been rejected from performing his main stage show at Anthrocon, several of his opinions on race, sexual predators, and victims of suicide came to light. He would eventually join the alt-furs, a furry faction of the far-right group alt-right, and most of the fandom has distanced themselves from him ever since.

Despite fears that the party would not break even (RapidoFrog had to pay upfront to host it), it was a sold-out event. Many of the attendees enjoyed it, posting how much they loved the boat and how accommodating it was for both regular attendees and fursuiters; they also appreciated the affordable drinks and 2 Gryphon's performance. The only criticism that could be found was that after the party finished at midnight, attendees were left on their own to find a way to their homes or hotels in the incredibly early hours of the morning.

Regardless, the amount of positive feedback was enough to persuade organisers to repeat the fun and make it even bigger than before. The boat party came to be known as the Red, Blue & White.

In April, RBW 2007 was announced, and it would be held 1–2 December. The theme was "Furs-In-Black" after the 1997 sci-fi comedy film *Men in Black*. In hopes of doubling the attendance, the entire event was expanded. Instead of a small party boat, the M.V. *Golden Jubilee*, a two-story boat with a dance floor, was booked. The boat could accommodate 240 people and included fully staffed bars[151]

In June 2007, RapidoFrog brought on Foxbearance as joint chair of RBW and confirmed that plans for RBW 2007 were being finalised. It was not going to be just a boat party:

> Not only do we have a super boat trip this year, but we
> also have many varied events in and around our venue.
> I won't go into full detail now about them. But what
> I can tell you is that I've tried to wangle some super
> prizes to give away along with making sure it's not just
> the fursuiters that get all the fun![152]

Along with the M.V. *Golden Jubilee*, the Calico Bar was set as the main venue for the daytime. The Royal National Hotel was reserved to provide overnight accommodations, which would be a boon to those furries who had a hard time the year before with getting home or to any place for rest in the wee hours of the morning. Along with the return of 2 Gryphon, LondonFur's furry artist UltraViolet and fursuit maker FatKraken joined the fun as guests of honours.

Vendors such as United Publications sold merchandise at the Calico; fursuiters competed in the Fursuit Commonwealth Games for prizes, showing off their talents at the Masquerade; panels on fursuit creation and drawing by the guests were held, and so much more. StarPaw (Jason Karlson) put together a conbook for attendees with interviews from the guests, artwork, and stories all centred around the theme.[153]

Hype around the event was considerable, resulting in a sell-out event by August 2007. In total, 242 people attended RBW, including 21 foreign furries such as Uncle Kage (Samuel Conway), Steve Gallachi, and Lance Ikegawa.[154] This made it the largest gathering of furries in the United Kingdom up to that time, and the second largest in Europe, surpassing prior LondonFur and NorthernFur meets. Some 197 furries went on the Golden Jubilee Party boat, enjoying another performance by 2 Gryphon and having a grand time despite a very choppy river and returning to the wrong pier, necessitating a long walk back to the hotel.

In addition to the fun, money was raised for a good cause, partially from the convention vendor sales but largely from the Sunday charity auction. Each of the guests of honour donated an item to bid on with most of the proceeds going to Mammal Trust UK. UltraViolet provided an A1-sized, signed print of the cover art she produced for the conbook, FatKraken provided a partial fursuit, and 2 Gryphon provided a dollar bill that he had signed.[155] Lance Ikegawa, a professional fursuit maker himself, also donated a fursuit for auction. In total, £1,775 was raised, with 75 percent (£1,331.25) going to the Mammal Trust UK.

RBW 2007 ended with a preview of what was to come next year. This included plans to make it a fully residential furry convention with the theme of "Masters of Alchemy." In January 2008, the Anthropomorphic Representation Foundation (ARF) was founded to run future RBW events.

RBW started to have internal issues when RapidoFrog stepped down from both RBW and LondonFurs in the summer of 2008. He left RBW in the hands of FoxBearance, Graafen Blackpaw (Garry Whale), and UltraViolet. Although he claimed to have already done a lot of preparation and organising for RBW 2008, he said there was constant disagreement between him and FoxBearance, so he resigned "to prevent the con from failing due to disputes."[148]

The Royal National Hotel became the setting for both the hotel and the convention, boasting several large rooms, including a grand event hall that could hold over 400 people. The boat party was expanded again to be aboard the M.V. *Erasmus*, which could hold up to 310 passengers as it sailed the River Thames. While early plans suggest 2 Gryphon and fursuit maker Latin Vixen were planned to be guests of honour, sched-

The Royal National Hotel in Woburn Palace, Bloomsbury, London, has 1,630 rooms.

uling conflicts made that impossible. They were therefore replaced with EuroFurence chair Cheetah, artist Zen Tiger, and French fursuiter Timduru[156]

Excitement over RBW 2008 quickly spread, and three days after registration opened, news hit that RBW had already confirmed over 100 attendees[157] and the dealer's den had sold out. When the convention was a few weeks away, it was confirmed that RBW had surpassed its previous attendance count with over 250 people making reservations. The final attendance count ended up being shy of early projections of over 300 attendees, but it was still an impressive 290.

Taking place 27–30 November 2008, the bigger, now residential, furry convention and boat party ended up not being so grand as anticipated by attendees. While the fursuiting events were well received, all the convention staff and attendees were friendly and approachable, and furries enjoyed the live stream of the main stage events as well as the boat party, the rest of the convention ended up being described as "chaotic."

Materials like the convention T-shirts and the final events schedule were not available when registration opened. It proved unhelpful when the only available event schedule on the first day was a draft that had completely different times, misleading attendees to miss events they wanted to go to. Even if they attended the events they wanted to, some ran late, and one panel had no presenter to run it at all.

The hotel provided a much smaller room for the dealer's den than promised,[158] Marcony also recalled how rushed the dealer's den situation was close to the convention's opening:

> With about three weeks to go, I asked who was in
> charge and it turned out nobody was and there was
> no floor plan or table allocations. In the end, I offered
> to run it and sorted the whole thing out in two weeks,
> mostly based on what we had worked out for Britfur.[99]

Even the boat party had issues. The boat company made a last-minute decision to change the pick-up point from Embankment Pier to Blackfriars' Pier, requiring everyone to take a longer journey from the hotel to get there.

Rude hotel staff and unprepared security were also problems at the convention, although some felt this was due to the number of regular guests at the hotel compared to convention attendees. The hotel even assumed they could rent out the convention space to another event whilst the boat party was underway, meaning the tech crew had to temporarily tear down the stage for the evening only to set it up again the next day.[159]

Even the charity auction did not go down as well. Despite having more items to offer, many did not receive a single bid. Bids picked up eventually when a custom RBW Monopoly set going for £160 was offered, along with a Husky fursuit going for £760.[160] While there is no exact amount on record for what was raised for the chosen charity, the Wildfowl & Wetland Trust, most sources give an estimate of £1,100.

The mixed reception left a sour taste for a lot of furries, but when RBW closed for the year, ARF moved ahead with plans to make the next year's convention better. Senior staff considered rebranding it entirely, yet the team was already committed to the RBW brand, and so they decided to keep the initials but change the name to Rather Brilliant Weekend.[161] After Foxbearance stepped down, it was also decided to not appoint an official chair and instead impose a more collaborative team effort.[162] This was despite Tryst (Robert Barnes), Kittiah, and Miyabi of the LondonFurs Committee being defined as the team leaders in a Staff Profile post titled "Chairman Meows."[163]

The new team secured the M.V. *Erasumus* once again for the traditional boat party. However, the hotel and venue were moved to the International Britannia Hotel by the Canary Wharf situated in the heart of London's Docklands. Advantages to the move included assurances that the Dealer's Den would have a better room not far from the lobby,[164] and an allocated block of hotel rooms (instead of hotel rooms being scattered across the hotel) would be reserved. There would also be a short walk to the Canary Wharf pier to enjoy the boat party[165]

Even with these changes, convincing furries to attend remained a struggle. Whereas RBW 2008 achieved over a hundred registrations in three days, RBW 2009 took three months to reach the same number.[166] There were a few factors behind these numbers, such as the reception of the previous year, the date being too close to other big furry conventions in Europe and America, and information such as events and special guests being either unclear or only available on the official RBW LiveJournal as opposed to the official website.

The key element that was putting some furries off was the price of attendance, which was increased from £55 (£66 to include the Boat Party) to £100, not counting the cost of accommodations at the hotel. The official reasons given for the increase were the economic climate (the 2008 economic recession) and the need to properly budget the convention to operate with at least 200 attendees.[167] Some speculated that the true reason was to recuperate losses from the previous year, but although it was confirmed that RBW 2008 operated at a loss, it had already recuperated with the help of anonymous donors. Considering the convention was hosted in London, it was argued by SouthPaw that £100 was a bargain, considering the size and location of the convention at one of the city's major convention centres.[168]

With less than three months to go, the RBW team made a plea to the fandom that it would all be worth it in 2009. They promised that all the issues from the previous year were not going to be repeated and emphasised that those who attended would enjoy a high-quality convention.

> We know that last year the events schedule was a joke. You can expect to see our provisional events schedule published right here imminently. All events that appear on the schedule have been confirmed with the panellists involved. No ambiguity here!

> We've gone out of our way to find a venue that matches the kind of high-quality convention we would like to run. The UK deserves a convention of a quality equal to any American or European con, despite the smaller scale. The new hotel is a lovely venue in an iconic location with staff who really want us there.

> The one thing that every single member of RBW staff is passionate about this year is making sure that everyone gets what they've paid for: a brilliant convention in a fantastic location.[169]

Even though it was not endorsed by RBW, Makali offered to personally upgrade members to sponsor level if they convinced five people to register. Sponsors got mentioned in the conbook and received a free official T-shirt and an exclusive print from last year's guest of honour, Zen, for the price of a regular membership.[170]

The plea worked, RBW 2009 opened on October 30, and a total of 226 attended.[171] Unlike 2008, RBW 2009 was positively received with plenty of attendees praising a lot of the activities and the much larger Dealers' Den. While the staff at the hotel was described as curious by some, attendees described them as being friendly and helpful. The security staff of Canary Wharf was praised for their cooperation during the fursuit walk and boat party, helping to stop traffic to let everyone cross safely and remaining in the background while everyone has a grand time.

In fact, the only complaint was that the hotel was humid due to faulty air conditioning during the weekend. Other events throughout the convention were largely considered fun and enter-

RBW 2009 Conbook Cover by KaputOtter.

taining, such as a masquerade with talented dancers and a magic act and a charity auction with the con staff in a strip show. But the Fursuit Games were criticised by the fursuiters and the audience for being a boring event.[172] This year, the charity raised money for the UK Wolf Conservation Trust, collecting £1,868.45 in total (£1,546 during the convention with an additional £322 during the closing ceremony), which exceeded the expectations of the staff.

RBW would return to the Canary Wharf on 5 November 2010 with the theme of "Space Cowboys" as an obvious tribute to *Cowboy Bebop* down to an official trailer recreating the anime's infamous opening title sequence.[173]

The traditional Boat Party on the M.V. *Erasmus* returned, and the Britannia International Hotel's dedicated Nightclub was also going to be used on Friday night, with the theme-fitting name of The Engine Room. To run with the sci-fi Western theme, the RBW Codex was introduced to encourage attendees to create stories and space journals, with the best ones published in the conbook. While RBW's ability to raise £3,185 was impressive enough, the convention's Master of Ceremonies, Bariki (1982–2021), got Microsoft UK to match the total fundraising amount through an employment scheme, resulting in the charity total for Sled Dog Welfare of £6,396.[174]

Flyer for RBW 2010. Artwork by PoorPolarBear.

RBW was a major success. In fact, according to a mailing list announcement, it was the most successful RBW to date, financially breaking even without anonymous donations for the first time since 2007. This positive news made it a real shock when it was announced that RBW 2010 would be the last one. The main reason given was that despite the critical success, attendance numbers failed to reflect any potential for growth. While the reception of RBW 2009 appeared promising after 100 tickets sold in the first 90 minutes of registration and a third of the total available tickets sold within seven days,[175] the final attendance count was still only 216. This was nowhere near the 290 count of 2008, which did put strain on the organisers.

One of the odd things about RBW is that everyone who's been loves it, but we never seem to get enough interest the following year. Not enough people want a 3-day residential convention in London to make it a sure thing—for the last three years we've been left worrying right up until the last month or two whether we'll have enough attendees to cover the cost of the event.

We'd hoped that the successes of previous years would fix that problem, but the number of attendees hasn't changed significantly. We suspect that one of the reasons for this is that London's already very well served by the thriving LondonFurs community, with its own special events that rival some full conventions. In sales speak, the market is saturated. We think that means it's time to try something different.[176]

The boat party would supposedly remain for 2011, which did reassure many of the disappointed furries that were hoping to return to RBW, but after months of waiting for news, further disappointment came to light. Miyabi made an unofficial announcement on a UKFur thread that the LondonFurs Meet Committee was unable to get the M.V. *Erasmus* for any of the dates they proposed, as well as being too committed to other events to make it happen.

> We've sort of dropped the ball on this—we're all quite
> enjoying the time off; not having massive heart palpita-
> tions and not being plunged into huge personal debt
> is a really nice feeling. We're also pretty busy managing
> LF stuff (well, most of us are, anyway).

> We'll probably make an official announcement soon
> but for the time being don't hold your breath for a
> 2011 boat party—think 2012 instead. We couldn't get
> the *Erasmus* at all for the dates we wanted this year,
> which wouldn't be a huge problem, but we'd like to
> keep the vessel the same.[177]

Although there was a promise to bring the Boat Party back for 2012, furries would end up having to wait another year, when the M.V. *Erasmus* would be the venue for the first day of the LondonFurs Summer Weekender on 19 July 2013.[178] While RBW was no more, the M.V. *Erasmus* continues to provide a partygoing experience to furries in London every July during the Summer Weekender.

RBW, regardless of whether it means Red, Blue & White, Rather Brilliant Weekend, or nothing at all, is usually looked back on fondly. Why attendance numbers did not increase is up for speculation, with some citing the economic situation or it being hosted in London, a city well known for being expensive. Others would agree with the official reason of there being other worthwhile events to go to as the new decade began.

There is also the possibility that RBW simply could not escape the shadow of 2008, when the numbers were at their peak, but the overall reception was poor. Although RBW's run was short, the team behind the convention deserves a lot of praise for not only bringing a convention to the United Kingdom but also saving it from a much quicker demise.

CONFUZZLED

Meanwhile, up north, FurbleFox started discussing within his own group of friends the possibilities of running their own furry convention. In 2002, he was critical of the first BritFur, accusing the main organisers of internal bias after they voted on Ruin's name of BritFur for the convention over his name of Furtannia in an internal meeting.[179] He condemned the organisers for not listening to suggestions given from outside the core LondonFurs group.

With him and his friends being furmeet organisers of NorthernFurs, he believed their collective experience was enough to get a convention off the ground. Rocky Raccoon, the Sheffield Furmeet manager during that time, recalls being in one discussion about a furry convention at the Queen's Head Pub with the other Sheffield Furmeet organisers, Avon, and Blue Phoenix:

> I think it was the actual year I went to University, 2003.
> It was about where [the convention] should be and
> trying to get the confidence to do it. [We] decided the
> best place would be either Sheffield or Manchester, as
> its central UK, but Manchester had the airport. Plus,
> we were NorthernFurs so we weren't London centric.
> I'm fairly sure Furble may have first come up with the
> name ConFuzzled at that meeting. I wasn't a fan of
> the name to be honest, I didn't like the idea of con-
> fused or confusing.[180]

According to Rocky, the idea ended up not going anywhere until FurbleFox brought it forward a few years later. This would occur at Eurofurence 11 at the Nuremburg Castle in the summer of 2005, when he approached a friend of his by the name of LevLion (Matthew Johnson): "[FurbleFox] said he was thinking about putting a con together but didn't know what that would involve, and he knew my work in the events industry and festivals. He also knew I had the equipment to put on a small stage, so I guess that helped."[181]

On board with the idea, LevLion and FurbleFox would spend the convention discussing over plans, recruiting friends like Wolfie Fox (Phillip Skyes), Nidonocu (James Shaw), and Anthropuppy[182] over the rest of the year into a team to make the convention a reality.

Their first biggest challenge was securing a venue. Recognizing how new running a convention was to them, and unable to guarantee a big attendance, the team had to set their expectations low: "As boring as it sounds, we had our paws firmly on the ground and worked to what was possible, not what we dreamed we could do. I have a feeling we decided we needed eighty or there abouts but hoped for a hundred people."

Fortunately for them, their main locale was the city of Manchester, a large and rather central city with easy transport connections. While they didn't have the budget for a hotel, there happened to be a hostel that was recently refitted, and when the team checked the place, they knew they had found their venue.

According to SouthPaw, who joined the original team in 2006, FurbleFox approached the YHA International in Manchester and paid a holding deposit of £144, a total of £1 for each bed at the youth hostel. After another meeting where the hostel was measured up, a contract was signed, and the convention was an official go.

News of an announcement was made when the team launched a new website for their furry convention in the summer of 2006.

> It's A Journey. Let's make pawprints into history.
>
> ConFuzzled is the first fully fledged UK Furry convention to date and is going to take place in June 2008 at the 4 Star YHA International, Manchester....
>
> ConFuzzled is going to be the biggest, fun filled, exciting gathering of people who share an extraordinary appreciation for anthropomorphic critters in the UK, and we'll be breaking a record as we'll be the first to do it outside of any usual furmeet.[183]

The news was spread through LiveJournal and Second Life communities, the NorthernFurs Furmeets, and furry fandom news websites such as Flayrah and the now-defunct FurteanTimes.com. The announcement did raise some eyebrows with its promise, as NorthernFurs was a large and popular community within the British furry scene, and the team also got advisory support from experienced convention organisers such as Cheetah (chair of Eurofurence), Timduru (organizer of FranFurence), Chairo (co-founder of Further Confusion) and Kiran Lightpaw (founder of Furry Weekend Atlanta).

Not all were optimistic, however, as one furry from the MidFurs mailing list stated in one of the earliest public comments that could be found about the convention's website, bluntly writing: "That site's been up a while, I think. As far as I'm aware, no-one believes it's really going to happen."[184] But the scepticism around the concept of a British furry convention still appeared to hold water for a few furs in the community. What did not help were how up-front the team was with its goal of being a British furry convention. Early promotional T-shirts were made with the controversial slogan "The First British Furry Convention," one of which was later auctioned in 2009.[185]

Cambridge furry AlexFox criticised the convention's initial reveal for how it promoted itself when little more than a venue and date were set in stone. He expressed a particular gripe at how other staff members were credited, regardless of their involvement.

According to his LiveJournal post, he questioned LevLion about his involvement with the convention, noting that the website listed him as one of the core staff of stage A/V management and as a co-founder.

LevLion's alleged response was that the only thing he was doing for the convention was lending equipment for the main stage, and that his role and credits listed on the sites were the first he ever heard about them:

> Wow! Promoting people without their knowledge, that's a good sign that things are going well. ConFuzzled has a core staff that mostly doesn't realise that they are core staff members? I wonder if they think that the money to do this con will suddenly appear from out of the blue too.
>
> Anyway, quick note to furry convention and event holders in the UK, please don't put a website up advertising your event until 75% of the stuff you need to do (i.e. the event is going to happen) is done. Else if it all falls through then you're just adding to the big joke that is associated with the words "British furry convention."[186]

ConFuzzled marched on for the rest of the year, becoming incorporated as a limited company on 27 March 2008,[187] and registration going online on 22 April with 42 paid customers on the first day.[188] News continued to spread about the convention thanks to social media, with the premiere of Confuzzled's own forum debuting in May, as well as a magazine-style newsletter called *Confuzzled Focus* getting published in October.

FurbleFox (with the laptop) and some of the team outside the YHA Manchester on the day registration went online (photo by WolfieFox)..

May 2008 also saw the debut of one of the convention's most unique elements, a mascot character. Furry conventions prior to Con-Fuzzled were known to have anthropomorphic characters in their official artwork, but FurbleFox wanted a standout character that was recognisable and quintessentially British. Slovakian furry artist TabbieFox (Josef Zsapka) was commissioned to draw concept art of FurbleFox's idea.[189] The result was Brok the Badger, a round and loveable mustelid with an affinity for cookies.

One of the sticking points around this time was the price and package options. ConFuzzled had no option to attend only, meaning potential attendees had to pay for a room at the Youth Hostel whether or not they wished to stay there. This was understandably off-putting for some. The standard price for the hostel was £170, with an early bird price of £160, and you had to pay even if you were a local who didn't need a room. And, since it was a hostel, one had no control over roommates, and there could be up to five people in a room.[190] ConFuzzled's official explanation for the mandatory room sharing was due to the contract with the Youth Hostel, which required all 144 beds to be paid for.[191]

There were also concerns of a North/South division in the fandom because, it was suggested, NorthernFurs and LondonFurs were now competing against each other in running their own furry conventions.

Internally, there was no such competition outside of a playful rivalry amongst friends. In fact, Graafen Blackpaw, Matt Lion (Matthew Hood) and Shep Shephard (James Anness) were on staff at both conventions as head of convention operations, first aid, and security, respectively, with several other organisers working at the two conventions. Regardless, talks on social media persisted enough that on 1 August, both ConFuzzled and RBW made an announcement on their respective websites refuting any claims of a serious rivalry:

> RBW and ConFuzzled have the same goals:
>
> To create a great event for everyone in the furry community where people can have fun and be with friends.
>
> Together, we are collaborating on new approaches in marketing and event planning.
>
> We aim to put aside any differences you may have heard about in the past and work together on making the future better, for all involved.[192]

Included in the statement were quotes from both chairmans expressing support for each other.

"I'm delighted to be working with the great guys on the ConFuzzled team to build a bridge of trust and co-operation so that no matter where you are from, or who you know, one thing is common—FUN, FUR and FRIENDS!" said Foxbearance, RBW's co-chair.

:We are very excited to be working with RBW as this brings us closer together to our goal of making the UK fandom better for all, and also making two world-class events people will want to attend," said Furble-Fox, ConFuzzled's chairman.

By January 8, Confuzzled was officially sold out,[193] with 136 paid and registered attendees, along with three who paid to support the convention as opposed to attending.[194]

YHA INTERNATIONAL

Britain's first fully residential furry convention took place on 20–23 June 2008. All attendees received a conbook produced by Twll (Martin Jenkins)[195] with its cover drawn by TabbieFox. Any attendees who went for the sponsor membership would get their name in the conbook as well as a pin badge, a limited-edition art print, a care basket with food and drinks, and a T-shirt designed by AzraFox, who won the honor in a contest with 21 entrants.[196]

The convention featured a single guest of honour, BigBlueFox, who, along with being a furry artist and fursuiter from Germany, was also

Group photo from the ConFuzzled 2008 Fursuit Parade (photo by MikePaws).

a professional TV cameraman. He conducted a workshop on "How to Film Furries" and provided plenty of high-quality video footage of the convention through his channel, BBF-TV. There were plenty of other events going on throughout the weekend, some of which would remain traditions for future iterations such as a pub quiz, karaoke, frankensuits (contestants are tasked with creating a fursuit out of scrap materials in a short amount of time), and MotorFurs, where attendees can show off their vehicles and pose for photos.

There were some who would describe the 2008 convention as more of a "fursuit convention" due to the number of fursuit specialty events that went on during the weekend, such as photoshoots, workshops, roundtables, games, and even a similar event to RBW's Fursuit Commonwealth Games called the Furrylimpcs. This would not be a surprise as the ratio of fursuiters to attendees was considerably large. Out of 136 attendees, according to the furry news website FurteanTimes, 67 were fursuiters.[197]

Confuzzled also had its own art auction and Dealers' Den for attendees to shop and raise money for the Badger Trust. According to reports from ConFuzzled's event team staff member Tungro (Thomas van der Elsen), every item that was submitted in the art show went to auction, most with a 20 percent split to charity with the rest going entirely to charity. The combined charity total came to £1,610.

Even AlexFox, one of Confuzzled's early sceptics, had a complete changed of opinion after he returned:

> I have to say that I was very disappointed with the run
> up to Confuzzled (as I am sure people are aware from

my previous LJ postings). However, I am willing to say now that I take it all back.

Confuzzled turned out to be really good, almost life changing for me. For a start I now consider myself to be a full furry artist. I think once you've sold an item at auction, or done a paid commission you earn that title, and last weekend at the confuzzled convention I did both....

As for the con, yes, I know I've been putting it down a lot, but the crew did do a good job, the hostel was OK, and Manchester is a much nicer place than I remembered from a few years back. I have to admit that I didn't see much of the events (since I was dealing this time), but what I did I enjoyed. Working was fun if tiring, and the [parties]/dances were excellent.

There were a few things that could have been better, like the organisation of the art and dealers' room could have been a lot better, and the timing was sucky (I wish that I could have gone to the art workshop but I couldn't due to the fact that I was dealing at the time. Oh, and the bar was a bit expensive, closed early and sold only bottles (although it was good beer!).

Either way I am planning on going back next year! Roll on Confuzzled 2009![198]

It would not be long before ConFuzzled 2009 was confirmed for 22–25 May. In fact, registrations for ConFuzzled 2009 opened on July 31, little more than one month after the 2008 convention ended. This would also be the first ConFuzzled with a theme: "Victorian England." The overwhelmingly positive reception got people's interests, with a hundred registrations reached in a little over a week,[199] and rooms sold out by the start of September.

Now with the confidence of being able to sell out their venue, ConFuzzled also offered around 50 attending-only tickets for those who wanted to go to the convention without paying for food and accommodations at the hostel itself. By January, even the attending-only tickets were sold out and a waiting list was in place.[200]

ConFuzzled officially announced the event schedule at the end of October. The activities were similar to the previous year and included an opening day BBQ and the WikiFur Pub Quiz, but there were also a few exceptions.[201] TabbieFox, the artist behind the convention's mascot and conbook, and Cheetah, the chair of Eurofurence who was credited with providing advisory support in the convention's first year, were made guests of honour. Both provided their own events in the form of a cartooning workshop and a panel on running a furry convention.

PawPets

Another new event was the very first PawPets UK Show production, titled "The Great James Mountbatten-Windsor's Magnificent Zoological Extravaganza (or The Mancunian Play)." A PawPet is the fandom's fancy name for a puppet. The word originated from a regular live internet show run by American furries in Florida called *The Funday PawPet Show* that started in November 1999. The show's popularity led to several regional "PawPet" groups forming in the USA that contributed to the main show. A German PawPet group was also set up by a local puppet fan called Fairlight (Marcus Hess). It took its inspiration from work done by Paw-Pets West (a group in the San Francisco Bay area) and eventually worked with his team to produce PawPet shows at EuroFurence beginning in 2000.[202]

According to the ConFuzzled 2009 Official Conbook's article "PawPet of Dreams," the ConFuzzled staff always had the idea of a PawPet show for 2009 on the table, even hinting at a show in the previous year's conbook, but as autumn arrived, preparation for such show never left the table. That was before Utlah joined the ConFuzzled staff as part of Convention Operations.

He pitched a show to the rest of the team that would be based on Jules Verne's *The Time Machine*, which would keep it in the spirit of the Victorian theme as well as allow time travel to different time periods to allow for pop culture references. He also had FatKraken on board with the idea, as she was already working on a puppet version of his fursuit character, Vin the weasel, and was willing to build an entire cast for the convention. As a result, Utlah had the support of the entire staff, but he indicated some slight regret in accepting the task when it dawned on him how big a task he had taken on:

> At the following ConFuzzled staff meeting, we discussed these options and asked who was going to direct the PawPet show. This soon went to a vote amongst the staff. The opinion would have been unanimously in my favour had it not been for my own panicked vote against it! I found myself the director of the show despite having very little experience

with either stage shows or puppets, but I was up for the challenge regardless of the very steep learning curve.[203]

Fortune was luckily on his side as Fairlight had relocated to England a few years earlier and was more than happy get involved and share his experience of working on the Eurofurence PawPet shows. Along with the help of Nidonocu, Frost T Wolf (Dean Langford), and FatKraken for the puppetry work, LevLion and Tungro led the stage works, YagFox helped write the script, and the entire team was able to put together a working production in six months.[204] Although the *Time Machine* story concept was scrapped early on for a simpler and more self-aware story of a bunch of animal people trying to put together a stage show, adding audience participation and cameos from FurbleFox and Uncle Kage, the debut show was incredibly well received amongst the attendees.

Like Eurofurence's PawPet productions, ConFuzzled's PawPet production would become a main event every year, getting bigger with a growing production team. Characters such as the Foxhound Jim (originally voiced by Fairlight, currently by Bungle), the grumpy rabbit Coney (originally voiced by Frost T Wolf, currently by Felix) and the sophisticated goat Sir William Bellicose (voiced by Nidonocu) became regular characters in the shows. The trio would later be joined by a mad scientist cat named Frank (voiced by Nall [Mat Beswick]), and his loopier canine friend, Floofy (voiced by Twll), and they would interact with many other colourful characters over the years.

The second year at the YHA was a massive success with 182 attendees[205] (56 of whom were fursuiters) and £2,000 being raised for two charities: the returning Badger Trust and the Manchester Dogs Home. However, the limitations of the Youth Hostel became evident. Events had to be held, at times, at awkward locations, and the kitchen staff was unable to cope with the number of attendees during breakfast).[185] While the hostel staff loved ConFuzzled, it was clear that for it to grow they needed to move.

BRITANNIA COUNTRY

During the closing ceremony, a preview video was shown that revealed that next year's convention was moving from the Youth Hostel to a 3-star Britannia Country House Hotel in Didsbury.[206] Although it was a five-mile drive south of the Manchester city centre, it promised many more room options such as single, twin, double, and triple beds with the ability to choose who to share with, as well as facilities like a swimming pool, gym, and games room. Importantly, the convention space rivalled that of RBW.

ConFuzzled 2010 was confirmed to run from 7 to 10 May 2010, with the theme of "Science." While registration was initially planned for July 31, it was delayed until 17 August 2009. Along with the change in venue, there was a small price increase of £10 (£60 for attending only and £170 for residential); single rooms required a small extra charge, while a triple room had a slight price reduction. There was also an increase in available rooms to 250.[207]

By October, almost all the rooms were sold out. People could now register with attending only spaces all the way up to a few weeks before the convention itself.[208] In total, there were 346 registered attendees,[209] nearly twice the number of 2009, making it the fastest-growing convention at the time. The convention was also gaining more of an international presence, with representatives from 17 different countries (although a large majority were British, followed by Germans).

That is not to say the run up was smooth going. On November 26, it was officially announced that FurbleFox had resigned as chair[210] for personal reasons. This was accompanied by the usual speculations and rumors for his "real reasons" for leaving. An election was held amongst the rest of the ConFuzzled staff, after which it was officially announced that Matt Lion would take on the role.[211]

Furries attending from abroad were potentially at risk for flight delays and cancellations when a volcano in Iceland erupted on 20 March, causing major airline disruptions for nearly two months. Flayrah reported that United Kingdom no-fly zones were being put in place as the volcanic ash clouds were potentially making their way towards the nation. Fortunately, the ash clouds moved west, and all airfields were cleared for use.[212]

Despite all this, the first ConFuzzled at the Britannia Hotel was a massive success. Many attendees loved the new venue for its large nightclub and dealers den spaces as well as for there being more bars. The attendee count doubled as did the number of fursuiters.

Most of the events were science-themed, such as a talk by a physicist from the Large Hadron Collider, as well as a science lab event in which people could try out a Van der Graaff generator and a heat-powered wheel. Adding to the atmosphere of science fun was the presence of many people dressed in lab coats.

> Frustratingly, the name of said physicist is unrecorded on the ConFuzzled conbook, and none of the staff members who were around at the time could recall the name of the physicist.

The biggest event of the convention, though, was the charity auction to benefit a wild cats private nature reserve. One of the auction items sold for £550, which made it the country's highest winning auction. That is, until a certain tablecloth went up for bidding.

For context, the guest of honour for ConFuzzled 2010 was TaniDaReal (Tanja Freese), a furry artist, fursuit maker, puppeteer, and crew member for the EuroFurence PawPet show in Germany. Her artwork was immensely popular at the Dealer's Den, and her commissions and stock of printed illustrations and badges all sold out.

Wanting to submit an original piece of artwork to the auction but running out of paper for it, she decided to draw a piece on the cloth used to cover her table at the Dealers' Den. It was placed in the charity auction with a starting bid of £50, but a bidding war quickly ensued, escalating the price to £200 in just a few seconds. Two of the bidders, ConFuzzled staff member RizzoRat (Colin McKay) and American furry Beshon Stapovic, were the lead bidders, going back and forth on their offers. The crowd got on its feet with roaring applause as RizzoRat made a £1,000 bid, but even this was not the end. Beshon continued to bid higher, and TaniDaReal was brought onto the stage.[213]

The auction ended with Beshon's winning bid of £2,000,[214] the news shocking everyone while attendees posted the news on Twitter with the hashtag #TaniCloth as the tablecloth was being escorted away by convention security. Thanks largely to the Charity Auction (of which £5,248 of the £7,789 went to charity), the final amount of money raised for the Wildlife Heritage Foundation was £6,200.[215]

As a result of the positive reception of the Britannia Hotel venue, more furries were eager to go to ConFuzzled 2011, and the organisers had a goal of taking over the entire convention hotel, which was willing

The charity auction tablecloth by TaniDaReal.

to do so if a certain target of 400 registrants could be achieved by the end of the year. Although over 200 people registered throughout the rest of 2010, this was not enough to meet that goal, but it was impressive enough for the hotel to extend the deadline by two months.[216] Just a few days shy of the deadline, ConFuzzled was able to reach the registration targetand secured exclusive access to the hotel.[217, 218] Hotel rooms remained available up until the end of March and attending-only tickets until the end of April.

ConFuzzled 2011 took place from 6 to 9 May with John "The Gneech" Robey, a furry cartoonist best known for his webcomic *Surburban Jungle*, as the guest of honour. Based in northern Virginia, USA, he was ConFuzzled's first guest of honour from outside of Europe.

The theme of "The Roaring Twenties" had a heavy emphasis on the American mobs of the time, so the conbook featured short biographies of the era's most notorious criminals with artwork by various British artists. Attendees got goodies that included artwork from The Gneech featuring Brok in both gangster mob and police detective attire on the T-shirt and sponsor mug. RizzoRat dressed as "the don" with fellow staff members dressed in mafia suits and packing toy Tommy Guns.

The PawPet show was once again a popular main event. The show poked fun at the neighbouring EuroFurence PawPet shows, mocking the characters trying to hide their German accents and their use of single-hand puppets over the ConFuzzled PawPet show's two-handed stage puppets (the EuroFurence PawPet show would later adopt these more complex puppets in future productions).

ConFuzzled 2011 conbook coverart by Nanook123.

ConFuzzled 2011 saw the debut of the Fursuit Dance Competition, an event that has been popular amongst fursuiters and dancers it debuted at Furry Weekend Atlanta and Anthrocon in 2008. Dance competitions are now regularly seen at conventions throughout the world.

The winners of the ConFuzzled 2011 Fursuit Dance Competition were duo fursuiters from Kent named Kiyo and Zakari, who performed a specially made mashup that included LMFAO's Party Rock; second place went to Dutch fursuiter Spark Wolf, performing to Hoobastank's Crawling in the Dark. Kiyo, Zakari, and Spark Wolf would continue to compete in future conventions, with Kiyo and Zakari winning four years in a row at ConFuzzled, and Spark Wolf winning in 2013.

The closing ceremony revealed the final attendance stats at 499, officially cementing ConFuzzled as not only the largest furry convention in the United Kingdom but also the second largest outside of North America (and behind EuroFurence).

The fact ConFuzzled was one person shy of a 500-attendee count was not lost on the convention, as the sound of groans could be heard amongst the applause when the figures was announced.[219] At the ConFuzzled 2017 opening ceremony it was joked that the count was due to one attendee cancelling, but the official attendee list and statistics would say that there were actually 498 confirmed attendees.[220]

The amount raised for the convention's charity, the International Otter Survival Fund, was also announced during the closing ceremony as £5,149.89, although the final total did not stop there. As with RBW 2010, Microsoft UK contributed to the total through their employee-match scheme to bring the total to £6,249.60. It was later revealed, however, that Microsoft had more than tripled their contribution to £4,400,[221] and an additional late donation brought the grand total to a round £10,000.

HINCKLEY ISLAND

The news of next year's convention was already set in motion at the 2011 closing ceremony, and an incentive was for those who had attended ConFuzzled for all five years. The theme of "Hollywood Glitz and Glamour" and a popular American fursuit dancer known as Mangusu were already confirmed for 2012.

As the Britannia Country House Hotel was now considered too small for the convention's projected growth, it was announced on 12 August 2011 that ConFuzzled was moving not only to a new hotel but a new location entirely. Saying farewell to Manchester, ConFuzzled moved south to the Barceló Hinckley Island, a four-star hotel in Leicestershire.[222]

The move was well suited to the con's needs, not only from a logistical standpoint of having the capacity to accommodate almost a thousand people with more function rooms for events, but also for its place as a main event for the British Furry Fandom. While ConFuzzled never remained the sole convention in the United Kingdom, the end of RBW and rise of ConFuzzled signified a turning point in the UK fandom.

Even with a hotel twice as large did not stop all the available room types selling out less than a week before residential registrations closed at the end of April.[223]

Although for many years there were furries willing to travel great distances, there was a perception of a North/South division going back to the early days of NorthernFurs and LondonFurs. Both groups had a role in creating their own conventions. When RBW ended, the choices were either to go abroad, travel to Manchester, or not go to a convention at all. With ConFuzzled moving closer to the centre of England there was less reason for northern and southern British furs to be separated.

ConFuzzled 2012 conbook cover by Tani-DaReal

The ConFuzzled team had gradually increased over the years from the initial 17 members in 2008 to 32 crew members in 2011. More people were recruited for the following year, leading to a staff restructure in which each department had leads, deputies, and crew for organisational purposes. The team size grew to 74 (45 staff and 29 crew), which didn't include the number of volunteers who helped out part time.

ConFuzzled 2012

ConFuzzled 2012 opened on May 25 with 726 attendees. The 49 attendees who had been attending every ConFuzzled since the beginning were each given a plaque as well as a gold-coloured con badge as a sign of gratitude.

The opening ceremony was made particularly memorable when Matt Lion escorted everyone out to witness the grand entrance by helicopter of the guests of honor, Mangusu and Colson, as well as Brok the Badger, the convention mascot. Brok was unveiled as a fully fursuited mascot created by American fursuit manufacturer CritterCountry and performed by fursuiter and 3D animator Deezlberries.[224]

Brok the Badger in the Helicopter at ConFuzzled 2012. Taken by SeanC.

Colson performed twice at the convention: once during an evening concert on Friday with music provided by Scottish musician Fox Amoore and again on Saturday at an unplugged session. Mangusu served as a judge along with Colson and Fox Amoore at the dance competition, and he was a DJ on Friday evening set at the nightclub, where he performed for sponsors at an exclusive lunchtime buffet.[225]

The convention had a pronounced impact on Mangusu's life because it was at this time that he met and started a relationship with a British furry named Dash Tiger. Despite initially being denied entry and detained by UK Immigration,[226] Mangusu would later move to England, and the pair were married in 2015.

The hotel was outside a busy A-road, and when lorry drivers witnessed the furries as they drove by, they contacted the hotel to question what was going on.

To fit with the theme, the staff put out a ConFuzzled sign resembling the Hollywood sign on a grassy hill. By the end of the convention, one attendee humorously changed the letters around to make it read "COFNUZZLED."

The convention took advantage of the hotel's multi-story rotunda, where rooms were located, by flying large banners featuring artwork of anthropomorphic characters from various films. The rotunda also offered the perfect photo opportunity for a large group photo of the fursuiters at the end of the annual fursuit parade, and it served as the venue for the closing ceremony.

The charity, the Nuneaton and Warwickshire Wildlife Sanctuary, received a total of £7,650[154, 209] by May 28. It is worth noting that this was the first (and only) time in ConFuzzled's history that the charity total was lower than the previous year. This was because there was no corporate donation to the charity that year, but attendees *did* donate more to the charity that year than they did in 2011.

ConFuzzled 2013

ConFuzzled 2013 returned to what was now called the Puma Hinckley Island Hotel on May 30. This time, the convention was extended to a five-day event. The theme was unveiled earlier in September as "The Middle Ages: A Mediaeval Fayre," with the author of the webcomic *Dangerously Cute*, Melissa "Gab" Douglas, and prolific furry author Kyell Gold as the guests of honour.[227] A total of 872 attendees registered. The main hotel was sold out, so an agreement was quickly made with the nearby Hilton Leicester to act as an overflow hotel with a free transport link.[154]

A key moment in the opening ceremony came when the Hinckley Island Hotel's executive general manager, Tony Hill, introduced his staff and expressed his love and gratitude for the furries of ConFuzzled with a few words:

> I don't think I've ever been so inappropriately dressed
> in my life, and that's a compliment. I'd just like to say
> … thank you so much for coming back, and you are
> very welcome here and we look forward to seeing you
> next year.

Some of the hotel staff showed their love for the furries by commissioning furry artist Neo to make their own furry-themed T-shirts, wearing them throughout most of the convention. Operations Manager Barrie Thomas contributed some entertainment with a poem specially written for ConFuzzled and its medieval theme titled "Ode to ConFuzzled":

ConFuzzled 2013: A Mediaeval Fayre

Lots and lots of people, with very fuzzy hair.

Truckers on the A5, wondering "What's going on there?"

The mystery, the magic, no wonder they stop and stare.

ConFuzzled 2013 conbook cover by Johis

Brok the Badger sits on his throne,

Welcome back to your Furry Puma home.[228]

Unlike previous years, Con-Fuzzled's event staff and volunteers were able to compile a schedule that featured several events specifically tied to the theme, along with the pre-existing non-theme events such as the PawPets show.

For context, Tony was wearing a smart business suit, whilst everyone else wore shirts with animals on them or fursuits. The remark got laughter and applause from the crowd.

The first two days had workshops for making your own chainmail and painting shields. On Friday, there was a demonstration of mediaeval combat with various weapons, and Sunday had a panel based on re-enactments and a workshop with role-play sparring.

The charity that year was STA Ferret Rescue, which benefited from the money raised by the popular Ferret Racing event as well as the auction and dealers' den contributions. By June 3, the charity had raised a total of £11,484, exceeding the 2011 record.

The love and support from the venue made it a bit awkward when Matt Lion added an announcement at the closing ceremony:

So, as you all may have noticed, we've gotten big! There's quite a few of you, and that has put a lot of strain on venue space and our staff. It's really hard to run a convention with this many people and we had to make a tough decision for the convention going forward.

What followed was a video explaining the future of ConFuzzled, and while the dramatic and suspenseful trailer hinted at the possibility of the convention being no more, something else entirely was in the works: ConFuzzled was moving to a new hotel.[229]

HILTON METROPOLE

Despite the sad news of the convention leaving Hinckley Island, the trailer was incredibly well received. It revealed the newest venue to be the Birmingham Hilton Metropole, the largest hotel at the Resorts World entertainment complex, which was adjacent to the National Exhibition Centre. It was bigger at over 790 guest rooms and easier to get to with its close proximity to both the Birmingham International Train Station and the International Airport—all for the same registration prices as the year before.[230]

ConFuzzled 2014

The extra-large capacity was needed for the 1,082 guests at Con-Fuzzled 2014 from May 23 to 27. According to Fred Patten, this made it the fourteenth furcon to pass the one thousand mark. Unlike previous venues, the Hilton Metropole's size meant con attendees had to share the major airport/resort hotel with regular guests and airline employees.

The theme was "The World of Tomorrow," representing the future as predicted by TV shows and movies of the Sixties and Seventies. The theme choice was also fitting for representing the future of ConFuzzled and its new environs.

The guests of honour for this year were Rick Griffin, an author and artist most famous for the multi-award winning webcomic *Housepets*, and Alexis Rudd, a fursuit and puppet maker who has had many of her creations on TV, including as a contestant on the American reality show *Jim Henson's Creature Shop Challenge*.[231]

The charity was the Cat Survival Trust, which received a total of £14,265 from the con. The charity expressed its gratitude at the closing ceremony, but also surprised everyone by revealing that the charity's director had commissioned a fursuit from FarukuCostumes.[232]

ConFuzzled 2014: The World of Tomorrow by Greevixor

ConFuzzled 2015

Confuzzled 2015
May 22nd – 26th
Theme: Wonderland
Attendance: 1223
Charity: Fat Fluffs Rabbit Rescue and Rehome, £13,552

ConFuzzled 2015 became the first ConFuzzled to feature a guest of honour from outside the furry fandom, veteran game designer and programmer Jeff Minter, alongside Dutch furry cartoonist Henrieke.[233]

Although there was much emphasis about Minter being an outsider, he had prior awareness of the furry fandom, as evidenced by his inclusion of furry fanart in one of the levels for his PC demo of his *Space Giraffe* game back in 2008.

In a talk he did at the convention titled "History of Llamasoft Games," Minter stated that he would have identified as a furry had he known about it back when he was developing games in the 1980s and '90s. He would often reference ruminant animals such as llamas and sheep in his games, and also used the nickname "Yak" on forums and informal credits.

ConFuzzled 2015 conbook cover art by Alector Fencer

At the closing ceremony, Minter expressed his thanks to convention staff and the attendees for being friendly and welcoming during his time at the convention even though he was no an active part of the fandom. He added, "[B]ut you know what, after all the fun I've had, the suits I've hugged and the people I've met, it made me realise that I am a furry!"[234] This inspired a round of applause, as well as people in the crowd cheering "ONE OF US," a common chant towards those outside the fandom who showed their support.

Zootopolis Inspires Awoo at ConFuzzled 2016

ConFuzzled 2016
May 27th – 31st
Theme: Carnival of the Night
Attendence: 1451
Charity: Prickles Hedgehog Rescue (£21,946)

This wouldn't be the only chant that originated from the convention. Before the 2016 iteration, the Disney animated feature film *Zootropolis* (aka *Zootopia* in the United States and other countries) was released to cinemas. The film was a huge deal for furry fans, being as it was the most furry-like movie Disney had made since perhaps 1973's *Robin Hood*. As a result, many furry fans were hyped for the film worldwide, and some organized trips to cinemas to watch it, some arriving in fursuits.

One of the many outstanding moments in the film is when the main characters—con artist fox Nick Wilde and bunny police officer Judy Hopps—attempt to sneak into a top-secret facility guarded by wolves. It was established in an earlier scene that wolves had a habit of howling at random as a group, so in an attempt to distract and avoid being spotted, Judy Hopps decides to howl. As a result, all the wolves begin howling in response, even when they desperately try to stop each other.

During ConFuzzled 2016–, one of the events was an exclusive screening of *Zootropolis* at the nearby Cineworld cinema. In a nod to the howling scene, a staff member designed a British-style road sign at the Con-Ops desk stating "Do not Awoo"; violators were threatened with a £350 penalty. This had the inverse effect, naturally, inspiring furries to howl "Awoo!" in unison during main stage events and group photos. This became a trend that spread to furry conventions around the world.

Following a mock campaign on Twitter called #LegaliseAwoo, ConFuzzled gave special "Awoo Permits" to sponsors and issued "Awoo fines" to anyone who lacked a permit.

ConFuzzled 2016 conbook cover art by Rachez.

ConFuzzled Continues at the Hilton

ConFuzzled has remained at the Hilton Metropole as of this writing (2022) and has continued to grow at a steady rate. The scale of the venue and its prime location has qualifies it as one of the world's big conventions alongside the likes of EuroFurence, Anthrocon, and Midwest FurFest.

Even as it grows, ConFuzzled strives to remain true to its roots. This was most evident during ConFuzzled 2017, which took place on 26–30 May as the tenth convention. It celebrated the milestone with a fitting time-travel theme of "Most Excellent Adventure" (after the 1989 movie *Bill and Ted's Excellent Adventure*), featuring plenty of artwork and props from past cons. ConFuzzled even brought back the Badger Trust as the convention charity and, considering that the charity was stunned when it received a £1,610 donation from the convention back in 2008, imagine the reaction when it received £21,113.36 in 2017![209]

The opening ceremony was notable for featuring both a dramatized recreation of the founding of ConFuzzled and an animated story of the past ten conventions. These two features were entertaining for the convention audience, but anyone who had actually been present for these events would have to say they fell short on historical accuracy.

The dramatization starred LevLion and Wolfie Fox sitting in an "undisclosed European convention" in 2006. The pair suddenly talk about setting up a convention, suggesting ideas like its name, mascot, and where to promote it in comedically prescient ways. As a dramatic recreation with actors replacing the actual individuals involved, some liberties were expected.[235]

Given that LevLion was one of the two original furries present, he commented regarding the first discussion that "apart from it taking place in a stairwell at the hotel, it was pretty much how it went down," although there were two discrepancies: first, LevLion and FurbleFox stated the discussion depicted occurred in 2005 not 2006; secondly, the "undisclosed European convention" was incorrect. Instead of using Nuremburg Castle, the venue of Eurofurence in both 2005 and 2006, the footage was of Eurofurence 13 at the Ringberg Hotel in Suhl in 2007. This can be forgiven since there was a lack of usable footage from Nuremburg Castle, and the Ringberg was possibly more recognisable to furries from the period.

The animated story was done in a form of infographic with signpost figures and simple graphics. It had a good sense of humour, and the information provided was technically correct, albeit simplified.

One example of this is when it states that the first ConFuzzled was created by the "small group of dedicated friends" represented by 17 figures. This refers to the original 17 members of the ConFuzzled staff, but it ignores the other organisers who had a hand in the creation of ConFuzzled such as SouthPaw and Rocky Raccoon, not to mention the chairfolk of conventions in Europe and the USA, who also had a hand in getting ConFuzzled off the ground.

Although not explicitly stated, the animation also suggests that all the original team had remained for the past ten years. Six of them had

ConFuzzled 2017 Conbook front and back covers by Skaifox.

stood down at that point, however, while the team had been joined by many more with additional help from numerous volunteers that eventually totaled 161 members.[236]

CONFUZZLED 2018 TO NOW

ConFuzzled managed to keep its momentum with a video-game-themed iteration in 2018. With 1,908 attendees, £26,037.40 was raised for the Vale Wildlife Hospital. The guests of honour featured artist Dark Natasha and writer Ryan Campbell, and the con introduced the "CFz Game Jam" for game developers.

> Those who arrived at the convention a day earlier had an amusing encounter with smartly dressed guests, as it turned out to be the last day of the Meat Management Industry Awards.

The next year, ConFuzzled made significant changes. As more and more attendees registered as sponsors in 2019, an option was added for "super sponsors," who were given access to more exclusive events and incentives, a tactic inspired by Eurofurence. It was also the first year since 2008 not to have a PawPets show. The show went on hiatus to allow for an extra year of preparation. Along with the guest of honour, an animator and layout artist named Joaquin Baldwin who had worked on multiple films for Walt Disney Animation, the con introduced the "Community Spotlight" award to honour furries in the local furry community. The premier prize was awarded to comic artist Gem Squirrel.

The charity fundraiser was particularly memorable. The Grentleshaw Wildlife Centre had suffered a fire two months before the convention began, resulting in an estimated £12,000 worth of damages,[237] so when the convention raised

ConFuzzled 2019 conbook cover by Garnetto.

£30,300.69, the wildlife centre expressed overwhelming gratitude and even named a Harris hawk after Brok.[238]

Speaking of Brok the Badger, the mascot was given a redesign by Made by Mercury that was revealed at the opening ceremony.[239] It was also the final year that Matt Lion would run ConFuzzled as chair. He announced at the closing ceremony that he would step down and take on the role of master of ceremonies.[240] Graafen Blackpaw also stepped down as head of ConOps.

As of this writing, ConFuzzled continues to be run by Crimson and Russet and the board of directors, along with a team of over 160 staff members. The convention remains the largest in the United Kingdom, the second largest in all of Europe, and twelfth worldwide.

SCOTIACON

Scotland's furry fandom has followed a trajectory similar to ConFuzzled in the way it was inspired by the World Science Fiction Conventions held in Glasgow in 1995 and 2005. As mentioned earlier, the country had its own mailing lists and discussions in the UKFur Forums. Scotland also had its own furmeets, which used the rotational format in Edinburgh, Aberdeen, and Glasgow under the ScotsFur banner before splitting into separate, city-based furmeets.

In the late 2000s, there were two key differences between Scotland and England when it came to the furry fandom: numbers and the lack of a convention. The population of Scottish ranked second after England, though it was higher than in Wales and Northern Ireland.

While it is impossible to find hard data to estimate the population of furries in individual countries, a snapshot of the UKFur Forums in 2007 shows the discussion activity in regional groups. At the time, there were 85 topics and 1,047 replies in the Scotland-specific subforums while England-specific subforums totalled 396 topics and 5,869 replies; the Welsh subforums had 18 topics and 187 replies in total.[113]

Original logo for ScotiaCon 2010 by Ixis.

There was still no furry convention in Scotland in the 2000s, but this was about to change.

ThrashWolf, who was running the regular furmeets in Aberdeen, formed a small team and announced a new convention called ScotiaCon, opening the official website in April 2009.

It was slated to be held at the Ramada Jarvis Hotel in the northern city of Inverness in April 2010, with ThrashWolf acting as chair, Ixis as vice chair and public relations director, Zenon as treasurer, and TigerFire as head of security. Software engineers Kanibal Thorne and Kytheraen were to handle the convention's own Web forum. In an interview with the *FurteanTimes*, Ixis gave a detailed description of the convention and made it clear that the intent of ScotiaCon's existence was to bring more furry events to Scotland:

> ScotiaCon is our attempt to create Scotland's first
> furry convention, simply, but it means a lot more to
> all those involved. We feel Scotland has been left out
> a little bit when it comes to UK furry events and we
> want to put that right.[241]

She also emphasised that ScotiaCon, being Scotland's first furry convention, would build its theme around Scottish history and heritage. A Scottish Terrier named after the legendary hero William Wallace was their official mascot, and early ideas for events were based on Scottish history and culture:

> We want to theme some events with English furs vs.
> Scottish, just for fun. Think foam swords.... That's an
> example of the history we'd like to embed within the
> con. We don't intend to give a history lesson of course
> — we're just proud of our heritage and want to make
> our event unique!

Thanks partially to Ixis' connections with the rest of the British furry fandom, she was able to get FatKraken on board as a guest of honour, as well as interest from 2 Gryphon as another potential guest.

Yet, in July, it was announced that the convention would be postponed until April 2011. By the end of 2009, the staff had increased to 11, Scottish furry musician Fox Amoore was confirmed as a second guest of honour, and the convention had donated its first ticket to the charity auction of RBW. It sold for £90, which was a little less than the price of their sponsor ticket of £99.

The following year would see a lot of staff changes, with the most visible change occurring in July when ThrashWolf stepped down as chair for personal reasons.

Blackwolf and Smirnoff, who both initially joined the team in March as vice chair and public relations director respectively, became co-chairs of ScotiaCon. They relaunched the website and social media presence for the con and announced new dates of 15–17 July 2011.[242] By the time ScotiaCon opened, Ixis was the only staff member who had been on the original team, serving as editor of the conbook and as one of the general volunteers.

ScotiaCon opened successfully with 50 people making the journey to the very north of Iverness, Scotland, to attend Scotland's first ever furry convention. FatKraken provided a talk on how to make good fursuits as well as leading an event for attendees to make terrible fursuits out of paper, cardboard, bin bags and scraps akin to ConFuzzled's Frankensuits. The other guest of honour, musician Fox Amoore, performed live and gathered other musicians and brave singers for a morning show. More music would be had at the karaoke show, FurryVision, modeled after a famous continental song contest.

There were a couple of events that represented the theme of Scotland. Eat Scotland offered attendees the chance to try some local dishes such as Cullen Skink (a smoked haddock soup), Haggis, and deep-fried Mars Bars, the last of which proved immensely popular with attendees rushing to grab a piece.

For the fursuiters, there was the Fursuit Highland Games in which seven fursuiters competed against each other in games of darts, bowling, caber tossing, hunting, and dancing. Other fursuit events included charades and a pool tournament.

Outside of fursuiting there was the usual dealer's den and a "Professor of Science" who gave lectures on the furry related science.[243]

... and like with ConFuzzled 2010, the name of this professor was not recorded.

The fursuit walk took place on the Saturday with 14 fursuiters and two puppets going on tour around the city centre. The staff worried about the weather impacting the fursuit walk, but the weather managed to hold up just long enough for a group photo featuring the Inverness Castle and a visit to Johnny Foxes' Pub.[244]

Although there was no charity for the event, there was an art auction that featured plush toys and artwork for sale. The highlight of the auction was a limited-edition bottle of whiskey signed by the ScotiaCon staff. After a bidding war, it sold for £450.[245]

The convention concluded with a group photo, an official convention cake, and a trip to Loch Ness. Everyone who attended praised the convention for its relaxed nature and fun events and were willing to forgive minor issues that were anticipated with a first-year convention such as event timing and organisation being a bit rough around the edges.[246]

SCOTIACON 2012

ScotiaCon would return to Inverness on 27–30 July 2012, and the positive reception from the first year meant that the confirmed registered attendees rose to 107, despite a slight increase in the price. While the events were roughly the same (the return of Eat Scotland, the FurryVision Song Contest, Failsuits, the Highland Fur Games, the nightclub called the Highland Fling and Fox Amoore performing a live set), other things changed now that the convention was firmly established. The Ramada Jarvis Hotel became the Mercure Inverness Hotel, the convention was plastered with the theme of "Keep Calm and Sing Along" with a conbook cover drawn by the guests of honour, Nimrais and Kajito, of the convention mascot Wallace depicted in a scene reminiscent of The Sound of Music.[247] There was also a new charity, Highland Tiger, which thanked ScotiaCon afterwards for the impressive £2,080 raised[248] to help with conservation and recovery of the Scottish wildcat.

The convention remained in Inverness for one more year, with the 2–5 August 2013 convention theme being "Science Fiction." TaniDaReal returned to Britain to be the guest of honour, this time alongside her partner and Eurofurence vice chair, Nightpaw, and fellow artist SpiritRaptor.[249] The now traditional Eat Scotland returned, albeit as an additional ticketed event.

Unfortunately, not much information about this con is known, although the data obtained by Fred Patten suggests the convention underperformed compared to previous years. There were only 89 confirmed attendees and only £615.85 was raised for charity.

Possible reasons for this underperformance were its date and location. July and August was the time for big events like EuroFurence and the LondonFurs Summer Party. Also, the hotel rates rose.

Because Inverness was on the northern coastline of Scotland, it was difficult to get to, especially for those traveling from England or Europe.

Scotiacon 2013 conbook art by TaniDaReal.

It is likely that new co-chairs SilverFoxwolf, Ceilfox, and Graafen Blackpaw had convenience on their minds when they announced that the 7–9 November 2014 convention would be moved three hours south to the Mecure Livingston outside of Edinburgh..[250]

ScotiaCon 2014 had the theme of "Superheroes (and Supervillains)" and featured the fursuit maker Made by Mercury as guest of honour. Main events returned like Eat Scotland, Fursuit Games, dances, and music. Some efforts were made to be in keeping with the theme such as a Green Lantern Corp canvas being produced for the auction. The overall decision to move paid off, as 105 people attended and £655.81 was raised for World Horse Welfare. While the hotel itself was described as a little unprepared for hosting a furry con, the Mercure Livingstone appeared to be the ideal home for ScotiaCon for future years.

The convention continued to grow in attendance year after year, starting off in 2015 with 152 attendees and £2,089.40 raised for the Scottish Owl Centre.[251, 252] This continued with 2016's convention hosting 176 attendees, although the charity total raised for the Scottish Waterways Trust dropped to £1,750.[253]

2015—Theme: Wasteland. Guest of Honour: Kerijano
2016—Theme: Winter Wonderland. Guest of Honour: BoosieTheDragon
2017—Theme: Pirates. Guest of Honour: Faruku. Charity: Parrot Trust Scotland (£3,250)
2018—Theme: Murder Mystery in Medieval Times. Guest of Honour: Syber. Charity: Saints Sled Dog Rescue (£3,000)
2019—Theme: Steampunk. Guest of Honour: Pocari Roo. Charity: Five Sisters Zoo (£3,500)

The convention surpassed 200 attendees in 2017 with 290 attendees. It surpassed 300 attendees in 2018 with 346 attendees. And it surpassed 400 in 2019 with 482 attendees.[254]

With this consistent growth and a consistently reliable set of scheduled events, it did come as a bit of a shock at the 2019 closing ceremony that there be no ScotiaCon 2020. As time had passed, more events competed for the winter season, so ScotiaCon's 10th instalment moved to February 2021.

The convention also moved from Livingstone to a much bigger city: Glasgow. A trailer was shown at the 2019 closing ceremony revealing the newest venue to be the Crowne Plaza, which is adjacent to the Scottish Event Campus (often abbreviated to SEC), the country's largest exhibition centre.

The new venue, which offered double the number of rooms the Mecure had, and with several other hotels available for overflow, ScotiaCon could now claim to be in the same league as ConFuzzled, but it would also bring the history of the Scottish furry fandom full circle.[255]

It had all begun with a small gathering in Glasgow at what was then the SECC during the World Science Fiction Convention in 1995, and it now returned to the same city and venue with a huge potential.

Scotiacon conbooks: 2015 character art by BooshieTheDragon and background by Heartlily; 2016 art by BooshieTheDragon; 2017 art by IndiWolf; 2018 art by Tazara; 2019 art by Syberwuff.

PITCHING A TENT

With the cancellation of RBW, the British Furry Fandom had two conventions by 2011: ConFuzzled in England and ScotiaCon in Scotland. But these cons were not the only fun options for furries in the UK.

Furries in countries like Canada and the United States had been enjoying camping together for years. The first and oldest annual camping event is Camp Feral, which is based in Ontario, Canada, and was founded in 1998. Rather like an outdoor convention, Camp Feral offered activities involving art, music, and dances, as well as various outdoor games such as Capture the Flag.

Archived photo galleries reveal that camping events organised in the United Kingdom as early as 2004,[256] although these were clearly sporadic and infrequent.

This changed in 2008, when a Doncaster furry and musician named Kodiak organised a camping event on the UKFur Forums. Going under the straightforward name of UKFur Camp and taking place in the latter half of July at Knotlow Farm in Buxton, Derbyshire, the first camping trip included 16 furries. Setting up tents in the fields, they indulged in activities such as drawing, Capture the Flag, walking around the countryside, and socialising in general.

Furstival logo art by IcyDragon

Although one account from an attendee going by the name Nate recalled that there was quite a bit of rain, some of the tents fell apart, and a furry named Aetherfax nearly choked to death by inhaling rice, the camping trip was considered a huge success.

UKFur Camp returned the following year, growing to 24 attendees. Fortunately, the weather was kinder and the campers were better prepared. More fun was had, and some furries made cocktails and discovered a nearby.[257, 258]

SouthFurCamp logo and mascot by Jesslyra.

With more people enjoying the camping, Kodiak and co-organiser Icey decided to expand on it, eventually renaming it Furstival. Despite chatter that Kodiak might enlist in the army and that he was looking for someone to take over for him, interest in Furstival grew. The event was scheduled for 21–25 July 2011.[259]

The camp organisers have managed to maintain the small and simple event, running it for five nights in the latter half of July. Due to restrictions from the campsite, tickets are usually limited to fewer than 50 people. Attendees receive a dogtag exclusive to the event, and in later years a sponsor category was added to include an exclusive T-shirt.

Activities include Capture the Flag and Scavenger Hunts, along with the art, quizzes, and anything that fits the year's theme selected by attendees ("Hawaiian Islands" for 2013, "Barebones" for 2014, "Picture Show" for 2015, "Medieval" for 2016, "School" for 2017, "Space" for 2018, and no theme for 2019). Many furries enjoyed the Peak District setting, with its beautiful nature walks and riverbanks.

As of this writing, Furstival has continued to operate as the only currently running, annual, furry-themed camping event in the United Kingdom. While it has evolved further to have exclusive merchandise such as T-shirts, it has remained rather small and simple in its structure, even limiting the attendance each year to anywhere between 30 to 40 tickets.

It is not the only furry camp, however. Taunton furry artist Jess Lyra (Jess Hayes) runs her own furry camp in the Taunton countryside under the name SouthFurCamp, which has taken place in July every year from 2008.[260] The first year had only eight people, but it eventually grew to over 50 people, according to Jess. It was cancelled after 2015, likely because of a staffing shortage. Jess remarked in an advertisement for the penultimate event that she would be running it all by herself.[261]

As of writing, JessLyra is looking at reviving SouthFurCamp for some time in 2023.

FURRY RAVERS IN THE UK

In the spirit of furry conventions having a nightclub meet in the evenings, which was either called a Furry Dance or a Furry Rave, there have been attempts in the fandom to run an event dedicated to music. Like what most people would expect from a rave, there would be DJs and plenty of lights and smokes to stoke up the atmosphere. This would last for two or three days and have a furmeet style atmosphere during the day.

The furry news site *Dogpatch Press* has a page that tracks all known furry raves, and while it shows that more than half of these events are in the United States, it implicitly credits Germany as having the first furry rave: Cologne Furdance, which debuted on 14 June 2008 and ran biannually until 30 July 2016.[262]

Remarkably, Britain had its first furry rave less than two months after Germany, thanks to a furry named Jasper Foxx. A fursuiter hailing from Bristol, he attended clubs that played hardstyle and hardhouse music, as well as participated in the bright and colourful Candy Raving scene.

One day in 2008, he attended an event at Club Cavern, a small basement venue of his local pub situated at the St. Nicholas Market called The Crown. After enquiring about hiring the place out, he discussed the idea of doing a furry rave night with his friend and furry DJ, Swolf.

> Candy raving is a counter-culture of raving where people dress in brightly coloured clothes and bracelets, in contrast to the common dark image of raves in the '90s and early 2000s.[263]

FRANTIC EUFURIA

Foxx advertised it as a "UKFur Rave" on the UKFur Forums with a date set for 27 July 2008,[264] although it would later be moved to August 1 for scheduling reasons. Because it was intended as a privately organised event, Jasper restricted who could access and discuss the event on

UKFur, so it is difficult to know how many people attended. It is, however, known through calendar event listings that UKFur Rave had another iteration on 7 November, as well as a third iteration that took place on 27 February 2009.[265, 266] Jasper Foxx himself consistently recalled the event being successful not just for him but for Club Cavern itself: "Club Cavern operated a process where I put back a £100 deposit, which was refunded if my guests spent a minimum of £500 at the bar. We never lost a deposit, and equally, I never got it back…. I always rolled it over to the next event and this did rather inspire confidence."[267]

In 2010 Jasper Foxx rebranded the UKFur Rave to appeal to more furries. Given his interest in hard dance and rave music, he renamed it after one of his favourite music anthology label, Frantic Euphoria. The first rave under Frantic Eufuria name took place on 1 June 2010 and continued to be a biannual event, with attendance doubling at Frantic Eufuria 2 on 16 October.

Even though the formula remained virtually the same as the past UKFur Raves, feedback following FE2 lead to a decision to include rock music by having electronic dance night at FE3 on 2 April, as well as Frantic Eufuria (Rock) on 14 May 2011.

As wonderful as Club Cavern was for a venue, its size was a problem for the growing furry rave. It could legally operate at a maximum of only 60 people. On 15 May 2011, it was announced on UKFur that Frantic Eufuria would be expanded, first by being incorporated into a limited liability company with Jasper as chair, Ravell (Alexander Bennitt) as vice chair, and Anthropuppy as treasurer.[268] Second, the rave would move to the Bristol YHA, where it could not only host electronic and rock music at the same time also provide on-site accommodations.

Group photo of Frantic Eufuria 1 in 2010 (photo by Kai Wulf).

Hard Mode DVD set for Frantic Eufuria 2. Taken by Awkore.

The new venue debuted at FE4 on 5 November 2011 and returned for FE5 on 7 April 2012. While the bigger venue and multiple dances meant there was more to organise, Jasper Foxx reflected on how less stress inducing running the rave was compared to a furry convention: "A single night rave was probably a comparatively easy thing to run. There was only the DJ scheduling to deal with, the YHA bookings and making sure that everything is in place before the one big night. It was a good starting point in running something between a furmeet and convention." [267]

Plenty of photos and videos recorded the raves and associated activies. So much video footage was collated that DVDs were produced by furry filmmakers Awkore and Equium for each Frantic Eufuria from FE2 to FE5.[269]

There was one stressful challenge Frantic Eufuria had, however, that was on a par with conventions: getting and keeping venues. Although the YHA suited well, the intention was to have a proper event space for the music and dances. FE6 was intended to occur at the Warehouse Club, a large event space that was opposite the YHA. Announcements were already made, and everything was prepared, yet three days before Frantic Eufuria was scheduled to take place, one of the bartenders was caught pedalling drugs at work and the venue's license was revoked. FE6 therefore returned to YHA, as the fallback venue on 20 October.

FE7 would also use the YHA as their complete venue on 20 April 2013, but as attendance kept growing, the the space was becoming cramped, as well as both hot and humid for fursuiters and non-fursuiters alike. With the Warehouse Club no longer an option, it was time to look outward. According to Jasper Foxx, the event's size meant Bristol was no longer an option without costs being exorbitant.

On 8 September 2013, it was announced that Frantic Eufuria would move from Bristol to Weston-Super-Mare's Club Tabu on 15 February 2014.[270] To the organisers's minds, this was a good idea, and the club's owners eagerly promised a hundred attendees to the local bed & breakfasts. But for other furries, this was a horrible idea. There were rumours and scaremongering spreading around that Weston Super-Mare was a dangerous place for furries and fursuiters because it was an area associated with chavs (or non-Brit readers, a "chav" is a lout or uncouth, aggressive youth). Unfortunately, all posts from the dedicated Frantic Eufuria subforum on UKFur about this have been deleted, but Jasper Foxx recalls these stories among the community.

This widespread panic put a heavy toll on FE8, and attendance dropped from reportedly over 140 the year prior to only 38. The owners of Club Tabu were not happy and promptly refused to host Frantic Eufuria again, leaving the organisers with a tarnished reputation.

Although there were attempts to try again for another event someplace else, internal politics left the organisers divided, and on 27 April 2014 it was officially decided to cancel Frantic Eufuria. The event had lost its way, starting as a humble, single-night furry rave and turning into a mini-convention, which lead to its absurd growth and made it too difficult to find an affordable space to host it.

WHAT THE FLUFF AND OTHER RAVES

The cancellation did not stop the demand for furry rave events, but the timing did conveniently line up with a new furry rave event that had been planned by fursuiters Weremoco, Skitz, and Freddypanda since 2012. What the Fluff, as it was called, ran bi-annually in Southampton as a meet followed by a fursuit-friendly dance night with free entry.[271-273] It ran successfully from 1 November 2014 to 27 February 2016 at The Strand before moving to Eastleigh Football Club on 24 September 2016[274] and having its last event on 2 September 2017 at the Talking Heads.[275]

Meanwhile up north, there was an unsuccessful attempt by FurbleFox in 2011 to start FurDance UK, a furry rave inspired by Cologne FurDance. It would not be until March 2017 that the MancFurs managed to arrange an event with Club Alter Ego called Club Animalz, the British nightclub for animals. As of this writing, it continues to be held immediately after the MancFurs Summer and Winter Parties.

What The Fluff 6 promotional poster.

FURRIES OF THE NORTH

Although the United Kingdom was able to establish two ongoing conventions as well as other major events, the mid-Noughties saw increasing demand for conventions throughout the year. Furries were increasingly seeking alternatives to ConFuzzled because although reception to ConFuzzled has remained positive overall, the size of the convention had become problematic for many seeking a more intimate experience.

Big conventions do have their downsides such as long lines for registration and main stage events, finding friends to catch can be difficult, and it's pretty much a guarantee that attendees will miss out on at least one or two events because of scheduling conflicts. Even when ConFuzzled was at the Hinckley in Leicester from 2012 to 2013, and later, Birmingham since 2014, long lines for the opening of the dealers' den, dance competition, and Pawpet show were becoming more common. This possibly explains why the ratio between sponsors and non-sponsors has changed since early entry to these events is one of the incentives.

THE GREAT FURSCAPE

For a few northern furries there was also the fact that ConFuzzled's move to the midlands meant it felt less local. Outside of Scotiacon, the next convention for northern furries was the Great Furscape, which was organised by Beshon and Shadow Seerclaw on the last weekend of October 2012 at Alton Towers resort complex outside Stoke-on-Trent. Although it didn't explicitly call itself a convention, the Great Furscape had many of the same features, such as the Splash Landings Hotel as its main venue for fursuit games, a buffet, and a nightclub,[276] as well as providing registered guests with a conbook and badge.

The main draws, however, were the attractions at Alton Towers, including its waterpark, which attendees had exclusive access to for two hours on Saturday[277] and the theme park, where along with the rollercoasters and amusements was live entertainment as part of the resort's Halloween-themed Scarefest.

With at least 37 furries attending, it was successful enough to run again on the third weekend of October 2013, with at least 48 furries attending a pirate-themed weekender. There were plans for a third event on the third weekend of October 2014—with a formal ad even being placed in the conbook of ConFuzzled in 2014—but that same year the official website was updated with the simple message: "Unfortunately Great Furscape has had to be cancelled this year. Please await further announcements."[278]

That announcements never came, and so the most northern furry convention-like event was no more.

FURVENTION

Even though the Great Furscape billed itself as a northern furcon and its location at Stoke-on-Trent was north of the midlands, it was still south of ConFuzzled's former home in Manchester, which many northern furries wouldn't consider north at all. A proper northern convention wasn't far away however, as a website and an online forum were set up in January 2014 and business cards and flyers were distributed later at ConFuzzled 2014 for a new furry convention in Liverpool called FurVention.

The product of ScouseFur organisers such as Fang (Steven Hatton), Pet (Peter Vaughan) and Matt (Stuart O'Shaughnessy),[279] FurVention was planned to be a northern furry convention situated at the Holiday Inn Liverpool on Lime Street in January 2015.[280] Its presentation and advertisements were very focused on appealing to furry fans of technology, computers, and video games with its theme of "All Systems Go." They even invited video game composer CoLD SToRAGE (Tim Wright) as guest of honour.[281]

Organising went awry when, on 3 January 2015, it was revealed that the original hotel was going to be renovated, forcing a move to the Aloft Hotel. The change in venue also meant the length of the convention was cut from four days down to three.[282]

FurVention succeeded where other early proposed conventions did not, running from January 23 to 25 with a total of 64 people registered, which was a fairly good number considering ScotiaCon started with 50. With the event schedule for this con lost, it's uncertain what exactly went on, but videos from the convention show there was a nightclub, dealers' den, and a fursuit walk[283, 284] As was traditional for most furry conventions, money was also raised for charity: a total of around £100 for Cancer Research UK. Comments from attendees were positive, and some described it as being no different to a large furmeet at a hotel.

The convention was confirmed to run the following year on 5 April 2015, and registration opened on August 3 for the 22 to 24 January 2016 con.[285] The theme would be "Wastelanders." Yet on September 2, it was announced that the convention was cancelled, and the excuse was technical issues with the registration system. According to the FurVention Facebook page: "This is due to technical difficulties we have been experiencing though the last few months which has resulted in us not being able to take registrations or keep things running, because of this our future is also unknown. We do not know if this is merely a hiatus of running or a permanent closure."[286]

Although the convention's Facebook and Twitter accounts hinted at the return to the Aloft in 2020,[287] no further news has been issued since then.

WILD NORTH

For the north of Britain, there would not be a new convention until 2018 with the test run of Wild North, an all-inclusive weekend convention hosted by Ziegenbock, Tyde Ratmeat, and Kivuli Rider from the NewcastleFurs.

Its beginnings mirror those of Eurofurence. Its premiere was organised amongst a small group of furries online, with 12 of its 14 registered attendees spending a relaxed weekend at the Joiner's Shop Bunkhouse in the quiet borough of Chathill, near Alnwick.

All attendees were given a goodie bag containing drinks, snacks, and a personalised letter.

Group photo outside the Joiner's Shop Bunkhouse in 2018. Photo by Greskhil Vulfhart.

Fitting with the northern English nature of the event, the beverages and snacks provided were locally produced. These included Kendal Mint Cakes from Cumbria and Fentimans from Hexam, Northumberland.

Although there were plenty of group activities at the Bunkhouse, Wild North also had excursions to the Alnwick Food Festival and the Beamish Open-Air Museum.[288]

The test run was considered a success, and it was announced at the closing ceremony that not only would there be a full-fledged iteration the following year but it would take place at the much larger venue of Featherstone Castle near Haltwhistle.

The new venue provided many more rooms for indoor and outdoor events, and the Haltwhistle area was a short drive to heritage sites like Hadrian's Wall. Although most of the promotion was limited to the Telegram group, the new convention was able to achieve double its previous attendance with 24 furries. As with the first year, attendees got a goodie bag with drinks, snacks, and a conbook. The convention ended with a trip to the Beamish Open-Air Museum. There were also £187.93 in donations raised at an auction for the charity Pawz for Thought.[289]

Group photo inside Featherstone Castle for Wild North 2019. Photo by Greskhil Vulf-hart

CONVENTIONS DOWN SOUTH

For furries in the south of England, their closest convention was RBW in London before its unfortunate end. There had been proposals from around 2013 to 2015 for a new furry convention in the south, such as one in Devon called Furviera that was proposed for October 2015 by Rorschfox, but it wouldn't come to fruition due to lack of interest and various difficulties with organising such a convention.

One of the more infamous failures was called Fur Isle, a furry convention with the concept of taking place on the Isle of Wight that was proposed by Kitual. Although interest in it was remarkably high, a few setbacks, including difficulties raising funds for a hotel, miscommunication between staff members, and waning interest from fans after several poorly received seasonal events, led to the convention being cancelled less than three weeks before its planned date in October 2015.

> Kitual would propose another furry convention in 2017 called Further South under his new company Wyvern Events Ltd. Although it opened for registration in 2018 with plans to run in Brighton, as of writing it has remained on hiatus.

Fortunately, two proposals did succeed, and coincidentally they are both situated in the southwest of England.

FURCATION

Before he cancelled it, Jasper Foxx initially wanted Frantic Eufuria to grow into an event similar to the Tidy Weekender, a rave festival in which thousands of clubbers would spend a weekend at a campsite in the north of Wales. Even with Frantic Eufuria's demise, the campsite event remained lodged in his mind and recognising the demand for smaller conventions motivated him to pursue the concept.

He began a plan under the existing Frantic Eufuria, Ltd. company. Bringing his friends Anthropuppy and Swolf on board to discuss ideas, they performed market research at other conventions like ConFuzzled to form their ideal approach. Although social media accounts were registered as early as July 2014, the event was officially revealed as Furcation on 1 December 2014.[290]

What made Furcation stand out compared to other big events was that it advertised itself explicitly as not a furry convention but rather as a furry seaside resort with entertainment akin to Pontins (a company that operates amusement parks) or Butlins (a chain of seaside resorts). The Warrens Holiday Village in Clevedon, North Somerset, was designated as the venue, and Furcation was planned to take place from 11 to 14 September 2015. The Furcation website made it abundantly clear as to how and why it was not a furry convention:

> A Convention is a heavily themed event with multiple
> shows, events and seminars which take place under
> one roof. Furcation is a far more open and relaxed
> weekend where attendees can choose to either socialise
> on site or organise their own activities on or off site.
> While we will have a number of events running over
> the weekend, we will be trying to make them different
> to the usual convention fayre.[291]

Frankie Ferret. Artwork by Goldenrod.

Registration opened on New Year's Day 2015, and while we do not know the attendance figures from this time, a public post from February 12 showed 30 registered users with 10 tickets sold.[292] Apart from changing the price slightly to make breakfasts optional (following feedback) and a temporary suspension of ticket sales in March due to technical issues, progress appeared to be going well.

A mascot for Furcation was also revealed in early March: Frankie Ferret, which was designed by California furry cartoonist Goldenrod.[293]

Behind the scenes, planning was going well with the Warrens. Jasper Foxx described his interactions with their manager as being "absolutely lovely" and completely on-board with the concept and furries in general. Jasper even brought one of his fursuits to demonstrate at one of their meetings.

Then things went silent.

It took some effort to discover that the manager Jasper previously spoke to was sacked over a grievance, and the new manager was much less friendly in comparison:

> I'd tentatively enquired as to whether we were still on and was met with a response of "I'm not sure we want your kind of people around here." So that was that I wasn't going to take an event to somewhere we weren't going to be welcomed so the venue search started again.[267]

On June 4, it was announced that Furcation 2015 would not be going ahead.[294] On its official Facebook group, Jasper Foxx briefly explained the situation with the change in managers and the considerable drop in the level of communication and service as a result.

> Although a contract was in force between us and the venue for the event, we have decided not to enforce the contract as we feel we would continue to experience poor service levels from the venue which would affect the event we bring to you. The step we are taking is one of damage limitation and we would rather reboot at a new venue who are willing to accept our custom than put on a poor event at a venue that doesn't.

Furcation was able to refund tickets and promised on its website that they planned to find a new location and prepare for the next year. Ticket holders were offered a free upgrade if they wished to roll over their purchases.

A new potential venue was teased on the official Twitter account in October 2015,[295] yet it would only be confirmed much later on 1 March 2016 to be the Sandy Glade Holiday Park in the Brean Sands, which is owned by the John Fowler Holiday company. Registration opened in April, and along with this announcement came a new event date of 14 to 17 October 2016.[296] The newly christened Furcation 2016 eventually incorporated as Furcation, Ltd. in June 2016.[297]

The news was received positively, even by those who recalled what transpired the year before. John Fowler Holiday appeared to be more receptive, adding their own animal mascot characters of a badger, rabbit, and fox to an official trailer for what would now be considered the first proper Furcation. This didn't mean there weren't problems behind the scenes, though. When their bookings team listened to Jasper Foxx's intentions and booked them to their flagship site back in 2015, they hadn't taken into consideration the actual kind of event that was being proposed.

As Jasper Foxx explained in July 2016, the owners of the Sandy Glade Holiday Park were expecting to accommodate around 50 to 60 people, but interest grew so much that by June it had surpassed that estimate to almost 100 and the number of chalets the park was willing to provide was running out.[298]

Concerns mounted that the larger crowd would prove disruptive for their other patrons, so the sales manager at John Fowler recommended moving Furcation to their much smaller Combe Martin Holiday Park in North Devon. Although the downside to this was an additional 60 miles of travel for most attendees and more limited public transport, the major advantage was that Furcation had a more exclusive venue to work with.[299]

By the time registration closed at the end of August, it was confirmed that 90 attendees had registered, including 48 sponsors,[300] although the current website states the attendee count was 92.

Furcation was able to deliver exactly what it promised when the October opening arrived. There was a schedule of events that took place from within the clubhouse, including the opening and closing ceremonies, dances in the evening, a fursuit walk, and photo shoot opportunities, but unlike Confuzzled these were spread out to allow attendees to social-

Official group photo for Furcation 2016.

ise more in and around the holiday park. Major features such as a dealer's den and retro games room, which at other conventions would run for several days, were only available for one day for a short period of time.

Many attendees praised this approach, which provided plenty of entertainment while also creative a fun and chill atmosphere. Even the holiday park staff joined the fun, posting their own photos from the event on their official social media accounts.

While Furcation insisted on distancing itself from the traditional convention, that did not mean it did not want to encourage fundraising for a good cause. Furcation 2016 raised £530 for the Secret World Wildlife Rescue organisation.[301]

JUST FUR THE WEEKEND

Going back to 18 July 2015, LondonFurs held their Summer Weekender, where one of the regular attendees, Cueball (Alexander Clark), told other furries about a new furry convention that for the following year. Cueball's sales pitch for the convention brought a lot of attention. He promised it would take place in a four-star hotel with four restaurants, access to two lakes, and floors for partying.[302]

Another selling point was that it was to take place on Easter Weekend (25 to 27 March 2016).

Logo for Just for the Weekend 2016.

Both Good Friday and the following Monday were bank holidays in the United Kingdom, making for an ideal time when most people are not required to book time off work to go somewhere.

The origins of Just Fur the Weekend, as described on its website under a section titled "The Fox and Goose," was from a discussion amongst friends about starting a convention at a pub. The discussion led to a fully laid out concept and a search for venues. The Holiday Inn Filton in Bristol was secured, and JFTW UK, Ltd. (pronounced as Jefty) was incorporated with Cueball as chair and fellow cofounders Tokala (Gino Baldacchino) and Bristol Bigglesworth (Kelly Alexander) as vice chair and operations director, respectively.[303]

While the WikiFur page claims the convention was conceived back in June 2015 (supposedly on information from the official website at the time), the amount of preparation involved including finding a venue, designing and publishing a fully operational website, setting up a company, and designing the mascot Favian the Fox makes it very unlikely it all happened within the span of a single month. A tweet from the official JFTW account in September 2015, which was maintained by Cueball and Tokala, remarks that there had been five months of planning at that point in time,[304] which implies the convention was first conceived no later than April.

After videos were produced to promote the venue and its Motor-Furs event, registration opened on August 31.

Production of the MotorFurs video proved more dangerous than expected. Videographer Corey Coyote received a black eye from opening a car door,[305] and Tokala was rushed to the hospital after dislocating his shoulder from exiting a car and slipping off the tarmac.

Word of mouth through furmeets and other conventions sparked enough interest for one hundred attendees to register by the end of the year.[306] Registration closed on February 21 with a total of 152 attendees.

For a convention that was not exceptionally large, it had many of the same features found at the much larger ConFuzzled. These included main stage events, panels, a dealer's den, game rooms, a nightclub for fun in the evening, and open bars and restaurants for relaxation and socialising. There was also the MotorFurs event on Saturday for furries who wanted to show off their vehicles and a dance competition for the more active fursuiters.

One of the unique selling points of the convention had to do with the fursuit walk. Whereas other conventions' walks followed a direct route to and from the venue, Just Fur the Weekend offered a ticketed coach tour to different sites around the city of Bristol. Fursuiters and photographers were transported to the Clifton Suspension Bridge, Brandon Hill, Victoria Park, and the Millennium Square in the city centre for photo opportunities.[307]

The convention was a major success, and £1,116 was raised for the Holly Hedge Animal Sanctuary. Many attendees enjoyed the convention's more relaxed atmosphere afforded by fewer scheduled events and more rooms for activities. One of the best words of praise came from the convention's own guest of honour, Alex "Khaki" Vance, an award-winning furry author, publisher, and photographer. Vance lauded it this way:

> Intimate and exciting, wild, and relaxed, the energy was infectious and addictive. I made so many new friends, people from all walks of life who all inspire me to be better than I am. The hotel staff got into the spirit of things more than I've seen at any other con, and a few of them may become One Of Us before too soon.[308]

Both Furcation and Just Fur the Weekend were confirmed to continue, much to the excitement of the British furry fandom. When compared to all the furry events prior to 2016, however, the excitement from furry fans might have been more than what their organisers anticipated.

Just Fur the Weekend was the first to open its registration for their following 2017 which it did on 1 July 2016.[309] The theme was "Wonders of the Industrial Revolution" and furry artists Lapres and Garnett were the guests of honour. Enrollment was going rather well, and by early December it was revealed that the con had already reached 150 attendees. Less than a week later, it surpassed the first year's 152 attendees, and by the end of the year topped off at 172 registered attendees. But that wasn't the end of it. Halfway through January it was revealed that JFTW had reached 200 attendees, and by halfway through March that number increased to 300.[310] By the time registration closed on March 17, there were a total of 317 confirmed registered attendees.

FASTEST-GROWING UK FURCONS

To put this into perspective, that translates into a 108 percent increase in attendance. It is stated that at the time, this would have broken the record for the largest second-year growth of a furry convention, although this is rather disputed. After searching through the confirmed attendance data of every known furry convention documented by Fred Patten, Just Fur the Weekend had the fourth largest growth of a furry convention in its second year, placing it behind the USA's Oklacon, Germany's Mephit Furmeet and Taiwan's Infurnity.

It would not hold onto its spot for long, however. Furcation 2017 (with the theme "Pirates of Combe Martin") opened for registration on April 22, and by the time registration closed on August 31, it had a total of 215 attendees registered. This 133 percent increase for its second year

Oklacon: 149% from 47 to 117 between 2003 and 2004.
Mephit Furmeet: 176% from 68 to 188 between 1999 and 2000.
Infurnity: 279% from 62 to 235 between 2015 and 2016.

alarmed Jasper Foxx to the point that he acknowledged in the Furcation 2017 conbook that they were already discussing with John Fowler's about moving to one of the larger holiday parks.[311] It was an especially hard decision to make, and to this day Jasper Foxx keeps fond memories from the Combe Martin:

> Initially, I was sceptical but once I had driven down to [Combe Martin], I fell in love with the place. The view from the clubhouse, its size, the staff, the welcome we got, it was all perfect. Seemed like a fitting start to a new event being built from the ground up. John Fowler's love[s] our attendees and our staff and eventually when we need to move on from them, that's going to be a very, very sad day. I've never worked with a venue that has been as accepting, welcoming and warm as John Fowler's have been.

JFTW 2017 conbook coverart by Heartlily

Indeed, Just Fur the Weekend and Furcation both grew at a rate larger than all past local conventions by an exceptionally huge margin, for good reason. British furries who wanted a smaller and more relaxed furry event now finally have two that proved it was possible, and so with the addition of word of mouth as well as promotion at

(Left) Furcation 2017 Conbook cover art by Parsonda; (right) JFTW 2018 Conbook cover art by Ram the Dragon.

furmeets and online, these cons drew in more furries. Both conventions continued their successful runs in 2017. JFTW was held on Easter weekend (April 14 to 16) and Furcation ran from October 13 to 16. JFTW raised money for Fluffy Retreat Ferret Rescue (£1349.52) and Furcation for the UK Wolf Conservation Trust (£2,037).

The following year, the story of these two diverged. JFTW 2018 took place from March 30 to April 1 with the theme of "Pier Pressure," or more specifically, all things relating to the British seaside. In keeping with the theme, the fursuit coach trip went to the Clevedon Pier for photo opportunities. Guests of honours were Blu the Dragon, a popular furry YouTuber from Australia, and Ceil Fox, a longtime British furry and engineer best known for his contributions behind the scenes at conventions with fursuit lounge and main stage equipment (as well as being co-chair of Scotiacon). A total of £1426.94 was raised for the HEART animal rescue charity.

One bit of information that was strangely absent from both the lead-up and the convention itself was how many people were there. Then, almost three months after the convention was over, the underwhelming 2018 total was revealed to be 203 attendees.[312]

Many agree that JFTW had a noticeable drop in attendance not because of the quality of the convention itself, (it was received positively just like in previous years, and its organisation was smooth despite Cueball leaving the team due to creative differences), but, rather, the price increase.

It's not unheard of for any furry convention to raise prices due to a variety of factors such as rising costs for supplies and equipment, the economic climate, or the convention renegotiating its contract with the venue. In fact, JFTW already increased their costs between 2016 and 2017 by £10 to £185 for its cheapest option of a Double/Twin Room Residential.[313]

However, around August 2017, when the new registration prices were unveiled furries did not respond too well to them. The Double/Twin Room had increased to £220, which remained cheaper than a similar room offered at ConFuzzled for £270, but JFTW was a three-day convention compared to the five-day ConFuzzled. Scotiacon was also a three-day convention and was much cheaper in terms of a twin-room costing £150.

If an attendee wanted to arrive a day early and depart a day later this would translate into a five-day stay at JFTW for £370 compared to ConFuzzled at £380 for seven days and Scotiacon at £230 for five days. None of these prices, which were compiled in a UK Furry Convention Price Comparison chart by CosmoSnowMew, considered optional sponsor-level fees or any other additional costs.[314]

JFTW 2018 also included attendance-only tickets for the first time at a base price of £110, and as another furry named TimmyFox remarked, the price was

JFTW 2019 Conbook coverart by Alector Fencer.

equal or more than the cost of a sponsor ticket for other conventions such as Furnal Equinox and NordicFuzzCon.[315]

There were people who defended the price hike as JFTW, which still provided more in terms of food (lunch and breakfast were included) and free parking. Most also rationalised the price increase because of negotiations with the hotel and needing to spread the cost out to a much smaller crowd when compared to larger conventions. Other furries were not satisfied and vocally decided not to go to JFTW in favour of other conventions, whether they were domestic or abroad.

That is not to say that JFTW was on a downward slope. Attendance was up at 233 for JFTW 2019. The theme that year was "It Came from the Silver Screen"; professional artist and graphic novel author Alector Fencer was guest of honour; and the charity Raystede Centre for Animal Welfare received £1,968.06.[316]

Furcation was one of the other conventions cited in the UK Furry Convention Price Comparison, and as noted by CosmoSnowMew, even when picking the most expensive registration options, it summed up to only £74.52 for four days. Although it is not likely the only reason, it is very telling that when Furcation 2018, which ran from October 12 to 15 at the slightly larger Sandaway Holiday Park in Combe Martin, played host to a respectable 339 furries. Just as in the previous year, Jasper Foxx acknowledged in the conbook that they would need to reassess their venue plans with John Fowler's as a result of rising rates.[317]

Furcation 2018 conbook coverart by Linny.

The theme of Furcation 2018 was "Paw and Order," a pun on the TV drama *Law and Order*. But the theme was played more for fun in the spirit of modern police buddy comedy films such as *Hot Fuzz* and *Zootropolis*. Mascot Frankie was given a ferret partner named Clive. To fit in with the theme, they renamed and tweaked some of the events, so the Dealer's Den became the Cop Shop, Fursuit Games became Police Academy, and the toy-gun Nerf Wars became Cops vs. Criminals. A total of £1,677.20 was raised for the charity Pete's Dragons,[318] which provides support for those who lose loved ones to suicide.

Since Furcation had already grown too large for its new home, it now became clear that there was only one place that John Fowler's could provide to accommodate them in the following year. Furcation 2019 took place at the Sandy Glade Holiday Park in Brean, the chain's flagship holiday park. By now, the relationship between event and venue was more positive and welcoming than it was in 2015.

There were several other changes made for this Furcation as well. The date had been moved from its usual October weekend to November 8–11, and there were more events on the schedule, some being relegated to a nearby function building known as the Dune House, which doubled

Furcation 2019 conbook cover art by MuteStudios.

as a quiet lounge for attendees who wanted to relax.

Being in John Fowler's largest holiday park was not enough to handle the 592 guests, however. Ironically for a furry event trying to distinguish itself from the larger cons, this resulted in the staff and venue dealing with similar issues that plagued ConFuzzled when it started getting really big. rooms sold out in minutes prior to the opening date, there were long lines to get into clubhouse events like the dealer's den and the opening ceremony, the fursuit group photo was so large that it had to be done in batches of three so everyone could be photographed, and there were so many events on the schedule that conflicts arose.

This is not to say that it was received poorly—quite the opposite. The theme was FC:TV Live, which played a lot into the nostalgia of many of the attendees, particularly in the evening dances and the quiz based around music and TV-shows from the 90s and early 2000s. The staff at John Fowler's had a particularly good time as well, especially the general manager, who was caught dancing around wearing a fursuit on one of the evenings.

The biggest highlight of the event was the charity auction, which had plenty of items for sale. One of the big-selling items was a weekend stay for six at the Sandy Glade Holiday Park in one of their largest platinum suites, which ended up selling for over £1,000, but that was not the biggest item of the night.

One day earlier in the dealer's den, the fursuit maker Kloofsuits was selling a white and pink fennec fox partial fursuit that was snapped up by a furry going by the name of XavierFox, a London furry who was already well known amongst the MotorFur community for his collection of sports cars and armoured vehicles. He donated the fursuit to the charity auction, and after a bidding war ensued with another attendee, he ended up winning it back at a price of £3,000. This made it the second biggest selling auction item at a British furry convention, as well as the biggest selling live auction item outside of ConFuzzled.[319]

So why did he bid on his own donation for such a high amount? Because he wanted to donate money to the charity. In the end, Furcation 2019 raised a reported £8,592.33 for the Ferne Animal Sanctuary.

ART AND ENTERTAINMENT

FURSUITS

In the Nineties and early Noughties, fursuits were incredibly rare in the United Kingdom, and there weren't people skilled enough to make fursuits within the country. That did not mean there were not those who made the effort to make their own fursuits.

The Fursuit Database, a user-curated resource to catalogue fursuits made within the furry fandom, has several entries of suits well before the website's creation in 2005. Searching through the database, and filtering to locate only fursuits in the United Kingdom, does provide a few results.

The oldest British furry entry, dating back to April 1997, is a fox head named Shelby that was made by a Norfolk furry going by the name of Erin the Hound.[320] Not much about it is known aside from a single photograph, but another early self-made fursuit debuting in September 1999 made a bigger impression in the fandom.

Made by a Southampton furry named Blaster Hedgie,[321] this fursuit included a custom head and a body featuring spines on the back. The design was inspired by Sonic the Hedgehog. Although a rather low-quality fursuit even for the time, Hedgie wore it several times, from LondonFur meets to furry variety shows at American conventions such as Duckon and Further Confusion, performing furry-themed covers of pop songs.

In 2001, he was interviewed on *Rapid T. Rabbit and Friends*, a public access puppet TV show that ran on New York's PBS station, where they talked about cultural differences between the United Kingdom and United States, music, song writing, and what it's like being in the fandom.

While there was no exact period when fursuits started becoming more commonplace within the furry fandom, there is no doubt that how-to guides and instructions for building fursuits becoming more accessible to the public played a hand in the explosion of fursuit popularity. One source is the book *Critter Costuming*, written by Nicodemus (Adam Riggs) in 2004, which provided two hundred pages worth of photos and detailed directions for designing and performing in fursuits.[92, 322]

Another source is YouTube, which launched in 2005. While there were online tutorials published earlier and the furry conventions in America had fursuit building workshops, the ability for anyone to watch

FatKraken with her cosplay of Kiba (photo taken at MinamiCon2005 by ManyLemons).

a fursuit being made from start to finish to use as a guide was effective motivation for several furries to make one of their own and refine their skills. As such, it was after 2005 that fursuit makers started appearing to create fursuits by commission in droves.

One of the earliest fursuit makers in the United Kingdom was FatKraken (Karen Dawson). She had experience building cosplay outfits for anime conventions starting as early as 1999 and taught herself through various tutorials on the internet, although the very first costume she made was a werewolf mask in primary school.[323]

There is a written account from MinamiCon 2004 of a reportedly impressive cosplay of Inuki from the manga and anime series *X*. At the same convention the following year, she would return with her next cosplay, a white wolf fursuit of Kiba from the series *Wolf's Rain*, which also garnered a lot of positive reception. She later described her experience performing in the fullsuit in her own convention report:

> It was also the weirdest costuming experience I've had. Doing the proper "silent" performance in a full mascot suit is totally different from any other costuming I've done. It's both restricting and strangely liberating; the total face and body coverage lets "you" retreat somewhat and let the character you are performing take on a life of its own…. I'm really glad I did the face/ears set too. It let me stay a bit more coherent when it came time to de-head. Word of warning: dancing in fursuit is a KILLER. Even without the head, two songs in a row was absolutely exhausting but SO much fun.[324]

FatKraken also gained recognition from outside the furry and anime fandoms when she created a fursuit based on a wolf featured in

There was a claim that it appeared in an issue of Official Nintendo Magazine in 2007. After searching through every issue from 2007 and 2008 in the British Library, I could not find a single mention of it.

the video game *Legend of Zelda: Twilight Princess*. In the game, the lead character, Link, gets transformed into a wolf when travelling to a dark parallel world; the wolf form quickly gets the nickname of Wolf Link. It was worn at MinamiCon 2007, where it won the Masquerade Award.[325] When it was posted online in March of that year, it went viral within the video game community.

FatKraken was invited to be guest of honour at RBW 2007 in the fursuiting track for which she provided a fursuit building workshop that would continue to run annually until 2010. She would also build and perform with puppets at ConFuzzled starting in 2009 and was the guest of honour at ScotiaCon in 2011. She established KrakenKritters as her fursuit making business in 2009.

Although not the first established fursuit business in the country (Dasker Cicurel set up Blue Fox Fursuits in 2008), FatKraken was joined by other makers by the end of the decade. Fursuit makers such as Hybrid Studios and HeadOverTails started taking commissions in 2009.

Around this time, the fursuit population was growing to staggering proportions with furmeets often featuring multiple fursuiters. Furry conventions also saw an increase in fursuiters. Back in the United States, Anthrocon's fursuit parade participants increased at a rate faster than its general attendance figures, surpassing a thousand fursuits in 2012 and two thousand fursuits by 2016.

FatKraken's Wolf Link cosplay. (Photo taken by Nic.)

Advancements in Fursuits

As more creators emerged in the early noughties, more advancements in materials, technologies, and designs were integrated into fursuits.

On the one hand, advancements in the noughties were usually rather small and subtle such as having the jaw move to give the appearance of talking or having concave eyes as opposed to flat ones to create an optical illusion that the eyes are following you around.

On the other hand, improvements were developed that added realism to the fursuit creations, even with the fursuits that were meant to have a more cartoonish look. Latex, rubber, and acrylic materials started to be used to make the less fuzzy parts, including paws, claws, and noses. Creatively placed padding around the legs gave fursuits the appearance of being digitigrade (when animals walk on their toes instead of flat-footed as humans do, which is called plantigrade).

There were also advancements that had less to do with authenticity and more with visual peal and accessorising. These included the use of magnets, LEDs and hydraulics to aide in attachments, make parts of the fursuit glow, or animate ears to appear to move on their own, to give just a few examples.

Improvements to fursuits also included advancements to make them more comfortable for the wearers. Fursuiters are particularly prone to overheating, thanks to the raised humidity inside the fursuits, leading some fursuiters to install small fans inside the heads of their fursuits to generate a constant airflow.

A pricier, yet popular solution to help keep a fursuiter's body cool while performing is to have a cooling vest that keeps the body temperature low. A popular brand within the fandom is the EZCooldown, named after their creator, Dutch fursuiter and professional filmmaker EZWolf.

Digitigrade Wolf Fursuit of Elis, from MadeByMercury.

Fursuit Costs

Inflation, improved tools and materials, and higher labour costs offered has meant that fursuits have increased in price significantly over the years. According to its price guide back in 2010, commissioning a fullsuit from Blue Fox Fursuits had a base price of £340, with a partial starting at £210.[326] In 2019, the same maker charges at least £1,400 for a fullsuit, and if you want to save money and commission a partial it would at least cost £900.[327]

It is worth noting that for an established British fursuit maker this is the lower price range of fursuit commissions compared to other well-experienced makers such as MadeByMercury, Snow Gryphon Studios, Kloofsuits, Faruku Costumes, and Beauty of the Bass. These fursuit makers are also in high demand, often taking only a handful of commissions per year, and their commission queues are typically filled within days of opening.

The good news is that it is more possible now than ever to build your own fursuit if you are willing to do so. There are plenty of online tutorials, and you can take some shortcuts by, for example, buying base models for heads or getting premade parts such as tails, wings, and paws.

British furries will also save money by commissioning from local fursuit makers rather than from one in America or Europe. This is not only because commissioning an overseas fursuit maker adds the additional cost of import duty tax, but also because overseas fursuit makers charge more when factoring in currency rates. As of writing, the most expensive in-fandom

Two furries walking in Birmingham. One wearing a Fox-eared hat and the other a Fox tail. Taken around 2003.

fursuit was a $50,000 commission from Zuri Studios, a maker based in the Czech Republic, in 2021.[328]

FurScience, a group of scientists who study the social behaviour and culture of the fandom, estimates that only around 15% of furry fans own at least one fullsuit and 25% of furry fans own at least one partial suit, according to an international furry survey done in 2011[329] and a 2020 survey shows that as the number of furries has increased, the percentage remained the same.[330] Despite this, the abundance of photos both from attendees and social media—as well as articles from news and popular media—has led to a misconception that fursuits are not only incredibly common but an entry requirement.

Another contributing factor to this misconception is the number of fursuiters who appear at furmeets and conventions, especially European events like ConFuzzled, where roughly 45 percent of attendees also registered owning a fursuit at the 2018 event.

Another furry survey done at Furry Fiesta 2014 found that a majority of furries are more likely to simply own clothing accessories and paraphernalia, such as badges, ears, paws, and the most popular being tails, than fursuits. Even so, fewer than half of furries owned such items.

As to why fursuiters appear prominently in media, both Dr. Sharon Roberts and Nuka (Dr. Courtney Plante) of Furscience argue that, as with other fandoms, outfits and costumes are the more recognisable and appealing aspects of any fandom—for example, Star Trek fans wearing Starfleet uniforms, Harry Potter fans wearing wizarding robes, and football fans wearing jerseys. To any outsider, they accurately portray how they imagine a fan would look in contrast to how most fans actually look.

The expense of fursuits also has a knock-on effect of the owners being compelled to use them more often to warrant such an investment, which explains why they are more motivated to attend conventions and furmeets where they get the most use. This motivation and general outsider perception explains why the Furscience team found that furries who own a fursuit feel more like they are a part of the fandom than those who do not own one.

The truth is that the fandom is more than just wearing costumes; it is also about sharing and creating art of anthropomorphic animals, writing and sharing stories, gaming, and simply socialising with people who share interests.

DRAWING

Artwork—from traditional to digital art, cartoons to realistic paintings—remains a dominant pursuit within the furry fandom. An international survey in 2020 found that 34.7 percent of furries identify as artists.[330] A 2014 study that compared furries with anime and fantasy sports fans found the furries were the most likely to identify themselves as artists out of the three.

At this point, this should come as no surprise, as the furry fandom was built around sharing drawings whether that be at conventions or in fanzines. Nowadays, there are plenty of artists in the British furry fandom, so much so that furries have plenty of different styles to choose from.

If they wanted an artist who could draw your favourite film or TV character in a style that emulates the media they are from, there are artists such as Zen Tiger for that. If you want something cartoonish like it's from a Looney Tunes show, look for artists like MagFerret. If you want your furry character to look dark and scary from a twisted horror, there are artists like Beauty of the Bass.

Like with other aspects of the furry fandom, it took time for the British to gain recognition from the rest of the world, and it would begin with fanzines.

For the United Kingdom, there was *AnthropoMORPHINE* and the *Fur Scene Newsletter*, where the few artists such as Aspirin, Foxy, Prask, and Simon Barber had their work published alongside noted American artists like Terrie Smith and Monika Livingstone.

Once furry art was predominantly published online, British artists could easily present their work alongside other artists around the world, but local art discussions could also be had on the UKFurForums. Competitions, trades, commissions, and art requests could easily be made amongst artists in the same country thanks to online forums, and much later, social media.

Outside of websites, British furry artists often got a lot of attention at British events, sometimes gaining more admirers than the fursuiterss. Attendees from the early LondonFurs meetups often discussed furry art outside of costuming. Marcony, Ruin, and Ia'Kat all tried their hands at furry art, sometimes lending their gothic themes to their work.

Beyond furmeets, furry conventions are a main avenue for furry artists to show off their work and attract the interest of other furry fans. This is done by submitting artwork for convention conbooks and banners, selling artwork in the dealer's den, or submitting art for potential buyers at the art show and auctions.

Before 2007, artists in the United Kingdom had to go to European or American conventions to sell much art, but once RBW and ConFuzzled took off, British artists found a stage of their own to gain recognition. Outside of furmeets, artists at the time were limited to publishing their artwork to either the furry art portals like Velan Central Library (VCL), or broader-themed art websites like Elfwood and DeviantArt.

One example of a British artist making their way into the spotlight was UltraFox (Nick Cramp), He discovered the furry fandom in 1998 and joined the LondonFurs during its earliest meets, making friends with other noteworthy artists in the fandom such as UltraViolet, who would later be a guest of honour at RBW for her popular dark fantasy artwork.

Initially, UltraFox only considered himself to be a writer, including cowriting an adult furry webcomic titled *PlayFur* with a friend from LondonFurs, BhavFox (Bhavesh Patel), who was both a furry artist and a computer graphics artist in the games industry. UltraFox would occasionally publish his own short stories and taught himself to draw.

Unfortunately, all UltraFox's art from the early noughties appears to have been lost, which wasn't an uncommon occurrence during the shifting times in the furry art world. VCL, despite its limitations and strict prohibition of artwork featuring copyrighted characters, was the most popular furry art website before being taken over by a more modern website called FurAffinity in 2005.

UltraFox opened his account in 2006. His posted artwork was praised for its detail to anatomy and furry textures. As he gained popularity, he was able to earn money as a freelance artist, accepting commissions both online and at the dealers' den at the big conventions like ConFuzzled and RBW.

It wasn't just furries who commissioned UltraFox's artwork; according to his curriculum vita, he also found work doing logos and art pieces for the National Maritime Museum as well as companies like ENworld and Fitzberg.

Being a professional furry artist is incredibly competitivedue to the thousands of new art submissions and the hundreds of artists who attend conventions. UltraFox didn't have much of an issue getting commissions, but he wasn't in the spotlight either.

That changed with ConFuzzled 2013. Given the medieval theme, UltraFox produced a large multi-character landscape piece depicting a tearful princess receiving unfortunate news while surrounded by soldiers and nobility bowing to her. Titled *The King is Dead*, it was printed in the conbook as a two-page spread, and a large print was submitted to the art show.

Like with other entries at the ConFuzzled art show, it had a card for people to write in their bids. Furries were quick to place their bids, filling

The King Is Dead *by UltraFox*

up the bidding card to value of over £100. As per the rules of the art show, any piece gets the number of bids required to fill the card would automatically go to the live auction which happened in the evening on the main stage.

The print was the last item at the auction, and in a rare moment for ConFuzzled, UltraFox was given the microphone to talk about his work. He described how he wanted to tell a gripping and dramatic story in a single panel. Once he finished, the bidding started.

The value was already set in the hundreds, but the audience quickly went into shock as one of the furries there bid £1,000. The only time this had ever happened before was for artwork by TaniDaReal. A bidding war ensued between two furries, and the value kept rising and rising. Art auctions typically a portion part of the bids to charity. Five percent is normal, but it was doubled to ten percent.

After much back and forth—and the two bidders double-checking their bank accounts—the bidding ended with Dutch furry pyremoon-shadow paying **£3,500 for** *The King Is Dead.*[331] The entire audience erupted in applause, and UltraFox broke into tears of joy. His artwork broke the record set by TaniDaReal's £2,000 tablecloth in 2010.

Such a newsworthy event boosted UltraFox's name recognition considerably; he would go on to draw the conbook cover for the Switzerland Golden Leaves Con that same year. Along with commissions, he continued to produce large multi-character landscape prints for ConFuzzled each year, presenting his skills in sci-fi and fantasy genres.

In 2017 UltraFox began work on a new sci-fi webcomic, *Terror Drive*, which is about anthropomorphic lizards that are living machines fighting for survival. Working around his freelance schedule, he published new pages twice a week, separating the story into chapters. The last page of the webcomic was posted in December 2020, but sadly that would be his last piece of artwork.

Unbeknownst everyone outside of family and close friends, Ultra-Fox was diagnosed with cancer and had been fighting it for a few years. He passed away on the morning of 4 January, 2021.

There are plenty of artists in the British furry fandom, providing furries plenty of different styles to choose from, such as the artists mentioned in this book.

But UltraFox still stands out in the British furry art community. Although he may not have been a guest of honour, he's one of a select few artists whose work has spanned most of the furry fandom, from the earliest furmeets to the present-day conventions. To this day The King is Dead remains the most expensive artwork sold at a British furry convention. Even with his success, he was known to be humble, friendly, and welcoming to newcomers and helpful to others. He is missed by many who knew him.

WRITING

As with with furry art, furries create a considerable selection of literature, varying from fan fiction of existing properties to original stories of anthropomorphic animals living in humanlike societies. The writing can also vary in genres from comedy and drama to romance and horror. Writers can also be commissioned to write short stories and sometimes branch out into indie publishing with their works.

Like furry artists, early furry writers such as Simon Barber got their start publishing in fanzines until internet art websites like VCL and FurAffinity allowed fiction to be published in the form of text files.

Unlike furry art, the furry writing scene is far more insular.

SoFurry

An alternative avenue for internet furries was to publish their work on their own websites and get the attention of other furries by sharing the Web address with either webrings or link databases such as Mia's Index of Anthro Stories. However, the short-lived nature of these websites creating deadlinks eventually led to Tourmal Rakesh developing a website dedicated to hosting furry literature in 2002.[332]

> Webring is the name of a collection of websites that used a script so users could click a link to go to the next or previous site. When a user, for example, clicks the "next" website link enough times, they would go back to the first site they arrived at, hence the websites were linked together like a ring.

Originally called Yiffstar, an acronym of sorts meaning YIFFy STory ARchive, it would expand and relaunch under the name SoFurry in 2009. Like FurAffinity, it also accepts illustrative art submissions, yet written submissions remain predominant on the website, along with frequent writing contests and author spotlights.

Furry Writers Guild

Since the visual artform garners more attention over the written artform in the furry fandom, the writers within the fandom are a lot more dedicated to supporting one another. In April 2010, the Furry Writers Guild was set up, according to founder Sean Silva in his mission statement, with the purpose "to support, inform, elevate and promote quality writing and writers of anthropomorphic fiction."[333] To ensure quali-

the CÓYOTL awards
Recognizing Excellence in Anthropomorphic Literature

ty, membership in the guild is free but only allowed to those who have published or sold printed (i.e., in anthologies, magazines, or conbooks) fiction or nonfiction that feature anthropomorphic characters or themes.

The guild also hosts the Cóyotl Awards, which operate like the Ursa Major Awards except they exclusively honour writers and literature made within the furry fandom. While its first ceremony had six awards[334]— three for general literature and three for mature—every ceremony since then has had four categories: Best Short Story (less than twenty thousand words), Best Novella (twenty to fifty thousand words), Best Novel (over fifty thousand words), and Best Anthology (including single author anthologies).[335]

Most of the more prolific writers have originated from the USA such as the previously mentioned Sean Silva, Poetigress (Renee Carter Hall), and Kyell Gold, all of whom have won either the Cóyotl Awards or the Ursa Major's literary awards numerous times. There are a few notable furry writers of British origin, including award winning writer foozzzball (Malcolm Cross).

Foozzzball is an author from London who started off writing on another furry literature archive website, FurRag, in the mid-noughties, but he had

The Ursa Major Awards logo (designed by Foxenawolf)

his biggest success when he began writing a line of novellas in 2009 with Kyell Gold and Rikoshi for FurPlanet called *Cupcakes*. His cupcake novella *Dangerous Jade* was published in 2012 and won the Ursa Major Award in the Best Anthropomorphic Short Fiction category that year.[336]

He has had other stories published in anthologies, and most recently crowdfunded and self-published a sci-fi military novel called *Dog Country* in 2020.[337] Foozzzball was the first British furry writer to win an Ursa Major Award, and he is only one of two to do so, the other being Huskyteer (Alice Dryden).

A furry from the southeast of England, Huskyteer originally got her start in furry writing in 2001 by contributing fanfiction of the Disney

Dangerous Jade *cover art by Meesh.*

animated feature *The Lion King*, which had its own long-running, online fanbase and mailing list that overlapped with the furry fandom. She also wrote fanfics for other franchises, most notably Digimon, Pokémon, Doctor Who, Harry Potter, and *Dogtanian and the Three Muskehounds*. She was personally nostalgic for Dogtanian, hosting her own fansite for the animated series.

Huskyteer migrated to So-Furry in 2010 to write original furry stories and quickly built up a reputation that allowed her to move into getting stories published. Her first published work was "Tiger Light," a short story of four friends reacting to being transformed into animals because of some magic light. It was included in the *Saudade* ebook from Pink Fox Publications in May 2012.[338]

This was followed with "Bad Timing," a student thriller about a female mountain lion getting deep into a taboo romance with a possible murderer.[339] It was published in the mature audience magazine *Heat,* Volume 9, from Sofawolf Press in June 2012.

This was then quickly followed by "Magnificent Dogs,"[340] published in the fourth volume of the Bad Dog Books anthology *ROAR*, also in June 2012. This story was one of the earliest that focused on Huskyteer's main passion, aviation. More specifically, it's set in pre-WWI England during the height of early flight.

She continued writing short stories for various American publishers, one of her most successful being "The Analogue Cat," a science fiction romance told in second person following a genetically engineered cat named Tozer and his female robot companion. It was published in *The Furry Future* anthology from FurPlanet Productions.[341]

The story won both the Best Anthropomorphic Short Fiction category at the Ursa Major Awards and the Best Short Story award at the Cóyotl Awards in 2015, making Huskyteer not only the first British furry author to win both awards but also the only furry writer to date to win from both awards in the same year.

The Furry Future *front cover (left) and Gods with Fur (covers by Teagan Gavet).*

What is crazier is that she achieved this feat twice. The following year, Huskyteer wrote "400 Rabbits" for the *Gods of Fur* anthology for FurPlanet.[342] Based on the Centzon Totochtin, a group of divine rabbits who meet for frequent drunken parties, "400 Rabbits" is a comedy about one rabbit who questions whether getting drunk on a nightly basis is a good way to live. This story also won the Ursa Major Short Fiction and Cóyotl Short Story award in 2016.

When she is not writing for motorcycle magazines and websites, or attending numerous air shows, or practicing martial arts, Huskyteer, a guest of honour at the furry convention Fur The 'More in 2019, continues to write furry stories.

MUSIC

There is one other type of artwork that can be posted on all these furry sites and its audio. It is not unheard of for such a visual artistic fandom to have a sizeable music scene. For example, both retro gamer and *My Little Pony* fandoms have a history of sharing remixes, covers, and even original music based around their favourite media. While the furry fandom is not centred around one type of media, the fandom is home to plenty of musicians, some of whom perform at concerts or sell albums at conventions.

Members of Donutsh (from left to right): Shazomei, Klepsydra, Ullan, Camrath

Some even collaborate, as was the case after a New Year's Eve party in 2007, when a small group of LondonFurs made up of Klepsydra, Camrath, and Ullan decided to set up an indie punk band called Donutsh.[343] Klepsydra generally wrote the lyrics and played guitar along with Ullan, while Camrath played bass.

They would later be joined by Shazomei and Blacksnip in 2009,[344] and starting in late 2010 they performed regularly at furmeets, ConFuzzled, and at small gigs in and around London, where some of their furry friends came to show their support. They managed to release an EP in 2011[345] and continued to perform up until 2013, when Camrath departed the furry fandom.

FreyFox

Interestingly, two of the more prominent furry musicians within the United Kingdom both happen to come from Scotland. The first is FreyFox (Mark Alexander Smith), who, despite being better known in the fandom as both an animator and a cartoonist that has worked on multiple comics like *Transmission, Kat Venture*, and *Dead Dog Running*, also used to perform as a guitarist and bassist for several bands.

In 2006 FreyFox formed a music collective known as The Raccoon Gang with CaveDweller (Craig Scrimgeour) and The Colourless (John Wightman) that was somewhat on the experimental side. The trio released four self-published albums before John departed as he moved from Dundee, leaving FreyFox and CaveDweller to perform as a duo. They continued to release more experimental tracks, including a compilation EP in 2011,[346] until they released their final album together in 2013.

FreyFox continued working on solo projects, which usually followed electronic and rock genres, as well contributing to a local electric rock group named Tezite-Va, before deciding to contribute to a project closer to the furry fandom.

Another British furry musician named RascallyBandit (Mike Spencer), or Ras-B for short, wanted to support the charity for ConFuzzled and decided to get other musicians from around the world to work on a compilation album. The final album was

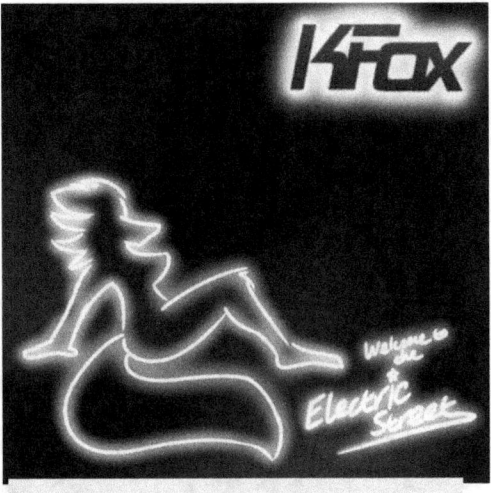

Album cover for the complete works of The Raccoon Gang.

called *Wildfire*, and both Ras-B (under his musician's name Sphatika) and FreyFox (as Subliminal Fuzz) contributed tracks to the 2-CD album, along with musicians from America and Canada, and it was sold at ConFuzzled 2017.

The album did rather well, encouraging a follow-up compilation album in 2018 titled *Tsunami—Furries of Music, Vol. 2*. This one boasted 30 furry musicians of different genres, including a few more British musicians like Equium, Regdeh, and Pascal Farful, and made over £300 for ConFuzzled[347] Ras-B and FreyFox have continued the tradition of releasing new Furries of Music charity CD compilations each year with the release of *Aftershock* in 2019 and *Avalanche* in 2020.

Fox Amoore

The second prominent furry musician to come from Scotland is Fox Amoore (Iain Armour). He started playing the piano at the age of five, learning on his grandmother's piano, before starting to play professionally at the age of 14. Outside of the fandom, he toured internationally for a Paul McCartney and the Wings tribute act called the GetBack Band, as well as composing music for video games and Web shows.[348]

Amoore started posting his music online in the early noughties, specializing in New Age and Orchestral music. He released his first professional album, *The Spirit of the Wolf*, in 2004. This album would be the first and only one to be released under his real name. Future albums would be released under his furry name, which stems from his love

Fox Amoore at Abbey Road Studios (photo by Nico)

of foxes and a twist on his last name (which originates from the French word Armour, meaning "Love").

After releasing three studio albums (*The Ballad of Midnight* in 2007, *Masked* in 2009, and *Fly* in 2010), Fox Amoore was brought on to produce music for *Bitter Lake*, a fantasy short film produced mostly by furries from the Netherlands, including its director, Shay, and producer, EZwolf.[349] The film garnered a lot of hype as it was a full furry production with actors performing in full realistic, theatrical styled fursuits from one of the most popular American fursuit creation companies, Clockwork Creature Studio.

Bitter Lake premiered at EuroFurence 17 in August 2011 to mixed reviews, but its DVD release still managed to sell out at the convention, and later internationally. It also proved to make a huge impact on Fox Amoore's career as it continued to get international attention.

After his 2011 album, *Feel*, and a 2012 collaboration with American furry musician Colson Grainger, he started his next big project in September 2013. An Indiegogo campaign was set up to raise funds to record his album *Come Find Me* at Abbey Road Studios.[350] The initial goal was set at £7,500 to cover the studio costs and invite other musicians to perform. He also had an extra-ambitious goal of £20,000 to include a full live orchestra. Within two hours, the first target was reached, and two months later the ambitious target was reached.

Recording at Abbey Road Studios took place on 25 January, 2014. Accompanying Fox Amoore were furry musicians like Colson Grainger, Alexander James Adams, Amadhia, and Lilpad (Nicola Kinsman), as well as the English Chamber Orchestra.[351] Amoore also had the grace of having it produced and mixed by Simon Rhoades, who was best known for producing music for the Beijing Olympics and the James Bond film *SkyFall*. *Come Find Me* was officially released at the furry convention Anthrocon in 2014.

Amoore returned to Abbey Road Studios in February 2017 to record his next solo album, *The Dreamcatcher*, following another Indiegogo campaign that reached $31,000.[352] This time it featured the City of Prague Philharmonic Orchestra, along with the Opus32 and Eclipse Choirs, the return of Lilypad and Alexander James Adams, inclusion of more furry musicians like RhubarbTheBear (Ned Wilkinson), Dolphin Boy (Joe Brisby), and Pepper Coyote (Jared Clark), and a cameo appearance from Tim Russ, the actor best known for the character Tuvok in *Star Trek: Voyager.*

Film poster for Bitter Lake

Fox Amoore inarguably remains one of the most prolific furry musicians in the world. Outside of his own albums, he has been guest of honour at furry conventions spanning five continents since 2011, including ScotiaCon (Scotland), RusFurrence (Russia), Furnal Equinox (Canada), FurDU (Australia), Infurnity (Taiwan), Argentina FurFiesta, Brasil FurFest, and Megaplex (United States). Even where he is not a guest of honour, he has been on stage either producing his own music, providing music for comedians, or producing the soundtrack to the EuroFurence Pawpet Show, a massive theatrical puppet show.

Most recently, he has teamed up with American furry musician, songwriter, and past collaborator Pepper Coyote to form Foxes & Peppers, starting in 2016 with their debut album *Hashtag.*[353] The duo has since toured together both at conventions and major venues like the Cavern Club in Liverpool, and even a musical for the Nevada furry convention Biggest Little Fur Con 2018 called *A Musical Tail.*[354]

THEATRE

Outside of the Pawpet Shows that feature on the main stage at conventions like ConFuzzled and Eurofurence, original live theatrical productions following furry themes are relatively rare both in and outside of the furry fandom. There are a few notable exceptions such as *A Musical Tail,* as noted above.

A Musical Tail

Fox and Pepper's 2018 musical follows three friends through their time at a furry convention. The songs follow a narrative about activities such as arriving and getting in line to register, watching the opening ceremony, going on a spending spree at the dealers' den, enjoying the parties, making new friends, and ultimately, trying to have the best weekend ever. The music was produced by Fox Amoore and Pepper Coyote, who played in the rear of the stage while fursuiters filled the roles of characters, acting and largely miming on stage.

Specifically made for Biggest Little Fur Con, which had the theme "musicals" that year, it only had a single showing at the convention and no productions at any other venues. Fortunately, the entire two-hour performance was live-streamed for those outside of the convention and remains available to watch on YouTube[355] as of this writing. The soundtrack is also available to purchase.

What few furries know is that this was not the first attempt to produce a fully staged musical with the furry fandom as its theme.

Yiff!

In 2005 a musical theatre student at Goldsmiths College using the pseudonym Mort L. Wombat (Tim Saward) had finished directing amateur musical productions of *Jack & the Beanstalk* and *Dr Jekyll & Mr Hyde* for the East London group the Woodhouse Players and began work on his third and newest project. He had been aware of the fandom through friends of his since 2002 and became fascinated with the size and appeal of the then underexplored community. He was inspired to use the furry fandom as the theme for this new musical.[356]

He decided to give it the name *Yiff!* As it was a common word within the fandom and also recognisable by those outside the fandom as a furry word. The exclamation point as a reference to a trend in musical titles at the time based on ostensibly unlikely subjects.

Using his production company *toomuchinfomation*, Mort documented his development of the show on a blog and ran polls for both musical and furry fans to get ideas for the musical. This included characters, themes, musical style, and stakes. He also attended LondonFur meets.[357] and participated in various IRC channels such as #NorthUKFurs over a period of months to build up a storyline. With the help of his prior experience as a science fiction fan, he was able to work his way around the fandom and get feedback directly from the furries themselves as a curious researcher.

Within a few months, Mort started getting help from those within the fandom to develop the musical. Soon after finishing the first draft, he brought on three furries from the United States to act as consultants: Vahn Fox, Syrras, and Stage Lion, the lattermost being a musical fan and a baritone. After posting an ad in the Further Convention 2007 conbook,[358] an Australian furry artist and animator named Edge (Kyle Evans) was hired to provide artwork and animated segments for the production.[359]

By September 2007, two drafts had been finished, and a cast was put together for the show's first 45-minute reading at the Goldsmiths Musical Theatre Showcase, given for the 27th and 29th evening shows.[360] Although feedback from both furry fans and industry professionals was positive, there were technical setbacks, and additional scenes needed to be added with the help of a classmate named Darren Wayte. These were presented in a follow-up reading at the King's Head Theatre on 28 January and 3 February 2008.

These two readings provided everyone with the first look at the synopsis.

"*Yiff!* Delves into the mysterious world of 'furries,' people who roleplay as animals," related a writer for the King's Head Theatre website. "Projected animations mixed with live action tell the story of Russ, whose childhood fixations seem to be crossing into distinctly adult territory, to the consternation of his religious mother. Some furries just like anthropomorphic cartoons or dressing up like tigers. Russ wants something a bit deeper and more adult: more sexy; more taboo; more … yiffy. Can he win acceptance and come of age, both online and in real life? Is a second life always a good thing? And how do you deal with the world's wolves? All the intrinsic comedy of the furry experience meets some serious questions about sexuality in a decade of easy fantasy in excerpts from this perky and comic new musical that is unmistakeably contemporary."[361]

Recordings from these readings provide more detail of the plot. It followed Russ, a nineteen-year-old loner from the English seaside town of Whitby who has a very Christian conservative mother concerned about his internet addiction. Through IRC, Russ learns about furries, and believing he has found his true calling, he creates a fursona named RedFox, gets into roleplaying, and even builds a relationship with a girl named JadeVixen. When his mother gets upset over this and cuts off his internet access, he runs off to a furry convention in the United States, where he hopes to fit in and discover new things about himself.

By the time of the second reading, Mort was halfway finished with the writing and songs, but he would place the project on hiatus to secure funds. Both Mort and Darren also started work on an indie commercial musical called *Faithful* in 2008 that contributed to the project's hiatus.

This would change in early October, when the pair were able to successfully negotiate a full production of *Yiff!* at the Scenic Route, a fringe theatre company that does productions in Islington,[362] with the condition that its title had to be changed. The new title was later confirmed to be <*furReality*> after one of the songs.

Several songs from the musical were performed at smaller cabaret shows at the Edinburgh Cellars in 2009,[363] the same year that Mort and Darren's relationship moved beyond professional to become a civil partnership.

On the 1 April 2010, a 30-minute preview was presented at the Loom Bar and Club in London. Unfortunately, this it was the last public showing of the musical as production was quietly and unexpectedly cancelled. Video recordings of the production that had been posted on YouTube were set to private viewing, reducing what little evidence there already was of the production's existence. The only recordings that remained were from the King's Head show in 2008 on Mort's Furaffinity page, as well as a capella covers performed at the convention Rainfurrest and uploaded to YouTube that same year.

It was a complete mystery as to the cause of cancellation until October 2017, when *Dogpatch Press* published an article by guest writer Duncan R. Piasecki on the musical after publisher Patch O'Furr had reached out to Mort.[364]

In short, Mort decided to cancel the production when it started moving away from his original creative intentions. This is understandable given that in a 2008 interview with *Clawcast*, a short-lived American furry podcast, he described <*furReality*> as both a student and passion project that allowed him to break away from the trends of a commercial musical production. When he felt the play began encroaching too closely to commercial trends in 2010, he pulled the plug.

As for the videos being removed, that was a demand from the cast, as well as the result of some online harassment. All the performers in each show were unpaid and had not agreed to being recorded, so there was a moral obligation to take the videos down. The harassment stemmed from an article from July 2008, written by the trolling community of *Encyclopaedia Dramatica*, ridiculing and trying to boycott it for its subject material and exploration of homosexuality. According to Mort, everyone was put off by the trolling, which gave him more reason to not keep the videos online.

After <*furReality*>, Mort and Darren continued production of their other musical, *Faithful*, which was taken on by Mercury Musical Developments and went into production at the Watermill Theatre in 2011. After that, Mort briefly experimented with pantomimes before moving on to his current profession as a theatre manager in Hillingdon.

As for what is left of <*furReality*>, in response to the *Dogpatch Press* article, Mort provided a near complete archive of sheet music, research notes, script drafts, as well as full audio recordings from both the 2007 and 2008 readings, including select songs from other performances. For the time being, at least, the furry fandom has all the documents to imagine what could have been, a full furry-themed musical for the London stage.

BROADCASTING LIVE

Furries are not limited to performing live in front of a crowd; they also perform for the camera or the microphone. Whether it be to share news, provide commentary, analysis, advice, or to entertain through skits, the fandom has always had those who are not shy to entertain through the internet.

One of the earliest examples of this is radio—specifically, internet radio. First pioneered in 1993 as a means for traditional radio stations to broadcast online,[365] internet-only stations started appearing in 1995. Internet radio allowed both professionals and amateurs to set up and run their own shows and play their own music with more flexibility than their traditional broadcasting counterparts, even after governing bodies started to clamp down on copyright complaints brought on by record labels.

One such amateur was Tae Kwon Do Tiger, who changed his name to TK Tiger (Thomas King). He had a problem with internet radio during the early noughties because at the time it was almost nothing but music playlists with no one presenting the show.

In an effort to do a better job with an online radio station, he decided to team up with Blaster Hedgie to create their own internet broadcast. TK already had a website that he used to host stories for the Lion King community called The Tiger's Tail (tigertails.co.uk), so the internet show naturally became *TigerTails Radio*, produced by TigerTails Entertainment.

Airing its first episode on 20 July 2004, *TigerTails Radio* set out with the promise that it was primarily a talk radio show between TK and Blaster, with some music introduced as broadcasts went on.

Incredibly, the show ran nightly from 9 PM to midnight. Some listeners also provided content to engage with the show, most notably Shep Shephard, who provide daily facts that he reposted onto his own Live-

Official banner for TigerTails Radio, featuring Blaster Hedgie and TK Tiger.

Journal, a tradition he kept up until 2012! When neither TK or Blaster could attend the makeshift studio, there was a selection of furries to take their place, including SouthPaw, Tungro, and Lazerus101.

While most of the shows had discussions of the daily happenings with occasional music, there were some noteworthy broadcasts that were documented. One was an Eighties-themed broadcast that ended up overrunning to a total of eight hours in length, largely because of nonstop eighties music that turned the studio into a disco. The event was captured on a webcam feed for all to see.

There was also a charity broadcast made for Comic Relief titled The TigerTails Radio Comic Relief Gunge-a-thon during which cast members had buckets of gunge poured over them for donations; this episode raised £301 for the charity Comic Relief.

After 365 broadcasts, exactly one year after premiering, TK announced that *TigerTails Radio* would go off the air. The final show was essentially a farewell party with the cast and listeners recalling their favourite moments. TK did a reprisal of a karaoke performance of a song called "Affirmation," an amusing reprisal as it was known amongst die-hard listeners that he hated singing that song.

Although the daily furry internet radio show was over that did not mean *TigerTails Radio* was finished. TK Tiger and Blaster Hedgie agreed to revive it for a second season, beginning on 22 February 2006. Unlike the first run, this new season had a sporadic schedule, which resulted in shows being archived for download for the first time.

Despite technical issues from both the broadcast and archive hardware impacting the show, which led to only 36 episodes of the planned 100 actually airing for the year, fans were still more than happy to see the show revived. When the cast did their second run of the Comic Relief Gunge-a-thon, they managed to raise £700, which was £200 more than their target goal for the night.

The third season began on 17 September 2007. The show settled into a weekly format at this point and also began to include themed and holiday shows. It was the last season to have Blaster Hedgie as a regular host. He resigned halfway through the season due to a busy work schedule, losing enthusiasm, and feeling he had become stale in his role. TK Tiger hosted the show on his own for most of the season until a Southampton furry named Eeve3 and TK Tiger's housemate, Xavier, both joined as regular cohosts and guests.

Another major development for British furry internet radio came in 2008. In the United States, several furries were creating their own internet radio shows, and some banded together to create their own radio stations with names like AllFurRadio, LT3M, and the Furry Broadcasting Corporation. In 2008, British furries AxleFox and Wolfpaw took inspiration from these stations and decided to create their own, and so BritFur. FM was born.

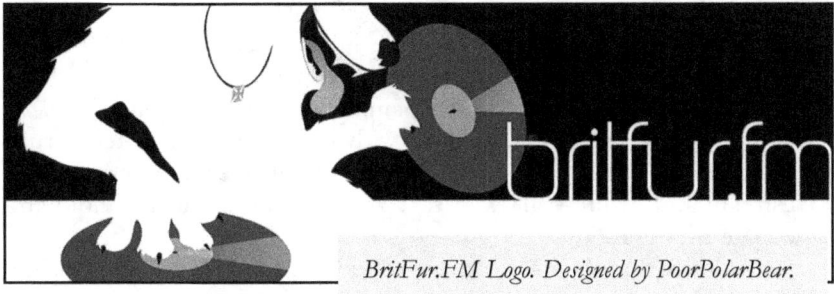

BritFur.FM Logo. Designed by PoorPolarBear.

For shows like *TigerTails Radio*, this meant they were now able to broadcast their shows using on a dedicated server for furries. TK Tiger, Eeve3, and Xavier continued *TigerTails Radio* on Mondays for BritFur. FM. They were joined by two rock-themed radio shows (Tryst's *Rock-Box* and Stuart Otterson's *Slaughter House Radio*), a technology show with dance anthems (*Virus Core Radio*), Japanese music (Dante the Jedi's *It Came from Japan*), and several others.[366]

BritFur.FM would not be the sole place for furry internet radio in the United Kingdom, however. *HardDrive.FM* originated from the station as an alternative music show hosted on BritFur.FM on Thursdays by Miyabi and Kittiah before branching off as a self-hosted entity. It grew in popularity as one of the more predominantly music-focused radio shows from the United Kingdom. It featured regular live DJ sets, mixes, and mashups to stand out from the musical playlists, later expanding its length from three to five hours due to heavy demand.

Meanwhile, in Swindon, a short-lived furry radio show was created by Snack Raccoon and Ollie Pup called *Furpile Radio*. It had its origins in an out-of-print furry magazine and had a failed pilot in 2006 before kicking off in 2007[367] as a weekly show with multiple segments based around news and humour.

The show was open about it being more tailored to mature humour, advertising that "Our show contains lots of swearing, drugs, sex and rock & roll!"[368] It ended after 36 episodes in September 2008, and Snack Raccoon tragically lost his life in a freak accident in 2011. According to Ollie Pup, Snack Racoon was into breath control fantasies, and died of erotic asphyxiation as a result of an experiment that went wrong.[369]

Podcasting and YouTubers

Although the furry internet radio scene was firmly established by the mid-noughties, there were already signs that the practice was losing its popularity. Podcasting, where audio broadcasts are downloaded rather than streamed live, was becoming more popular around the Web thanks to devices like the Apple iPod. Both *TigerTails Radio* and *HardDrive.FM* provided podcasting options alongside live broadcasts by 2009 either through direct downloads or services like iTunes.

Video broadcasting was also gaining popularity. While *TigerTails Radio* had previously played around with having live video feeds running alongside the radio broadcast, the advent of live video services like Livestream and Justin.tv allowed easy access to broadcasting audio and video live for eager fans.

It is likely that the rise of these services made stations like BritFur. FM largely unnecessary, considering both the broadcast station and its website quietly shut down in 2011. Fortunately, two of its most popular shows managed to stay up and running on their own. *HardDrive.FM* continued to broadcast both audio and video streams until it ended in 2014.

There was also one other service that provided an avenue for broadcasts: *YouTube*. *Furries* had already made use of the site by posting videos of slideshows, tutorials, animations, and more for years. While the broad YouTube community had its reservations around the fandom (a collection of online trolls banding together in 2007 to harass and hack into certain accounts owned by furries in what was comically dubbed the "YouTube Furry War"[370]), furries persisted and used the site heavily.

> The YouTube Furry War supposedly began when an American furry named Soki Twopaw published a video titled *Ultimatum Declaratum* to express disdain for online trolls posting negative comments on furry videos. An online trolling group called the Fried Chicken Trolling Crew responded by hacking multiple furry accounts.

TigerTails Radio first started archiving its video streams to YouTube in 2012 after moving to Google Hangouts for live video broadcasts. Hedgie returned as a regular guest starting in 2014, joining TK, Xavier, and Echo (Eeve3 left the show in 2012). It still runs to this day, celebrating its tenth anniversary in 2014 and hosting a party for its 16-year-anniversary episode on 20 July 2020.

Along with podcasts, YouTube was an innovator in vlogging. While the genre had been around since YouTube's inception, it never caught on within the furry fandom until 2014, when various members of the fandom like Blu Dragon started setting up channels to record skits, or challenges, or to discuss various topics in the fandom, whether itinvolved furries online space or at conventions and furmeets.

The vlogging movement started to explode a year later, as furries gained subscribers for these kinds of videos. Majira Strawberry, for example, is an Ohio furry who currently has almost 300,000 subscribers and regularly uploads content that receives tens of thousands of views. Other furry YouTubers also stand out such as Americans Ash Coyote with her professionally produced documentaries, and Adler the Eagle with quality animations, as well as Thabo Meerkat, a Dutch furry who produces furry, popular media, and animal-related news with an upbeat, positive spin.

Among the popular YouTubers from the United Kingdom is Artemis Wishfoot, who created his channel in 2015 and does various weekly videos. He performs in his blue-and-amber collie fursuit and commonly dresses smartly with a white-sleeved shirt and black vest. His videos vary in subject matter, most of them surrounding British culture and topics within the furry fandom with a British twist.

Artemis Wishfoot

Another YouTuber is Shadow Raccoon, a red-and-grey raccoon fursuiter who sometimes sports a Hawaiian shirt. Shadow started off in 2017 doing short film and game reviews. Then, in 2018, he purchased a new fursuit and created convention videos and skits, often collaborating with partner and fellow fursuiter Theodore Rabbit and friend Regdeh the Hoopoe.

But it is not just YouTube where furries perform for the camera. Artists who previously used Livestream use the likes of

Shadow Raccoon and Theodore Rabbit.

Twitch and Pictaro to stream their in-progress artwork. Twitch works well for broadcasting game play, while performers have gravitated toward TikTok.

What was once a niche in the fandom is now one of the fastest growing forms of fandom-driven entertainment on the internet. This popularity does have a double-edged sword, however, as Majira Strawberry pointed out in the documentary series *The Fandom* produced by Ash Coyote:

> On one hand, yes Furry YouTube impacts the fandom. It's exposing it to more people, but on the other paw, it's causing big growth in conventions, it makes it harder to get into hotels and it makes it harder to get the artists you like. It really depends on how you look at it.[371]

The most noticeable change is that the presenters are more likely to be fursuiters, with furry YouTubers who appear as themselves (e.g., Arrkay on the channel Culturally F'd) and ones who use hand-drawn avatars (e.g., BetaEtaDelota) being in the minority. Some have argued that this is only because audiences are drawn to a person's fursuit instead of the content they create. Combined with the impact these personalities have on the fandom, it has not helped the perception that the fandom is solely about the fursuits.

What could help is increased promotion and discussions of the fandom beyond the fursuits, which might be a daunting task but still very much possible considering this is a media-based perception that the fandom itself can control. As for media outside the control of furries, that has a more unfortunate history.

The award-winning documentary directed by Ash Coyote was released in 2020 and is free to watch on YouTube.

READ ALL ABOUT IT

The furry fandom has long been viewed as an entertaining curiosity to many journalists in the print and broadcast media. In the United States, there have been news articles dating back as far as 1991, from brief descriptions such as "that subset of science fiction fans who dress up as little Smurf-like creatures"[372] in the *Chicago Tribune* to full reports about artists who explore anthropomorphism through costumes, comic books, and illustrations such as on the Sci-Fi Channel.

In 1997, Minnesota news affilate KARE-11 followed a few local furries to California for ConFurence 8 to report on the growing subculture.[373] The report covered a number of features of the convention, including workshops, live music, and a room for posting on bulletin boards, but the cameras focused heavily on the fursuits.

The KARE story also showed the after-dark, adults-only parts of the convention, from "pet auctions" in which furries put themselves up for bid in return for favours to "strip shows."

Reactions from furries to the news report were mixed, ranging from the outright vitriolic to others who felt it was fair and accurate in a positive way. Either way, it helped bring attention to the furry fandom—and not just in the United States.

The British furry fandom wouldn't get any media coverage during the Nineties. It simply wasn't large enough to attract the attention. That would be until Emily Hohler, a reporter for the British edition of the women's lifestyle magazine *Marie Claire*, took interest in the KARE-11 news report and travelled with photographer Evan Hurd to San Diego Comic Con[374] to cover the "fursuit phenomenon."

She spoke to several people at the meet-up, including Welsh-furry Porsupah, which resulted in an article published on October 1997. Although the article is often cited as "Creature Comforts" in various places, its full title is the attention grabbing "I Married a Man Who Thinks He's a Wild Cat."[375]

The title is in reference to Kim and Ben Camacho, married furries who dress up as a monster and wild cat respectively in the fandom. They weren't the only ones featured, though. Cataroo and Topfox (Rachel and

John Cawley) were another married couple in the fandom to appear in the news story, and the article describes their fascination with animals and how they both wore fursuits at their wedding; they also wore them on excursions to the park and local supermarket with their eight-year-old child.

Relationships aside, Hohler decided to focus on the fursuits and furry as a lifestyle rather thanon the fandom as a whole, detailing the fascination furries have with being an animal. This included mentions of Topfox's love of foxes; Furlup, who believed he spiritually identifies as a wolf; and Byron Havranek, a feline furry who was quoted saying they experimented with licking themselves like a cat.

Even Mark Merlino and Rod O'Riley, the only gay couple inter-viewed for the article, had their part edited to show only their time talking about spirituality and getting in touch with your animal side.

"We think it deserves discussion.... Getting in touch with your furry side is 120 percent a positive thing," said Rod. "Being a mink has kept me sane, given me a good collection of snappy remarks. I don't stop and think about it: the mink has worked its way into my personality enough for it to become automatic."

That is not to say that there weren't lines drawn regarding furry as a lifestyle in Hohler's story. They commented on behaviours for which the furries had no patience. Nor is it to say that the article described the idea of pretending to be animals in a negative or sardonic way. Indeed, it described how dressing up as animals can help people lose their inhibi-tions and cope with bullying and being ostracised during their childhood.

Of course, with *Marie Claire* being a British publication, it did manage to squeeze in a reference to British members of the furry fandom, such as a brief mention of Porsupah, who "became so obsessed with the furries that he moved to California to be closer to them." Not only did Hohler note the growing British furry fandom, but she also encouraged it:

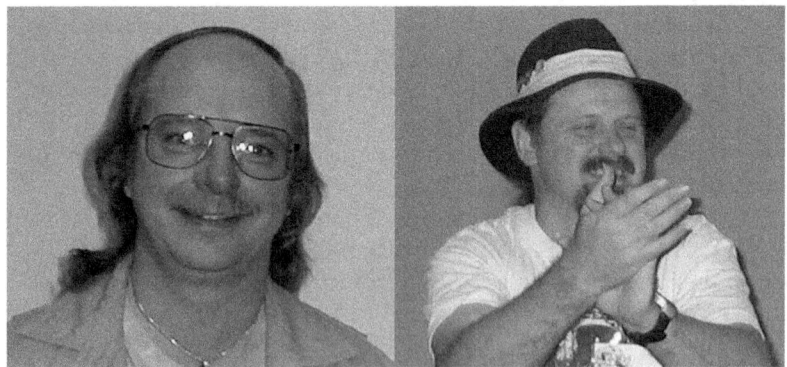

Mark Merlino (left) and Rod O'Riley (photos by RainRat) are two of the Founding Fur-thers of the fandom and were among those interviewed in the Marie Claire *article.*

Britain, famed as a nation of animal lovers, would appear to be ripe for Furry infiltration. Some US Furries have made pilgrimages to obscure British wildlife sites, and there are even a couple of dozen padding around South London, allegedly staging an undersubscribed event called UKFurcon. If anyone needs proof that stroking soft toys is for adults too, it's out there—somewhere.

Pressed Fur, an old website that reviewed and provided downloadable versions of mainstream media reports on the furry fandom, wrote that the *Marie Claire* article "seems more filled with a sense of wonder and pity about furries. It's fair and balanced, though the image painted still brings some unease."[376]

The image being painted was that furries are people who simply dress up and pretend (or worse, believe) they are animals was what brought that unease, potentially moving perceptions further towards it being a lifestyle over a fandom, something more about costumes and less about cartoons and comics.

Even the British newspaper *The Independent* reacted to the *Marie Claire* article by describing furries as "a fast-growing Californian cult of people who like dressing up as animals"[377] and highlighted comments by Furlup, Havranek, and even Rod O'Riley' remark about how being a mink "kept [him] sane." Although that wasn't the worst of it.

LOADED

At ConFurence 9 in 1998, attendees noticed a reporter and photographer walking around the convention. They were Bill Borrows and Robbie Cooper, who worked for *Loaded*, another British magazine that was owned by the same publisher as *Marie Claire*. Unlike Emily Hohler, there was a distinct lack of interest for the fandom from this pair.

Specific written accounts include entering a BDSM panel only to leave ten minutes later when it became apparent that they weren't going to get good photos and attending a late-night furry cabaret before leaving early because it was, to paraphrase. "crap."[378] Even those who spoke directly to the reporters were left with the impression they were expecting something more shocking than what was really happening.

Ian Stradling recalled that most of the British furries had avoided speaking to them altogether, which was most likely because they knew what kind of magazine *Loaded* was. It was a lifestyle magazine like *Marie Claire*, but what made it notorious was it was targeted to "lad-culture," a subculture of anti-intellectual young men who favoured the pastimes of straight sex, drugs, alcohol, and opposing political correctness.

The optimists saw the upcoming article as another instance of a British reporter writing an empathetic and curious look at the happenings over in the United States, the same as *Marie Claire* but with an appeal to young adult men instead of women. Ultimately, they had to read to find out.

Published in the April 1998 issue of "Heavy Petting,", the report opened with a self-insert story of the reporter witnessing convention attendees' rushing of the lobby because he mentioned that three dogs were outside. He was not kind to the attendees, comparing them to paedophiles and describing them as "overweight American computer geeks, freaks and 40-year-old virgins, thighs rubbing together and saliva dribbling down their chins."[379]

For some credence, the report acknowledged the furry fandom as "a broad church" and referenced literature explaining that furries could be anyone "from a person who simply enjoys viewing furry fanzines or films to those who actually believe that they are a non-human trapped within a human form." It quoted hotel staff describing the convention attendees as being "really polite and don't cause any trouble" in comparison to other conventions.

Borrows even managed to talk to at least two British furries at the convention, and he depicted them rather sympathetically even though the descriptions didn't refrain from ridicule:

> The British are instantly recognisable because they are
> slightly embarrassed and intimidated by all the hug-
> ging and scared to death by the animal noises and sex
> stuff. Despite fitting the computer geek template, the
> two twenty somethings from Kent and Skegness are
> at pains to distance themselves from the surrounding
> madness.

According to Borrows, the madness included claims of people selling graphic videos of real-life animals, and subdivisions of the furry fandom, including "plushophiles," "zoophiles," and people who wear fursuits to have sex in them. "There is also, for some reason, a preponderance of male homosexuals who fit into any number of the sub-divisions within furry fandom."

As with other articles published in *Loaded* magazine that ridiculed American football fans and film buffs at the Sundance Festival, it was unobjective sensationalist reporting with anonymous and unsourced quotes, baseless comparisons, and cheap stereotyping. Pressed Fur described it at the time as "cruel, scandalous, and very one-sided, but worst of all there's probably not a single actual lie in it." While it was obviously written to entertain, it was deliberately inflammatory to bring in viewers and had nothing to suggest what was and was not real.

Loaded wasn't the first publication to connect the furry fandom to fetishism and sex, but prior publications such as *WIRED*'s "Johnny Manhatten Meets the Furry Muckers"[380] viewed the connection as merely online role playing and fantasy, nothing to suggest it was a literal and wide part of the fandom.

Loaded, on the other hand, while stating the sexual aspects are extreme cases and not universally accepted, wrote about them being common enough at the convention to deserve more focus over the daytime events, the music, or other activities that prior reports covered, even providing an anonymous interview with three "zoophiles" to add to the sensationalism.

Documentarian and journalist Louis Therous hosted the show Weird Weekends *about various subcultures from 1998 to 2000 (photo credit Claire Boxall).*

Loaded was possibly influenced by *Marie Claire*, which in turn was influenced by KARE-11, and *Loaded* influenced other articles and TV shows. Documentarian Louis Theroux wrote an article for the *Guardian* newspaper in May 1999 titled "Weekend Pass" about various topics that he rejected for his series *Weird Weekends*.[381] One of the topics he covered was furries, and while not as explicit, his coverage made clear his view of the furry fandom had nothing to do with fandoms.

> A subculture of men and women who have a fetish
> for cartoon animals, like Bambi or Tweety Pie. They
> dress up in big furry outfits and go to conventions
> to pair off. I could see myself dressing up in a furry
> mascot-style costume. I could see myself prancing
> about with a man-sized honey badger to the strains of
> Disney's Hakuna Mutata and saying, "This is weird!"
> But then what? You've got the convention and noth
> ing else.

Although the worst thing the *Loaded* article influenced were the furries that saw these rare and extreme sexual aspects in full view and looked at whom to blame. Instead of blaming the publications for creating sensationalist reporting that falsely skewed what furry fans were into, finger was pointed at Confurence, specifically its founders and chairs.

One of the accusations was the convention having little to no enforcement of rules or code of conduct, basically allowing attendees to be as wild as they liked. In the 2020 documentary *The Fandom*, by Ash Coyote and Chip Foxx, Mark Merlino recalled in the early years that there were incidents where attendees got drunk and caused trouble, including a few that were evicted from the hotel. Still, he thought it was unnecessary to print the rules of conduct for attendees to hold on to for those first few years, as he once argued earlier in 2011:

> We always asked attendees to be polite and civil. Wasting pages in the con book (which no one ever reads anyway) with pages of "rules" served no purpose but to have something to point to if someone did something stupid.... Maybe we did expect attendees to behave better, but for many of them, it was the first time they had to "let their hair down." There is a social learning curve.[382]

The staff still intervened to complaints from hotel staff and other attendees, and whatever disputes didn't cause any harm to their reputation with the venue and local area.

Rules of conduct were eventually printed in the convention program, but perhaps it was done a little too late as some attendees weren't satisfied with the way they saw the convention progress.

One furry fan published an open letter after CF8 that went viral on alt.fan.furry. He vented his frustrations that his wife didn't raise enough money in the pet auction compared to those he deemed not to be furries, along with accusing Merlino directly for poor security, allowing new attendees with "alternative lifestyles" that alienated the old ones, and listing a number of extreme incidents.[383]

While the author claimed certain incidents such as finding "semen in the elevator" were corroborated by other attendees, several furry fans, as well as historians like Joe Strike, are doubtful that some even happened the way they were described, or even at all. "I don't think it's true. I think there were people who wanted to give the furs a bad reputation" Strike said in *The Fandom*.

Although the worst that Mark and Rod had to deal with revolved around their relationship, as at the time they were a couple and identified as bisexual. The pair were open about their relationship, and how the furry fandom helped them explore their sexuality, as well as the sexuality of other furries in the fandom. Mark Merlino expressed his views even in television interviews such as *EuroTrash* in 1999.

"A lot of furries seem to be interested in sexuality.... I discovered my bisexuality, and I think this has to do with the attraction of animals."[384]

This attitude rubbed some in the fandom the wrong way, the kind that didn't believe the LGBT were a part of the fandom, or shouldn't be open about it, and attacked the pair for bringing in "alternative lifestylers" and letting them run "inappropriate" events.

Furry historian and author Joe Strike has written two books about the fandom.

What's wrong was that the LGBT and events deemed inappropriate weren't "brought in" by anyone, they were always there. The staff and early attendees were also connected to the science fiction convention scene during the height of *Star Trek*, and so Confurence was structured based on those sci-fi conventions and had events inspired from them.

For instance, fursuit competitions were lifted from cosplay masquerades, as were dealers' dens. Pet auctions were a charity fundraising event inspired by slave auctions, which followed the same structure of people auctioning themselves for services, that carried on in the science fiction community long after it fell out of favour at furry conventions.[385]

What was also a part of the science fiction community was the LGBT and mature content. When the first recognised erotic fan fiction originated in the science fiction fandom during the 1960s, it was based on *Star Trek* and was homoerotic.[386]

Meanwhile, erotic cosplay was prominent, with nude cosplayers in the masquerades until they were banned in the 1970s.[387] Even if LGBT weren't a part of the furry fandom, it wouldn't have been any less sexual, considering the late-night "strip show" Fur-Le-Dance prominently featured male and female performers.

Mark Merlino himself shared his own thoughts for the growing LGBT presence at Confurence:

> The main attendees of ConFurence before 1993 were
> science fiction fans and the artists were cartoonists and
> illustrators who wanted to network. They appeased the
> few fans by doing sketches in their sketchbooks. After
> 1993, places like Furrymuck ... had become popular,
> and we did promote the convention there. The atten-
> dance doubled, and many of the new members were
> coming to meet their on-line friends in-person, and
> many were gay or bi. This freaked out the old-school
> artists and more, their fan-base. A small group decided
> it had to stop and started their sabotage campaign.[388]
> What a fantastic bomb to drop on us right before our
> vacation. This isn't the same old recycled BS that the
> homophobic fans generated to attempt to cancel our
> convention and any other con that welcomed openly
> LGBTQ+ members. The same small group has been
> responsible for creating scenarios and making stuff
> up to this day. They were involved in the RainFurrest
> convention disaster (though the staff were complacent
> for sure).

This sabotage campaign would include the police being tipped about
video piracy, a fake bomb threat, and anonymous hotel complaints of
pornography[389] among others, One even accused Merlino of advertising Confurence to fetish communities despite having no physical proof
other than the name of an obscure adult magazine.[390] Although the only
adverts to surface appeared in sci-fi magazines like *Starburst* and convention directories, this rumour persisted until 2015 when the magazine in
question was posted online, with contact information of the convention
and Ed Zolna's Mailbox Books but no advertisement to speak of.[391]

> That's it? This is what you, ... Crush Yiff Destroy
> and every other LOL Furries site has used to justify
> forcing this fandom to live in a state of complete deg-
> radation for nearly 20 years? I think this fandom owes
> Mark Merlino one hell of an apology. –Perri Rhoades,
> 2015.[392]

The ongoing attacks on the pair added to the stress of running
the convention, leading Mark and Rod resigning as chairmen after Confurence 10 in 1999.

FURTANNIA

THE BURNED FURS

While Mark Merlino's critics were bad enough, there were furries who thought even they didn't go far enough. A furry going by the name SqueeRat published a manifesto decrying the fandom for tolerating zoophilia and plushophilia, along with attacking furry lifestylers, therians, and even vegans as being psychopaths responsible for making the furries synonymous with perverts.[393] The rant got enough attention that she and four friends formed a movement in a follow-up post called the "Burned Furs." According to a post by C. Trotman:

> The name has a double meaning. Non-psycho furs can be called "Burned," because anyone with a firm grasp on reality would clearly feel slighted by the screamingly deviant direction the fandom has taken. Another way of looking at it is the example made of furs who have spoken up against fandom perversion and been "burned at the stake" for it.[394]

The Burned Furs' intended goal was to improve (or clean up) the fandom by calling out and vocally disassociating from parts of the furry fandom that go against the original intention of the fandom to celebrate the anthropomorthpic arts. They wanted to hold them to account for the negative media coverage, even citing *Loaded* magazine as a key example of their bad influence.[395] Along with vocally denouncing plushophilia and zoophilia, the Burned Furs advocated for adult artwork to come with content warnings online and to be separated and covered at conventions.

The group had some support from furries who agreed with their cause, but there were problems with the movement as well. One was their counterproductive approach to focusing on the negative aspects of the fandom rather than telling the public what furries are actually about.

The movement was also grassroots and leaderless by design. This resulted in certain members going against the positions laid out on their official websites such as what kind of furry art was allowed.

The founding members weren't positive examples either. SqueeRat distributed flyers encouraging suicide at the furry convention Anthrocon, claiming it to be merely dark humour.[396] Another founding member, Hangdog, made homophobic remarks about certain critics involving glory holes.[397] While SqueeRat was subsequently banned from the Burned Furs, Hangdog was allowed to stay and was defended by other members. This led to allegations that the Burned Furs was a homophobic hate group in which members targeted gay- or male-only adult furry art. The irony of a movement that had set out to improve a group's image by holding bad actors to account coming under fire itself for the same thing was lost on them.

VANITY FAIR

The Burned Furs ultimately failed in their cause, and negative coverage of the fandom continued. *Vanity Fair* published an exposé in its March 2001 issue on the furry fandom written by George Gurly and titled "Pleasures of the Fur." Mostly covering the first iteration of Midwest Furfest back in 2000, Gurly asked a variety of furries to describe many parts of the furry fandom, but he offered a patronizing view of most of them and gave particular attention to a known plushophile named Fox Wolfie Galen. Gurly also printed a testimony of a sex researcher that gave the perception that furries were sexually disturbed individuals, sardonically calling furries "furverts."

As a result, many complaints were written to *Vanity Fair*, most falling on deaf ears or being heavily truncated letters to the editor in the following issue.[398]

In another instance of a Burned Fur founder setting a bad example, Eric Blumrich posted his complaint online and included physical threats of violence towards Fox Wolfie Galen and a few other furries who were interviewed in *Vanity Fair*, saying that they should be publicly hung in Times Square and have their remains fed to dogs.[399]

The *Vanity Fair* backlash didn't work, and it ended up being so popular with the mainstream press that it would influence other media outlets to cover the furries in the same fashion, and that unfortunately included the United Kingdom.

In the same year, 2001, British media corporation Granada Media Group contacted Confurence about doing a report in which a British couple would go on a trip to their convention to talk about their relationship and how it applies to the furry fandom. Darrel Exline, a self-proclaimed Burned Fur and director of Confurence following Mark Merlino's resignation, warned people of red flags about the proposed report, claiming their contact cited the *Vanity Fair* article.[400]

Exline predicted after some research that Granada Media was looking to do a report for *Nightlife*, a midnight show done by the London broadcast arm of ITV called LWT. Although the plans to report at Confurence 12 did not go ahead, Exline's prediction still ended up true when *Nightlife* did a report on a few London furries on the Naked City segment of their March 30 episode titled "The Furverts".

The segment featured five furries active in the LondonFurs scene, and the first error it makes happens almost immediately: using the term "furvert" interchangeably with "furry." Clawz Skunk talked largely about his attraction to tails and was asked to talk about plushophiles, but host Jacqui Joseph never makes it clear that these are separate things.[401] The one saving grace of the *Nightlife* broadcast was that the entire segment only aired once on London TV well after midnight. But it didn't stop avid LondonFurs from recording and distributing the segment online. It was at this point that furries were beginning to get hesitant when it came to meeting the media.

For example, *The Financial Times* wrote a positive article on furries in December 2001 titled "Fursuit of Happiness," which focused on the cost and business opportunities of buying or making fursuits. However, photojournalist Mark Peterson's struggled to find furries willing to be interviewed, as reporter John-Paul Flintoff explained:

> Most furries, stung by prior encounters with the media, told him flatly to leave them alone. But Rapid T Rabbit, who runs a puppet show on cable TV in New York, allowed Peterson to follow him around for a while. In due course, Rapid T Rabbit introduced Peterson to his friend Thaddeus Fox.
>
> Both furries declined to be interviewed—as did the other furries Peterson photographed, with their consent, at a massive convention in Philadelphia but they did supply written statements.[95]

Not only were furries avoiding the press individually but so were the conventions and gatherings. Midwest FurFest introduced a zero tolerance, "no press" policy beginning with the 2001 convention,[402] and other conventions in America followed suit. Considering what the *Vanity Fair* article did to the furry fandom, who could honestly blame them for avoiding the press? Pressed Fur listed plenty of other articles written within months after the exposé, not just the *Nightlife* report, with a point scale indicating whether it was a pro- or con-furry report.

From the printed publications in the United States and Canada to the early web articles, all the way up to 2002, the media reported on the furry fandom, some calling them "furverts" and getting any willing furry to speak about fetishes. While Pressed Fur did feature a few articles that were on the pro side of the scale, most were either on the con side or somewhere in the middle.

Even though it took until 2005 for the British press to mention the furry fandom again, even four years on they felt the need to follow in the steps of the *Vanity Fair* article. "Is Your Team's Mascot a Furvert?" from the sports section of the *Guardian* claimed to question the sex lives of sports mascots. Ultimately, their findings weren't worthy of an article as only one professional mascot was quoted in the article. The one interviewee claimed that girls think they're too immature to go out with, making them "sexually frustrated" as a result.[403]

Journalist Steven Wells suggested that these sports mascots should instead pair up with the "incredibly horny furries." No surprises as to where he got that idea from:

> Furries, as you might know, are people who like to dress up in animal costumes. Some furries are also plushies … some [plushies] like having sex with people dressed as your team's mascots…. [I]t should be emphasised that not all furries are plushies…. But those that do often gather at Fur Conventions. Here the "furverts" might be found in a huge "fur pile," collectively "yiffing" or "skritching" one another…. I swear all this is true… It should be noted that, according to a 2001 Vanity Fair exposé of the furvert scene, a high number of furries are bearded and wear glasses.

In fairness, Wells did put in the effort to clarify that it was only *some* of the furries who did this. He wouldn't be the only journalist to shoehorn furries into sex-related articles needlessly, though. The tabloid newspaper *The Sun* brought up furry conventions in an article about a non-furry couple who dress up as animals when they have sex, and a porn star who made a viral video of himself dressed as a kangaroo. They didn't interview any actual furries, either, but the porn star Jim Slip was aware of them and described them as people "who dress up in animal suits and go to discos. For them it's a lifestyle, not something sexy to have fun with."[404]

Meanwhile, another tabloid newspaper, *The Metro*, decided to make up vocabulary to get furries involved:

> Forget dogging—the new sex craze is "furring."
> [There's no such word in the furry lexicon.]
>
> The practice sees people dressing up in giant teddy bear or other outfits and meeting in woodlands and forests for sex.
>
> Participants—sometimes called "furverts"—also dress as rabbits, squirrels or cartoon characters.[405]

Interestingly, although British furries were clearly aware of these articles, they took little to no interest in giving them any attention. Most critical responses to these articles at the time came from American furries, who wrote their criticisms directly to the website under the article.

In 2008, when the British furries had only just begun to run their own conventions, there was no explicit "no media" policies like those at the U.S. conventions, although they were as hesitant to allow the press to attend, including at furmeets. That didn't stop one journalist from trying.

Alix Fox was a reporter for the alternative culture magazine *Bizarre*, and when she wanted to investigate the furry fandom she was aware of the sensationalist reporting and its effects on the fandom. She wrote:

> As a consequence of bad press, role-playing forums are being spammed with aggressive taunts from bully websites like Godhatesfurries.com; fans of *Thundercats* and Disney's *Robin Hood* are being accused of bestiality; and any group of Furries meeting to socialise are automatically presumed to be furiously doing it like they do on the Discovery Channel, in an unrestrained orgy of claws and paws. Now it's time to tell the real story.
>
> I want to write an accurate piece about these super furry animals; to hang out with them for a few days and report back on what Furry Fandom is really about. That means fully immersing myself in the culture....[406]

Anticipating a flat-out rejection if her and photographer Tom Broadbent expressed their intentions to report at a furmeet, Fox decided to go to a LondonFurs meet incognito, ordering a red fox mascot costume from China. When that didn't arrive on time, she went with faux fur and body paint to provide the desired effect. She was apparently caught red handed. However, plenty of furs described her as being nice and transparent once the cat was out of the bag. A few furries were a lot more willing to talk and pose for photos.

Although some furries were still sceptical about Fox's intentions, the pair were deemed to be genuinely interested and trustworthy enough to merit attending an arranged smaller picnic gathering in Sutton. The result was a lengthy article titled "Super Furry Animals" featured in the June 2008 issue of *Bizarre*.

Furries did take some issue with the article itself, offering mixed opinions on her writing as "*Bizarre*'s pun-loving reporter." Some witty examples include "B.O. that could K.O. a buffalo" and "what the mutts might like to do with their nuts." Not to mention the groans inspired by her direct references to early negative media, including both *Vanity Fair* and *Loaded* magazine's "Heavy Petting." These issues are minor compared to what most agreed was a rather in-depth, honest, and positive article on the fandom.

Alix Fox spent most of her time speaking to TigerFire and Out-Kast, remarking on the craftmanship of the fursuits at the meet and how much effort and sweat goes into performing in them. She also provided descriptions of various fursonas she encountered, from a realistic dapper steampunk wolf to a draguinea ("an odd hybrid between a guinea pig and a dragon"), and details on how fursonas can be based on existing characters or the real-life personalities of the furries themselves. She also pointed out the furry fandom's higher than average number of gay and bisexual people, as well as its being predominantly filled with tech-enthusiasts to the point where some artists notice a load of programming in-jokes that go over their head.

Sex is brought up, partially because Fox saw lots of hugging and collars and because she was given a promotional item for a furry convention in the form of a condom. One of the furmeet organisers offered their belief that what happens in the fandom is no different to what happens outside the fandom: "I think in any gathering of people who share a common interest, there are likely to be some who pair off … especially if booze is involved. I don't think there's much difference between people's sexual behaviour as the evening goes on at a Furry meet than at any other party."

OutKast admitted in the article to wearing furry accessories in bed, saying she liked the feel of fur akin to someone liking the look and feel of PVC, but nowhere near a full fursuit, Alix herself remarking that the situation felt no different to her own experiences of dressing up as a bunny or cat girl for her partners.

Even the article's small section on furry lingo had a surprisingly high degree of tact and thought, mentioning that the word "yiff" originated as a word from the Foxish language meaning "an energetic 'Yes!' or a cheerful greeting" in online role-playing circles before evolving into a term used for sex.

In the end, Alix Fox enjoyed her time with the furries, finding them "chummy" and spending a lot of time role playing and enjoying the reactions of passers-by in their outfits, which was far different from what the press had told her before she made her arrival:

> Furries strike me as a highly creative and warmhearted bunch, and it's a shame that so many misguided people seem to want to dock their tails and neuter their apparently harmless fun. They may be breaking away from

the herd, but having seen things from the inside, I'm inclined to say that the world might be a chirpier place if a few more sheep dared dress in wolves' clothing.

Both Alix Fox and Tom Broadbent would continue to write about furries a few months later to cover RBW 2008, and then again while covering LondonFurs Summer and Winter Parties for the London City magazine *TimeOut*.

Although Alix Fox herself would later leave journalism to be an advocate and advisor for Netflix's show *Sex Education*, she continues to bring up the furry fandom in a positive light. Tom Broadbent published the book *At Home with The Furries*, featuring a collection of photos of fursuiters from around the United Kingdom interacting in their homes.

This nicer coverage also relaxed a few British furries who then opened up to the press more. This was the case with Foxbearance and Marcony when they spoke to Lisa Scott for the article "Unleash Your Sexual Inner Beast" in *The Metro* one year after its article on "Furring."

The lifestyle department of the newspaper didn't completely change their tune, however, feeling the need to include a Dutch porn filmmaker and vetting furry terminology with less effort than *Bizarre* did (three of the five words they provided were variations of "yiff.")[407]

However, they did allow FoxB and Marcony to talk freely about the two sides of the coin to the fandom. FoxBearance spoke of the purely fandom aspect of furries, relating how they became a furry thanks to the video game series *Sonic the Hedgehog*, how they find wearing a fursuit to be fun and energetic, and explaining how furries come from various backgrounds. Meanwhile, Marcony shone a light on the mature lifestyle side, acknowledging a sexual aspect but preferring to wear make-up and prosthetics and draw anthropomorphic animals in their underwear.

Like many furries, FoxBearance was inspired by characters in furry games and movies, especially Sonic the Hedgehog.

MURDEROUS INTENT IN LANCHASHIRE

One of the more positive and informative instances of news reporting on the furry fandom came from an article in the BBC, although oddly enough, the origins of the article came from a not-so-positive incident.

On the evening of 7 February 2009, a married couple in Lancashire were attacked by a knife-wielding young man. Fortunately, both survived with only minor injuries. The police arrested the young man as well as his co-conspirator, who happened to be the son of the two victims.

In the trial it was revealed that the two young men became friends online and had planned out the murder through chatrooms and private messages in the months leading up to the attack. While both men denied that the incident was anything other than roleplay gone too far, they were both found guilty of conspiracy to murder. The attacker was sentenced to seven years in prison, and the son of the victims was given an indefinite hospital order.[408]

Most of the press that covered the story did not go into any details of their online habits. The exceptions were the *Lancashire Evening Post* and the *Metro*, which revealed that the two met through furry websites and were into gratuitous roleplay.[409] The fandom quickly identified and denounced the pair as a result and found itself briefly in the centre of discussion in both furry and non-furry communities.

Sadly, Denise Winterman passed away from cancer in 2015.

In response to the trial, the *BBC News Magazine* decided to write a full-length article on the fandom, eventually being published in November 2009. "Who Are the Furries?"[410] published in November 2009 and written by Denise Winterman, answered the titular question in detail.

Impressively, the article included furries both locally and internationally, with interviews from Mark Merlino, TaniDaReal, and Fred Patten, as well as Dr. Kathy Gerbasi, a social psychologist and founder of the International Anthropomorphic Research Project, and Ian Wolf, an editor for the *FurteanTimes*.

As opposed to previous news articles, the focus was on the furry fandom as a creative community. It detailed their interests in various kinds of art: creating fursonas, roleplaying, performing in fursuits, meeting up in person at furmeets and conventions. It also gave a brief history of the fandom from its pre-internet days to present. Dr. Gerbasi also discussed the psychology behind furries, explaining why one would have such an interest in anthropomorphic animals:

I think most humans grow up interested in animals.
We grow up with teddy bears, pets, Mickey Mouse, etc.
Animals surround us in advertisements, nature, stories,
and fables.

Humans tend to anthropomorphise as a way of understanding and interpreting the world around us. Furries
just take this interest a bit further than most people.

Considering article originated from the story relating to adult on-
line-roleplaying, the sexual element is brought up and described as being
overplayed in the press. The amplified misconception caused furries to
want their fandom kept private, as Dr. Gerbasi discovered: "If you tell
people about furries they often think you are kidding or making it up.
Also, due to bad publicity, furries have not been cooperative about being
studied."

The article proved to be extremely popular, reportedly causing online traffic to the *FurteanTimes* website to nearly triple upon publication
and was very well received by furries and non-furries alike. It was nominated for an Ursa Major Award for Best Other Literary Work, the first
work of mainstream journalism to be nominated in the history of the
Ursa Major Award.[411] The team behind *BBC News Magazine* also had
pride in the article itself, ranking it as one of magazine team's ten favourite stories in a special article reflecting on the magazine's ten-year history
in 2013.[412]

The BBC continued to cover the furry fandom on occasion, including once in a televised news report in July 2012 that covered the
furry scene in the Mexican city of Monterrey. While the story focused
primarily on fursuits, it also showed furries drawing their fursonas and
recognised that wearing fursuits is primarily meant as a way to dress up as
cartoon animals for fun. All in all, it was a more general view of fursuits
compared to prior news reports.

Even in a country where sensationalist reporting and negative furry
stereotypes weren't as widespread, the fans in Mexico were aware of
people looking at them strangely. For example, Adrian Diaz is followed
as he goes out with his friends to a milkshake bar while dressed in a fox
fursuit. He commented:

Here in Mexico, when people don't understand things,
it bothers them. If something is strange or different,
people begin to bother you, or make fun of you,
because it isn't something common in everyday life.
There are many people that accept [furries] and think
it's fun, but the majority don't accept it very much.[413]

The comments reflect on the impact the press had on furries since the 1990s. The repeated misconceptions and lack of focus on what most of the fandom is actually about lead the average viewer to think that furries are not just strange but dirty and deserving of ridicule. Twenty years on, furries were suspicious and defensive towards the media; they would document all mentions of the fandom across the world on Wiki-Fur, LiveJournal, and even a thread on the UKFurForums.

The media looked to certain popular figures like Uncle Kage (Dr. Samuel Conway), the chair of Anthrocon, who is a comedian, storyteller, and recognised unofficial spokesperson for the American furry fandom.

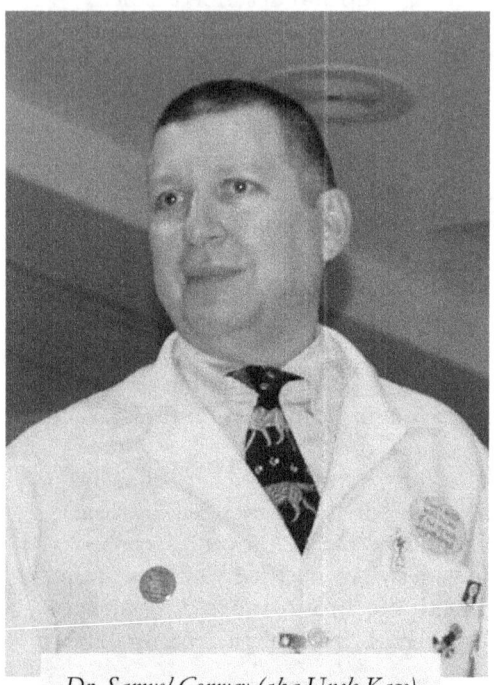

Dr. Samuel Conway (aka Uncle Kage)

He regularly did panels on how to talk to the media, something he was experienced in as someone trained to handle the press during his time working at the Red Cross. While he admitted being hesitant to speak to the media, he began appearing in local news reports covering Anthrocon in 2004, often directing the conversation away from sex and fetishes and towards more family friendly aspects of the fandom.

Kage once spoke to a radio station in 2006 next door to the United Kingdom, Dublin 98 FM, where he was able to evade attempts to direct the conversation towards the adult themes to focus on cartoons and animated films.[414] In this way, Kage told furries to "implant" positive images in the minds of outsiders.

Of course, not all furries agree with Kage's philosophy that sex in the fandom is a negative that should be avoided when talking to the press (or "whitewashing" the fandom, as Uncle Kage describes when talking about his critics). There's even a 2016 documentary called *Fursonas* in which director Dominic Rodriguez brings up Uncle Kage's refusal to participate in the film unless he had some creative control. Rodriguez points out how Kage ridicules certain furries who interacted with the media and presented themselves in ways that go against his viewpoint. It is no surprise that Kage indicated he believed the stories about Mark Merlino inviting fetishists to Confurence and that, while he never endorsed the group, he agreed with the Burned Furs "on principle."

Whether or not furries agreed with Uncle Kage's approach, there have not been many furries who could handle the press with much skill and aplomb. British furmeets and conventions have all but avoided any offers to be covered by local journalists, which explains why most reports focus on news and events internationally in such places as the United States or Germany.

How the current news reports depict the furry fandom can vary depending on the outlet. Sometimes the differences can be mistaken for black-and-white truth when read all over.

In August 2014, Eurofurence 20 was held in Berlin for the first time and hosted over two thousand furries from around the world. Attendees enjoyed the many events at the city's largest hotel from the fursuit parade, pawpet show, acrobatics, music, and raising €21,081 for a bat conservation charity.

Two days after the convention, *The Independent* published an article with the headline "Furrie Invasion: 2000 Fans Attended Eurofeurence in Berlin to Celebrate Their Love of Anthropomorphic Animals."[415] The author, Anna Hart, wrote a highly informative piece about what went on at the convention, its history, and what furries in general get up to, whether it involved fursuits or not. Although the article didn't avoid the subject of sex, it largely sided with the furries who commented on the link between sex and the fandom being largely overblown. Ass one interviewee named Liza put it: "If you think we're secretive and suspicious, it's only because we're sick to death of reading those furry conventions are all about sex." A survey was also referenced that claimed only 37 percent of furry respondents felt that sexual interest is important to their furry activities and that for most it's about a shared cultural obsession, an online community, and a burgeoning artistic genre.

Anna Hart wrote optimistically about the fandom's response from the press and the public:

> There were no muckraking reports in the press billing
> the festival as a sex party, and when the police showed
> up, it was only to examine and admire the prop patrol
> car created by organisers in keeping with the festival's
> "Crime Scene" theme. (Previous themes have included
> "Aloha Hawaii" and "Kung Fur Hustle.") Reception
> staff at the Estrel Hotel gamely accessorised their
> crisp work uniforms with cheetah-ears and giraffe-patterned fuzzy bow-ties.

Unfortunately, Anna Hart spoke too soon. The following day, the *Daily Mail* published its own report on the convention and headlined it with the less flattering "Cats Wearing Stockings and Bears in Satin Corsets: 2,000 Adults Dress as Sexualised Cuddly Toys at Bizarre Festival."[416] Anyone who wanted to argue that the headline was simply designed to get attention and that the contents were fair would be arguably wrong. This article was less focused on Eurofurence and more interested in writing about select furries wearing provocative outfits with their fursuit.

While the *Daily Mail* copied Liza's quote from the *Independent*, most quotes came from Dr. Kathleen Gerbasi (of Furscience). The article highlights her quotes to emphasize the sexual aspects of the fandom and how some believe they are part animal even though Dr. Gerbasi said both of these aspects of the fandom involve the minority.

British furries on the UKFurForums were appalled by the *Daily Mail* writing something so sensationalistic about the fandom but not surprised either. While one could argue that these two articles portrayed the furry fandom so differently to appeal to their readership and their general political stance, evidence can contradict that.

While the *Daily Mail* is considered a right-leaning conservative newspaper, and the *Independent* is considered a centre-to-left-leaning liberal newspaper,[417] that doesn't directly prove that right-leaning papers write about furries being sexual and provocative while the left leaning ones don't. *The Metro* has historically written about the furry fandom as being very sexualised, and yet, though it is owned by the same media conglomerate as the *Daily Mail*, it's considered a centre-left liberal newspaper.[418] *The Daily Mail* has also written factual articles identifying the demographics of the furry fandom from a FurScience report in 2017, including religious beliefs, gender, and sexuality, pointing out that 4% of the fandom believes sex is a top priority in contrast to 35% of the public thinking they do.[419]

Instead, the reason for the difference in reporting depends on whether the paper is a tabloid or a broadsheet. Tabloid news media such as the *Sun*, the *Metro*, and the *Daily Mail* will lean more towards sensationalistic reporting, which likely means that words like "fetish" will appear in headlines even if it's feels irrelevant. For example, from the *Sun* in 2018: "THIS stunning US Navy Woman Spends Her Free Time Masquerading as a Giant Husky to Entertain Her 23.6K Instagram Followers—But Insists It Isn't A Sexual Fetish."[420]

Meanwhile, broadsheet (and even Berliner) news media like the *Independent* and the *Guardian* will lean more towards in-depth coverage and down-to-earth articles. This can include anything from profiling professional fursuit maker Sarah Dee to an opinion piece on feeling welcome in a fandom that is often stigmatised.

Sadly, even though the fandom has seen more acceptance in recent years, the tabloids predominantly cover the fandom—and not fairly, either. When the *Daily Mirror* printed an article on their website about an amateur video recorded at Furry Weekend Atlanta of a couple doing suggestive movements,[421] the individual who recorded the video, Nikki the Husky, later complained on Twitter that the *Daily Mirror* used the video without permission. She posted a direct message conversation with a news editor in which she turned down their request.[422]

The result of all this is that there remains to this day a level of mistrust and scepticism among furries when it comes to news reporters. This leads to kneejerk reactions whenever word comes out that someone wants to cover the fandom. In the month prior to ConFuzzled 2019, for example, a woman working for the *Birmingham Mail* contacted a few furries over Twitter about covering the story and interviewing them.[423]

When one private message became public, there were some initial concerns, but a few decided to investigate the reporter further. They quickly discovered that, based on her social media profiles, she worked for the *Daily Mail*'s online division,. This led to an accusation that the reporter was lying about working for the *Birmingham Mail* to write a story for the *Daily Mail*, so people in the fandom were urged to be cautious about talking with the reporter.[424]

Although the air of caution may have been well-intentioned, the accusation of lying turned out to be unfounded. While the reporter did state she was working for the *MailOnline* on her social media profiles, including LinkedIn, and there was no mention of the working for the *Birmingham Mail*, she also stated that she was a trainee.

The *Daily Mail* had graduate trainee program that included in-house training at a regional newspaper, which would include the *Birmingham Mail*.[425] As of this writing, the reporter's LinkedIn profile was updated to state that she did a three-month placement at *BirminghamLive* (*Birmingham Mail*'s online division) between April and June 2019. The likelihood of interviews being passed on to the *Daily Mail* would have been unlikely but given the fandom's experience with the press, it would have been hard to shake off doubts.

While the furry fandom has made great strides in its relationship with the media, it will still take time before furries no longer feel the need to be apprehensive when faced with a news reporter.

ON THE TELLY

It isn't just print journalists and news reporters that furries have had to keep an eye out for, but television producers and personalities as well. Documentary makers and talk shows have found furries, with their artwork and full-bodied costumes, to make for fine entertainment for their target audiences.

EUROTRASH

British Television viewers got their first taste at what the furry fandom was about from a late-night magazine show called *EuroTrash*.

Word about *EuroTrash* first spread to the fandom in March 1999, when it was reported that a British furry was approached by producers to be part of a segment for the show. While they initially planned to produce the segment in the United Kingdom and Europe, they decided to go to Confurence 10 in California as they believed this venue would result in better content.[426]

Confurence staff member Darrell Exline confirmed that *EuroTrash* planned to cover the convention while following a German fursuiter around the hotel. Given the reporting from *Loaded* magazine and *EuroTrash*'s appeal to a similarly lad-based culture with sensationalist coverage of places and activities from around the world, red flags were flying. Despite the assurances of Confurence staff that the production team would be escorted by a press liaison some furry fans still suspected ulterior motives from *EuroTrash*.

The episode aired on October 1, 1999 and followed the German fursuiter, Skunki (Stephan Müller). Furries were likely on the edge of their seats as they were introduced as a fetish and shown pages of the *Loaded* magazine as well as erotic furry art and sexually explicit furry filk songs. Much of the segment did as promised and followed Skunki as he interacted with other furries at the convention, danced in the nightclub, and played golf while bouncy and wacky music played in the background.[384] Apart from narrator's constant use of sexual inuendo, most of the talking (in German) came from Skunki, although he did speak English in one rather amusing moment in which he revealed that he does not like performing around kids.

> Skunki: "Children especially like to pull [my tail] down and let it bounce up again."

> Other Furry: "Yes, I see how that can be a problem. How do you fix that?"

> Skunki: "Stay away from children."

Apart from Skunki, Mark Merlino was also interviewed about the practice of pretending to be an animal and Munich-based furry artist Dirk Schmidt spoke briefly about furry art.

Reactions from furries at the time were mixed. In general, it was considered to be another misrepresentation of the furry fandom, but many also saw it as mildly amusing and harmless. One of the issues they had with the show was how it referred to furries and fursuiters inter-changeably as if they were the same thing when the latter is merely an activity for the former.

Pressed Fur described it at the time as "wince-inducing" and a story of "moderate ridicule, but with less restraint and much less dignity" than other media coverage Some defended the show as being tongue-in-cheek, as was the general motif of *EuroTrash*. As SlyCat once described it on his website, "Some furs were offended by this show, but I say, if you can't laugh at yourself, you can't laugh at others."[427]

In hindsight, some were more relieved that the *EuroTrash* story was as fun and silly as it was compared to what it could have been.

BBC AND CHANNEL 4 COVERAGE

The Burned Furs were still a new and growing group in 1999 whena British TV producer contacted one of the few, if not only, British members of this fringe group, a Scottish furry writer known as Fionacat.

Although the BBC producer Vincent Beasley alleged he was working on a fair and balanced TV special and arranged an interview with Fionacat and furries on the Burned Furs IRC channel, it was quickly discovered he was an executive producer for the show *Ruby's American Pie*, a travel comedy program hosted by Ruby Wax. Heated drama surrounding the interview on IRC led to the interview and the TV special being cancelled, and while there was speculation that Beasely was making further attempts to interview furries,[428] the special never came to fruition.

Meanwhile, the independent Channel 4 featured the furry fandom in its late-night programming, although not all of it was in good-natured fun. Channel 4 had a reputation for covering niche, underground, and alternative subcultures compared to their main competitors, the BBC and ITV. An example of this was *4Later*, a late-night block of offbeat programming that, unlike *EuroTrash*, was dark and edgy in tone.

Frontal

Frontal was one such show on the 4Later schedule. It was an interactive live show that presented music videos banned from TV screenings, reviews of legal drugs and S&M equipment, and interviews with unconventional guests like the Lesbian Avengers, an activist group that

American-British actress, comedian, and TV host Ruby Wax (photo by J. J. Noordman).

used humor to try to get more media coverage of lesbian issues.

On 1 September 2000, the show covered furries. On the right of the table was Chik'ki, a lifestyler furry sporting an orange striped tail and a black T-shirt with a giant tiger print on the front. On the left were the two hosts of *Frontal*: Lisa Rogers and Natasha Bell, who gave this introduction: "Now I've known a few men who turn into right wildebeests when the disco stops, but furries are people who generally believe they're animals trapped in a human body."[429]

Chik'ki believed himself to be a tiger after an experience in the Sumatran Jungle four years prior. His life improved upon discovering the furry community and coming out as one, and two months prior to the interview he had married a woman named Louvé, who identified as a wolf. He said that he occasionally found recognition and bonds with tigers and other wild cats in captivity at zoos.

Days prior, he wrote on alt.lifestyle.furry that he was invited to talk on *Frontal*. While there was opposition and fears that he was "going to commit another *Loaded*" after the "Heavy Petting" article that was published two years prior, he defended his decision based on the transparency from the show's producers and how the topics were pre-arranged and approved between all parties.[430] Therefore, Chik'ka sat in his comfort zone and had no qualms discussing his personal beliefs.

Even as Lisa Rogers doubled down on defining furries as people who think they are animals in a previous life, Chik'ki corrected her without hesitation: "[Furry] also applies to people who just dress up as animals or enjoy animal artwork.... There are quite a few out there—I mean furries in total."

After the interview, Chik'ki stayed around to answer phone calls from viewers, and *Frontal* also showed the alt.lifestyle.furry newsgroup while Natasha Bell advised viewers to learn more by going to furries. com. While the representation was heavily focused on furry as a lifestyle and therian belief, it was a rather friendly broadcast given the kind of show it was.

The Other Side

Another 4Later show that made an impact was *The Other Side*, a documentary series in which each episode was directed by a relative newcomer and focused on niche communities and events. One of those newcomers was Emma Piquemal, who felt that the London furry community would make an appealing subject. After asking around, she was redirected to the LondonFurs Mailing List. Marcony recalled how most furries in the mailing list were weary of the media covering the London-Furs thanks to the earlier *EuroTrash* episode.

> There was quite a body in favour of the scene telling her as one to bugger off, but it was realised that if we didn't do it somebody else would and the kind of somebody that keen to be on the telly was normally the kind of person you don't want to represent your scene on the telly. As such, we let the director know that we would be happy to talk as long as the documentary focused around something other than porn and yiffing.[99]

Piquemal subsequently attended a LondonFurs meet to talk with some of the furries directly. This put many people at ease and facilitated the documentary's go-ahead. Recording was scheduled for a future fur-meet (ultimately taking place sometime in July[431]), as well as at various locations in London and the homes of furry fans.

The episode itself would air incredibly early on the morning of 27 October 2000, with several British furries hanging around on the UK IRC channel set to watch and discuss it live.

The documentary was titled "Human Furry Animals," and while several British furries were featured in the documentary such as Vexen Crabtree, Ia'kat, UltraFox, Fated Fox, and Lev Lion, three were given arguably the most screen time: Ruin, Marcony, and Lone Wolf.

Through the testimony of the furries themselves, the documentary defines them as "people who hold a stronger-than-average attachment to the more bestial side of all men, or the nature of animals," and explored how individuals would discover the fandom, express themselves, and interact with each other both offline and online. One of the

Saucy Jacks, a regular post-meet locale at the time, was another location used. The segment ultimately had to be cut due to a power cut that hindered filming during the evenings.

prominent features here is a video of a LondonFurs meet at the Devonshire Arms with several furries wearing tails or covered in body paint.

Thanks to the inclusion of self-identified therian Lone Wolf, the documentary also covered "Weres" (Therians), who are distinguished from furries as those who sincerely believe they are part animal . He was humorously introduced going up the stairs on all fours, something he was made to do for the sake of "good entertainment" even though it was an act furries don't normally do in real life. He recalled:

> And yes, I was running upstairs on all fours. Despite
> bitterly protesting about having to embarrass myself
> in front of a hundred thousand viewers like that to
> [Emma], she still insisted so much that I go ahead with
> it (to use as background to the speech) that in the end
> I had to give in to her.[432]

One of the more eye-opening parts of this documentary was when three featured furries all talk about what they tell their families about the fandom. A side effect of misrepresenting the sexual aspects of the furry fandom—as well as its open acceptance to the LGBT community—is that until recently it was common for furries to avoid or heavily downplay their involvement in the fandom.

Marcony and Lone Wolf talked about how they have told both of their parents about their interests in animals, but neither went into detail on either the sexual aspects or lycanthropy, although one of Marcony's old school friends acknowledged that the fandom had helped his friend become more outgoing and confident.

Ruin, on the other hand, related a sourer experience at her school when other classmates began spreading false rumours to teachers about her and her furry friends. She even got teachers and her own parents involved. Fortunately, Ruin said nothing came from whatever the teachers were told, and her mum was particularly supportive of her and the furry fandom. When Ruin's mum was asked, all she said was, "I don't like anything being really obsessive, but I don't think [Ruin's] obsessive. She's got her head on her shoulders."

Being broadcasted so late at the night (or so early in the morning) probably meant viewership of *The Other Side* was not as high when compared to some of the magazine articles that had been published about the fandom, but the effort put into letting the furries speak for themselves was surely appreciated. Piquemal later moved up in the television industry to become senior producer for ITV and the BBC for shows like *Strictly Come Dancing.*

MORE LATE-NIGHT DOCUMENTARIES

More late-night documentaries followed, although their quality compared to Channel 4's efforts are subject to debate. Anna Nolan, a television presenter whose claim to fame was the reality show *Big Brother*, worked for the BBC on a documentary series called *Anna in Wonderland* in 2002 for BBC Choice.[433] On the 30 August episode, Nolan wanted to learn what furries were, so shewent to Sacramento to meet a married couple named Ursus and Wabbit, a group of furries at a camp out, and Stalking Cat, a furry who became famous for having numerous cosmetic operations to make him look like a tiger.

The documentary had a particular focus on how welcoming and accepting the fandom is. Many of the participants mentioned how they were ostracised until they found friendship within the community.

For instance, Wabbit talked about how people in the fandom accept her as beautiful despite her weight because of her rabbit fursona. Nolan did try her hardest to get a full experience, even wearing a raccoon fursuit around a supermarket and during a fursuit walk in a cave. Unfortunately, based on the uncomfortable facial expressions captured by the camera, it looks like Nolan is not having the best time.

When she visited Stalking Cat, she found his multiple surgeries disturbing, comparing him to "a transexual, but instead of wanting to change into a woman, he wants to change his species."

She also had to be incredibly patient with the furries she was with because of their bad behaviour. One of them invaded her personal space by licking her face, others forced her into a fur pile, and another forced her to wear a collar and leash. It also didn't help that Ursus, who early in the documentary described yiff as a sexual term, proudly wore a collar tag reading "Yiff Beast." And he wanted to take the presenter to his furry den, where he and Wabbit had framed commissioned furry erotica on their living room wall.

Nolan's conclusion was summed up in the narration: "I was glad these lonely people have found love and acceptance through being furry, but being part of Ursus and Wabbit's sex commune was not my idea of animal rights."

Along with frequent comments on how she couldn't understand how men and women in their thirties were enjoying puppet shows, plush toys, and animal costumes, Nolan clearly didn't leave with a positive impression. However, it was apparent that Nolan tried to get along with this specific furry group, with Pressed Fur postulating that Anna Nolan was a lesbian and therefore part of a "sexual-interest minority", so it was produced with the best of intentions, which is better than what many other documentaries have done.

PLUSHIES AND FURRIES & MTV

Beginning in 1999, a filmmaker using the alias Pyewacket travelled around conventions like Confurence and Midwest Furfest to speak with furries. They became well known in American furry circles as a nice and polite person working on an independent film project.[434] But no one was sure whether this was to be a student film about furries or a TV special involving upcoming artists.

The truth came to light when the film *Plushies and Furries* premiered at the LGBTQ film festival OutFest in October 2001. Pyewacket was a Hollywood adult filmmaker and photographer named Rick Castro, who described his work as exploring "the various pleasures derived from bondage, S&M, kink, porn and street hustling."[435] *Plushies and Furries* was subsequently picked up by the channel MTV, where it aired as part of its *Sex2K* series (later re-airings would be under the name *True Life*).[436]

The documentary opens with the statement "wearing a fursuit can be sexually arousing" and goes downhill from there. Footage of fursuiters in provocative positions and exposed genitalia featured them confidently declaring that "anyone that says furry is not a sexual based fandom is really kinda fooling themselves."

Defining fursuiters as "people who get turned on by dressing as big stuffed animals" and featuring an overabundance of references to fursuit sex led to the documentary having a very negative reception. The infamous *Vanity Fair* article had come out not long before this, and this unfavourable and inaccurate representation of the fandom only served to increase the ire among furries.

What most furries don't know about the MTV documentary is that it was edited from the original film festival release. An unrated version aired only once in the United Kingdom on Channel 5 on 15 July 2003.

The documentary soundtrack no longer had the luxury of MTV's large library of music licenses, and footage showing genitalia had to be blurred out due to British broadcasting regulations, so while it's unrated it wasn't uncensored.

The late Robert Hill, one of the first fursuiters in the fandom

The most glaring change was the overall storyline, which followed a young furry named Yote (Mike Sano) as he receives his first fursuit, attends his first furry convention, and shares his furry interests with his mother. This ultimately helps their relationship despite her struggles to take the furry aspect of her son's life seriously.

Although Yote appears in the Channel 5 version, his role was reduced and scenes involving his storyline were absent such as those involving his mother and his first fursuit. The most likely reason for this change was to avoid the controversy that resulted from the original MTV broadcast.

Pressed Fur anonymously received emails from Yote, who alleged that the entire storyline was fake. According to these emails, for example, his mother already knew about the furry fandom for years and the convention he attended had been his second. Yote also wrote that Castro strong armed him into doing the story using peer pressure.[437] Although there's no evidence that Rick Castro responded to these allegations.

What the unrated version has in place of these narratives is an extended interview with the late Robert Hill, who was one of the pioneers of fursuiting, in which he presents his fursuits and illustrations and relates a story of a one-night stand he had with an erotic dancer whilst wearing one of his bear fursuits. For those interested in the early days of the furry fandom, seeing Robert Hill with his enthusiasm and charisma is quite compelling, even if the story of his one-night stand was uncomfortable to listen to. The editors also used interview footage of Yote giving overwhelming praise to Hill's artwork so as to connect the two storylines.

Another segment that was absent from the MTV cut but present in the unrated version takes place in an art gallery exhibiting fursuit photography, erotic furry art, and phallic animal sculptures. Castro himself gives a brief cameo during this segment in which he uses personal recordings from a fursuit masquerade from Confurence in 1997.

Despite his allegedly dishonest approach to filmmaking and research, Castro would use the success of his documentary to further his photography career, write articles about the fandom, and host his own furry art exhibition called "Furotica." British furries did at least have take comfort in the fact that this version had a limited airing in the United States and that British production studios were more willing to present furries with a more open mind.

See Hear

This was the case with *See Hear*, a monthly magazine programme from the BBC targeted towards people who are deaf or hard of hearing, which discussed furries in an 18 December 2004 episode.

Presenter Julian Peedle-Calloo and sign language interpreter Robert Skinner travelled to Washington, D.C., to meet Boogi (Robert Goodwin), a fursuit performer and builder who is also legally deaf.[438]

Julian and Robert got a tour of Boogi's home, where fursuits (most of them works in progress), animal masks, sheets of different fur, and equipment to build fursuits could be seen everywhere. Because of the challenges in interpreting some furry vocabulary into sign language, the report substituted some furry lingo into more general language. For example, fursuits are called costumes and furry conventions are "costume conventions."

Overall, the tone of this program was lighthearted. Everyone appeared to be having a good time talking about fursuits and having a good laugh at Julian putting on a full body wolf fursuit for the camera as he played around and tried to howl like one. Julian's only issue with the fursuit was humidity's effect on wearing it. In sign-language he remarked, "This is good because it's helping me to lose weight from all the sweating! It's hot!" The presenters had also planned to walk around the nearby town in costumes, but they had to cancel due to poor weather.

The show also went into how wearing fursuits has helped Boogi, as a deaf person, become more social because of how people change their behaviour when they wear one. Boogi commented:

> When you wear a costume like that, including the head, I've seen shy people become really outgoing, or a really outgoing person become a shy person. With one costume I have, I become a shy person.
>
> I wasn't really doing much.... I wanted to be out of the house, I wanted to work on my social skills, that kind of thing, and doing this has helped me.
>
> Because I'm deaf, sometimes I tend to be with other deaf people, but doing this helps me work with other hearing people.

There was also a brief discussion about goes on at the conventions in which Boogi describes how some people will wear costumes while others who don't still create and sell artwork, socialise, and make friends. The question is raised about whether people have made romantic relationships at conventions to which Boogi simply answers, "It happens."

This nice and informative look at fursuiters would ultimately be the last produced by British television for years. While scores of sensationalist articles continued to be published and there was a documentary proposed for the UKFurForums in 2008[439] covering furries in youth culture that never came to fruition, the furry fandom wouldn't appear on British television screens for the rest of the decade.

British furs were, of course, aware of some of television episodes featuring furries being produced in the United States such as episodes of the crime drama *CSI: Crime Scene Investigation* and the hospital drama *ER*. They also followed the news coverage shared by their American counterparts and were equally on high alert for any producers who wanted to cover the furry fandom.

THE 2010s

But with the arrival of the 2010s, broadcasters once again wanted furries on their shows. In February 2011, a thread was made on the UKFur Forums about an email sent around from a producer at ITV inviting furries to discuss the fandom. A paraphrased description of the email claimed that the production team was interested in the art and fursuiting and had with no intention of discussing the adult side.[440] Most of the furries in both the original thread and others suspected the claim to be unreliable, however.

OMG! on ITV!

There was an expectation that the show would be used to once again trash the furry fandom, especially when it was identified what type of show ITV was planning to produce: a talk show called *OMG! with Peaches Geldof* that focused on people and their shocking stories and habits. It was hosted by Peaches Geldof, a former model, TV personality, and daughter of Boomtown Rats lead singer Bob Geldof.

Outside of the email correspondence, ITV encouraged the public to send in their most shocking personal stories through its website for a chance to appear on the show.

> Each week, Peaches Geldof and her team of professional experts will aim to help find a resolution to your

problems no matter how big or small. From gamblers to gold-diggers, bad boys to break ups—this is your chance to tell your story and seek advice.

If you have an embarrassing story, confession, compulsion, obsession, or problem that you want to share and get help with, please email problem@itv.com for an application form.

The deadline for applications is 11:59 PM on January 31st, 2011.[441]

Heated discussions would be had on the UKFurForums. Furries had not been on a late-night talk show since *Frontal* back in 2000, and yet this one was bound to get more coverage given that it was hosted during prime time by a former model and TV personality.

Just two years earlier, American furries had similarly received emails from an associate producer asking them to appear on a talk show hosted by a former model and TV personality: Tyra Banks.[442] In the episode of *The Tyra Banks Show* titled "Is Your Sex Life Normal?" Chew Fox and her partner are featured sitting on a bed while dressed in nightgowns. One of the questions asked is whether they had sex in their furry costumes, and when Chew Fox confidently answers "Yes" in front of Tyra Banks and a studio audience on television,[443] furries watching at home completely lost it.

Chew Fox received countless threats on FurAffinity and was temporarily banned for arguing back and causing the website to crash.[444] They continue to receive animosity to this day.

Many British furries who recalled the American show feared that history would repeat itself, and yet there were some who were still willing to take on the offer after Birmingham furs Aigus and Xywolf made an offer on the forums to appear on the show with a trusted group of friends. On 9 March 2011, the second episode of Peaches Geldof's show aired on ITV2 along with radio presenter Aled Haydn Jones and psychologist

Peaches Geldof (photo: Dell, Inc.)

Emma Kenny as her regular panellists, alongside special guest panellists Dom Joly from the sketch show *Trigger Happy TV*, and stand-up comedian Eric Lampaert.

The furries were the feature of the second half of *OMG!*,[445] and while Aigus himself did not appear, his group of friends from both the Birmingham and Yorkshire, led by Xywolf, did. Other furries from the group were Meeple, Aetherfax, Jasper Wallace, Jingles (calling himself Chonkster on the show), and Nightwind, who showed up at the studio wearing a full grey, white, and cyan full-bodied wolf fursuit.

On the positive side, the show was rather relaxed with its talk show layout. Geldof and Kenny shared one sofa with Nightwind while the other furries sat on another. Geldof was quickly seen enjoying her situation, remarking that she wanted to cuddle up to the fursuiter, and she admitted that if she had a fursona it would be a squirrel.

Emma Kenny also remark that she felt she had been converted to the fandom because she liked seeing furries running around in costumes and entertaining kids. Kenny said, "It's fantastic to see a group of people who are all just really nice and kind. I can imagine after a really, really, hardcore night out coming home and finding someone like [Nightwind] in your house to just go …" and then she cuddled up with Nightwind.

The audience was shown smiling with amusement, with one of the audience members eagerly volunteering to be hugged by Nightwind and later saying it felt like "being hugged by a teddy bear."

Through most of the nine-minute segment, everyone appears to like seeing the furries—that is, with one exception. Dom Joly, who through most of the show is seen drinking from a wine glass, spends most of the segment rudely shouting over other people to try and convince everyone that the furry fandom was a sexual thing. He contradicts whatever the furries say and claims to know more than them. A transcript reads:

> Dom: Like, in America, you'd have trouble because you're not called furries, you're called plushies.
>
> Meeple: No, it's furries in—
>
> Dom: No, no, no! Trust me, as Trigger Happy, it's plushies and there's a whole scene where people like to have a little bit of sexual activity with you guys.
>
> Peaches: But that's different, that's the preconception that it's a sexualised thing and it's not.
>
> Dom: It is, in America! Trust me, it is, and I was a cult figure for a year.

Jasper: To be fair, everything is about sex in
America.

Joly's behaviour continues until he is shouted down by Lampaert
after several interruptions. In the end, though, none of the other hosts
took his statements seriously. Geldof herself wasn't happy with Joly's
behaviour, describing him as "a handful. He was difficult. I feel like he
was quite an embittered man"[446] in a *BBC Newsbeat* article published less
than a week before the episode aired. "I just feel like Dom Joly is, I don't
know. Like, if you're whole life revolves around stuff like I'm a Celebrity,
then it's a bit depressing."

Furries who caught the *OMG!* episode felt it wasn't bad, largely
because the furries who appeared tried to focus the attention on how the
fandom is about fun and creativity. They found Joly's attitude unsurpris-
ing, given that the expectation was for a deliberately shocking program.

There was also much more fun banter between Geldof and Kenny
than one usually witnessed from other talk show presenters. Lines like
Geldof admitting she's "really
into Nightwind" got laughs for
being an in-joke in some circles.

The most mainstream re-
sponse to *OMG!* came two weeks
later with the comedy TV-pro-
gramme *Harry Hill's TV Burp.*[447]
In it, Harry Hill uses furries to
either make fun of Geldof's lack
of big-name guests or to ridicule
Dom Joly and his "celebrity sta-
tus."

Dom: I know what
you're saying, be-
cause I was on [*I'm a
Celebrity, Get Me Out
of Here*].... It's about
as low as you can go,
isn't it?

Dom Joly (photo: Paul Bednall)

Harry: Well, appear-
ing on *OMG* with a big furry wolf comes a close
second!

RUSSELL HOWARD'S *GOOD NEWS*

Another comedian took a harder swing at the furries a few years later. Russell Howard's *Good News*, a comedy news show that aired on BBC Three between 2009 and 2015, had two encounters with the furry fandom. The first one was part of a clip show in the series seven finale on 13 December 2012, the series Christmas episode. In a segment in which two people debate why they should be in the news, one of the guests was Apes Lion dressed in a full lion fursuit with red hair.[448] Apes was mostly ignored during the program.

The other guest, Tim Cranmore, was a man who made instruments out of vegetables. When Tim demonstrated a carrot that he made to play like a recorder, Howard was dumbfounded. Apes was pretty much left in the background during the routine, ignored until the very end of the episode, when she got caught in a suggestive joke made by Russell.

Russell Howard

Tim: Because that's what a carrot is for. What else would you do with it?

Russell: There's many things you could do with that carrot.

Apes Laughs

Russell: Dirty b****.

Howard would not mention the furry fandom again until 16 May 2013, when he did a segment based on the BBC news report on the furry fandom in the Mexican city of Monterrey from the year prior. Howard's commentary on the story conflicts with the report, however. Whereas the reporter describes furries as people who create and design animal costumes based on cartoon characters to dress up and have fun, Howard ridicules them as people who think they are animals in human bodies: "What a bunch of dicks! 'Oh, look at me, I'm an otter!' Just be comfy in your own skin! You don't see gibbons [going] 'Oh I'd like to be an estate agent'"[449]

To be sure, making fun of nerd and niche cultures is one of the things Howard was known for on *Good News*. In the same episode, he compared *Star Wars* fans in America to an overweight YouTuber raging with a lisp.

Like the news report itself, Howard never indulges in stereotypes about furries such as their supposed sexual obsessions. But he does knock himself down a peg by cutting to a crude and tasteless scene in which he is dressed like a sheep being raped by a farmer, pretending to be traumatised while his audience laughs at his expense.

The overall reaction from British furries was more mixed, with commenters on the UKFurForums either finding it funny, insulting, or not worth their attention.[450] A few suspected that the only reason Howard decided to make jokes about furries at all was to set up the gag about him being dressed up as a sheep.

Comedians poking fun at furries appear in surprising places. On the 2014 New Year's Eve episode of the *Graham Norton Show*, the talk show host asked his celebrity guests about cartoon "sexual awakenings" in a response to English actor Eddie Redmayne admitting in an interview that his first crush was the lioness Nala in Disney's *Lion King*.[451]

Amusingly, Redmayne also confessed to liking the vixen Maid Marian from Disney's *Robin Hood*, and enthusiastically agreed with Bradley Wiggen's answer that Cheetara from *Thundercats* was hot. This might suggest that the actor of *Fantastic Beasts* might have more in common with the furry fandom than he realises. Graham Norton sardonically said Redmayne's crushes were "Wrong. That's so wrong," but actress Anna Kendrick went to Redmayne's defence, saying the Disney characters were drawn really sexy and admitting that she had a crush on Robin Hood (the fox character) herself.

MILITARY FURS AND *WORLD OF WEIRD*

Fortunately for the furry fandom, it is particularly good at embracing that fact. In 2016, the San Diego chapter of furries were featured in a short-lived Channel 4 documentary series called *World of Weird*, which covered various strange interests, businesses, traditions, and the like from around the world with a somewhat adult theme.

The show was not shy about covering fandoms, having covered a *My Little Pony* fandom known as Bronies in the pilot episode. Host Billie J. D. Porter met up not only with the local fursuit making business Mischief Makers but also with several furries who were both current and former U.S. military.[452]

Furries in the military were not an unheard-of subject to the British media. For example, the *Metro* newspaper did a story on Mark the Husky, an E-4 US Army soldier and Furry YouTuber. While the *Metro* article focused more on Mark's personal and social life, including how he became more extroverted as he easily found fandom social groups wherever he moved, very little was mentioned about his experience as a furry in the military aside from "his squad mates and comrades in Korea either didn't care about his obsession or thought he was 'weird.'"[453]

In comparison, *World of Weird* went into a bit more depth, with former U.S. Marine Chance the Dragon (Alex) stating: "Specifically, with the Marines, [the furry fandom] would not be well received. This is a wonderful escape from that. It's very freeing, very liberating to pretend to be someone or something else entirely."

The idea that the furry fandom would be therapeutic to those with similar backgrounds to Chance's was a common theme on the show. Porter suggested during her interview with Chance that furrydom can be cathartic, describing how dressing up and performing in fursuits allows people to feel more relaxed and more themselves compared to the strict routine and behaviour of military life or even "normal" society.

Porter also got an opportunity to wear a fursuit, the first time a reporter had done so for a British show since the *See Hear* report in 2004. Specifically, she donned a yellow wolf fullsuit owned by San Diego furry Keitelwuff. Porter almost instantly fell in love with wearing the fursuit and performing at the local furmeet, although she would complain about how hot and humid it was.

Ultimately, she found her time with the furries enjoyable, and while she said she would not wear fursuits as frequently as furries usually-would, she understood why they enjoyed performing and being part of the fandom.

The *World of Weird* might be considered the perfect kind of documentary programme for the furry fandom. It was a show that took strange things from around the world and sought to understand and embrace them for the good they could bring.

Although this does not mean there were not issues with it at all. There remained the one issue that still carries over from those early coverages of the fandom: the hyper fixation on fursuits. The media fuels the popular misconception about the fandom (other than its being a fetish) that you have to have a fursuit to be a furry.

FURSUIT OBSESSION

The *World of Weird* show was not the first time that the British media has focused in on the fursuits. Another example was when *This Morning* on ITV did a small talk on the fandom in 2017. Eamonn Holmes and Ruth Langsford spoke with Ani Boxer, Ed (the Poodle), and Dexy from the LondonFurs. All three guests were in full fursuits as they talked about their characters and expressing themselves. As they did so, a subtitle bar displayed the words "WE'RE GROWN ADULTS BUT WE LIKE TO DRESS UP AS ADULTS" and "WE'RE FANS OF FUR … BUT IT'S NOT A FETISH."[454] During the show, comments from online audiences were read aloud by Holmes and indicated that people might have thought the fursuits were weird but accepted them as harmless.

To be fair, Ed does attempt to explain that fursuits are not the only thing the fandom is about:

> The costumes are one part of it, but a huge part of it is celebrating art and the creativity. So, when we meet up, people can be drawing pictures, we have charity events we do. I like to go out and entertain the public, but I have also gone to different parties to entertain people, and it's really what you want to make of it is why it's special.

Nonetheless, fursuits are what grab an audience's attention, and the media know this. Even if the media show fursuits without mentioning them, their audience could recognize them immediately as was the case with the gameshow *The Crystal Maze*. On the fourth episode of the 2017 series hosted by Richard Ayoade, PuzzleCheetah, Ed Hamster, Murdock, Icewolf and his brother teamed up to take on the maze and its many physical challenges. After introducing each team member one by one, with all but one shown in their fursuits, furries watched at home got a laugh when their team's name was revealed to be "The Cosplayers."[455]

According to Ed Hamster, the production company set the name to Cosplayers, despite asking for it to be changed to "Team Furry". The name didn't fool anyone, as many took to social media to talk about the furries on the show.[456]

This attitude of focusing on fursuits and costume by the media continued with more local reports such as BBC's "We Are Bradford" project, a series of interviews with various people in the city of Bradford. During one segment, Cosmo (Sophie Robson) and Rook (Ron) were seen entertaining the public in a shopping centre and then working on fursuits in their bedroom while talking about how fursuits make them happy.[457]

As positive and embracing as these fursuit featurettes are, the rest of the furry fandom still hoped for more than a passing mention of the drawings, writings, music, and videos that come out of the fandom.

Another local report that went into the benefits of the fandom and fursuits took place farther south in Bristol. After a radio presenter happened to catch a fursuit walk organised by the BristolFurs, Sandy Brushtail (Frank Baldwin) talked to them and explained who they are. The interaction garnered enough interest in Sandy to be get them featured in a video interview for BBC Radio Bristol.[458] Here he relates a personal story about struggling with drugs. The fandom helped him overcome those issues, and he also received positive support from his family, despite his strict Christian upbringing.

Another interesting part about the Bristol report is that it included footage from both a BristolFurs' meet *and* from the furry convention Just Fur the Weekend. Unlike in the United States, the British media does not cover UK furry events very much, likely because of the long-presumed "no media" policies from con organisers.

Rare and intermittent reports on furmeets and fursuit walks occurred, though, such as the *BBC Sounds* show "The Why Factor" that partially covered a Cambridge furmeet, and the *Birmingham Mail* photographing the city's local furmeet. Nevertheless, not since *Bizarre* in 2008 had anyone from the media covered a British furry convention—at least not until BBC Radio One got involved.

Back in April 2018, a newly created account made a post in the "Newbie" thread of the UKFur Forums claiming to be a producer for the BBC working on an upcoming programme about the British furry fandom. It was to be a short documentary as a part of the BBC Radio One Stories series that features young people across the United Kingdom. The post included a link to an episode on teenagers in the Witchcraft community called "Britain's Young Witches" as an example.

The producer (who went by the pseudonym "jelly-lemon," which was possibly inspired by the British electronic duo Lemon Jelly) made their intentions clear that the documentary would focus on the positive impact that the furry fandom has on people, especially on the younger generation:

> We're looking for people who have recently joined the community to hear about the positive impact from becoming a furry. We're also keen to hear from those who are interested in the community but haven't attended a meet yet....
>
> The programme will be a very positive one—we want to teach the public about the furry community so

that there is greater tolerance and understanding, and address misconceptions....

I've spoken to lots of furries over the past couple of months to ensure the programme is a fair and accurate reflection of the community. But we're just looking to get a few more involved."[459]

An almost exact copy of this message would be posted a month later in the General UK Furry Discussion thread. After that, production proceeded quietly with virtually no open discussions of what went on behind the scenes all the way up to the *Meet the Furries* premiere on 20 July. What is known was that BBC Radio One approached Takk (Luisa Rose), an Exeter furry who joined the fandom around October 2017, to be the focus of the documentary.[460] Another furry, going by the name of AtlasTravelFox, wrote on Twitter that he was approached to help with the documentary and recommended the filmmakers go to ConFuzzled to get some insights.

The documentary talks about Takk and her preparations before going to her first furry convention in the United Kingdom. She had been introduced to the fandom by an American furry named Victoria with whom she had spent time at Anthrocon. Her fursuit of a blue African wild dog fursona was commissioned from Kloofsuits, and she quickly gained a following on Twitter and Instagram wearing it.

While Takk does have supportive friends and family when it comes to her being a furry, not everyone in her personal life knew. This leadis to a scene in which Takk introduces her fursuit to Ellie, one of her close friends. Ellie is understandably surprised and in some disbelief over the discovery and admits that her previous impressions of the fandom had been negative.

Takk acknowledges this, citing the media as responsible for giving furries a dark and sexualised image. She instead describes fursuiting to be more like being a mascot at Disneyland and the fandom as more about making friends. Ultimately, Ellie seems to like the idea, even suggesting she might get a fursuit herself for the fun of walking around the supermarket and shopping centres. Ellie also comes to believe that it is good that Takk has found a community in which she has fun and make friends.

Even so, Takk was still nervous about going to ConFuzzled on her own, being a shy person and not enjoying social situations. However, she believed her confidence from wearing her fursuit would help with anxiety, and she presented a voice message from another attendee, Skunk Mantra (Martin Roberts), wishing her a good time.

At this point, the rest of the documentary takes place at ConFuzzled. To follow the convention's media policy, the BBC had to work within certain requirements, which included coverage being limited in time and scope, footage obtained at the convention being used in one continuous segment, and no footage or photographs of the art show, art auction, or dealers' den.[461] As such, the only footage from the convention itself were of Takk's hotel room at the Birmingham Hilton Metropole, various corridors, the main stage (of a furry dance), and outside the hotel grounds.

Although there were many British furries present in the documentary through footage sourced from YouTube and Instagram, only a few were interviewed. At least one comment suggests the ConFuzzled administration did block select furries from talking with the BBC. Azy (Chris), Candyfloss (Tina), Kasumi (Emily), Sasha, and Gari (Mike) all gave testimonies about the furry fandom, while TacoTeko, Fatality Husky, and Skunk Mantra appeared in supplemental footage.

The end product is arguably the best example of portraying the furry communit in popular media, and it garnered many positive comments on both the shortened YouTube version and the responses from furries on Twitter. Probably the most shining light of praise came from ConFuzzled's organizers, who recommended everyone watch *Meet the Furries* and praised Takk for her involvement:

> Everyone go watch this BBC film, featuring [Takk]
> on her journey into furry & ConFuzzled. She's a great
> ambassador for the community! The film is so positive
> and a great portrayal of our community![462]

EVOLVING MEDIA ATTITUDES

The furry fandom has had a long and difficult relationship with journalists, documentarians, and presenters who have painted the community with a broad, dirty brush. It started with one news report covering activities at a furry convention and snowballed into a general portrayal of furries morphing from fans to perverts.

Thus far, the fandom has persevered, and in the last decade there have been several outlets that have taken the effort to show the fandom from different perspectives, whether that be by describing furries through the voices of furries from around the world, having open discussions about what the fandom is about, or bringing forward the positives of being part of a friendly community and doing outdoor activities like fursuiting.

Shows and articles in the last decade like *World of Weird*, and *Meet the Furries* are, by their core premises, similar to *EuroTrash* and *Plushies and Furries*, and yet the contrasts in how they perceive the furry fandom and what they decide to focus on are like night and day.

EuroTrash showed strange, and sometimes very adult, things from around the world and depicted the furry fandom as a fetish that enjoyed erotic art, suggestive fursuiting activities, and not much else. In comparison, *World of Weird* showed similar furry images, and yet it decided to portray furries as a community of people who dress up for fun and to escape the stresses of normal life, focusing on how it benefits those from military backgrounds.

Furries might disagree with comparing something as wonderful as *Meet the Furries* to something as horrible as *Plushies and Furries*, yet both documentaries are at their core about introducing the furry fandom to a mainstream audience. Both follow the story of a relative newcomer to the fandom who introduces the fandom and fursuits to friends/family and then makes their way to their first convention by themselves.

What is clear is that *Plushies and Furries* was produced by an adult photographer and filmmaker who, for lack of a better way of describing it, dragged furries through the dirt to advance his own career. In contrast, BBC Radio 1 found a young adult furry who had been in the fandom for less than a year and shared their genuine firsthand experience of attending a local furry convention. The result was a documentary that fulfilled the series' intention of telling authentic stories of young people throughout the country.

Ultimately, we have furmeets, conventions, and regular members to thank. Their serious efforts and those of a few media outlets have finally resulted in the fandom being shown in a positive light.

That is not to say media representation the furry fandom is perfect. It's still overly focused on fursuits, neglecting the many other aspects of the fandom. And they still exploit the fandom for entertainment purposes—that is, they have a rather mocking slant such as in the scene in *Meet the Furries* in which Takk is shown doing gardening in fursuit while not that far off Lone Wolf was directed to go upstairs on all fours.

Today, most furries are still defensive about their fandom and are hesitant to work with the mainstream press. However, if the last decade has proven anything, it's that the furry fandom has gained acceptance by the media as something that is fun and not perverted.

Only time will tell if they can look beyond the fursuits.

WHEN THE PARADES STOPPED

This book was originally written to tell the history of the British furry fandom from its beginnings up until the end of 2019, with the time from 2020 onward being left open ended to allow the reader to wonder what will happen in the future. Time, however, did not want to wait for changes to happen.

In early 2020, conventions were still running throughout the world, and in the United Kingdom the furmeets were running through January and February like it was another regular year. Just Fur the Weekend (JFTW), ConFuzzled, Wild North, and Furcation were all preparing behind the scenes for hundreds of attendees who had eagerly paid in advance to have fun with their friends. There were also ongoing conventions in Japan (Japan Meeting of Furries), Hungary (Fursang), Sweden (NordicFuzzcon), Poland (Gdakon), and several in the United States.

But plans for any social gatherings were about to face a giant roadblock: an outbreak of a coronavirus in the Chinese province of Wuhan was spreading in the background. The virus was initially discovered in November 2019, which is why it is called COVID-19, but information on and cases of the virus were not internationally confirmed until January 2020. News spread throughout the United Kingdom and the world in February, and it was declared a pandemic on 11 March, 2020.

COVID-19 cases produced flu-like symptoms around two weeks after someone was infected. It was highly contagious, so social gatherings became a serious health risk and were discouraged by health experts.

Although a few conventions tried to assure attendees that their events would be safe and sanitary, as soon as March set in, conventions were being postponed or cancelled. Depending on the country, they either blamed COVID-19 and the health risk as a factor of their decision or a legal imposition put in place due to the virus such as a national lockdown or a ban on large events.[463]

Meanwhile, in the United Kingdom, furmeets were considering cancellation for health and safety reasons, too, particularly after March 16, when Prime Minister Boris Johnson advised the public against non-essential travel, as well as telling people to avoid pubs, clubs, and theatres.

Four days later, this was made stricter when the government announced the closures of public venues, including pubs and nightclubs.

Conventions, on the other hand, could not act so quickly. In their official statements, they argued that they could not do anything but act as if they would run on schedule. On March 5, the ConFuzzled directors Rizzorat, Crimson, and Russet issued a statement addressing the COVID-19 outbreak, which had spread to 79 countries, stating that while there was a genuine possibility that ConFuzzled 2020 would be cancelled, there was no immediate plan to do so at that time.

On March 15, the directors further explained that postponing or cancelling the convention was easier to say than to do. Along with contractual obligations with two hotels, they had to consider other financial expenses and stress on the events staff:

> While postponement to later in the year might seem like the easiest solution, we need to consider things like both venues having the space available or suppliers availability aligning with our new dates. Additionally, we would need to consider the stress this would put on our team of volunteers who would effectively be delivering two conventions within a six/seven month time window when taking into account next year's event....

> While we are of course insured for ConFuzzled, there are specific sets of criteria that must be satisfied in each given situation to invoke this process. Currently, owing to the HM Government's position to not ban mass gatherings as an example, we cannot take the business decision to cancel the convention without there being heavy financial penalties that would jeopardize the future of the event."[464]

Even when the government announced that public venues would be closed it was not enough to cancel or postpone ConFuzzled because the closure did not include hotels or event spaces. JFTW also faced this issue, only it was under more pressure because the con was scheduled for April 10 to 12. They gave similar excuses to those of the ConFuzzled directors, including finances, lack of a proper event ban, and lack of transparency over venue closures.

It was not until 23 March, 2020, that Prime Minister Boris Johnson would announce lockdown measures, including a stay-at-home order and public venue closures that included hotels. ConFuzzled announced its cancellation a day later.[465] JFTW confirmed on March 30 that it would postpone its con until 2021.[466]

Around this time, the total number of COVID-19 cases in the United Kingdom was around 5,000. Wild North, scheduled for late September, confidently announce on March 20 that its event would run as planned, stating "We see no reason to cancel the con as it is still six months away, and a lot can happen in that time."

Yet, the outbreak got worse as the number of cases and fatalities kept increasing. By the end of June 2020, when the total U.K. case numbers soared to over 300,000, the November event Furcation was cancelled.[467] Less than two weeks later, Wild North officially announced that it would postpone to 2021.[468]

So it was that the Covid-19 pandemic halted almost all planned furry events entirely.

But there were at least two known exceptions to this during the summer when the first British lockdown ended and pubs and restaurants briefly reopened.

Stafford Furmeets returned once on July 11, but there were significant restrictions in place due to government regulations and rules set by the Bird in Hand pub. The pub required people to book in advance, remain at specific tables only shared with others from the same household, take food and drink by the wait staff only, wear masks, and no fursuiting was permitted. The group had attempted to run other meets, but concerns around sharing the venue with other guests and future possible lockdowns led to physical meets being cancelled for the foreseeable future.

The other exception was Andover Furs, who ran a furmeet once on August 8 at the White Hart pub. As with the Stafford Furs, the meet and the pub also required face masks when not at a table and social distancing when seated. However, attendees could order one at a time at the bar, and fursuiting was permitted in a function room that was restricted to 30 people maximum.

They would plan a future furmeet in September, but it was subsequently cancelled when the government enforced a tiered lockdown system that forbade gatherings larger than six people at any public venue.

Also, unlike Stafford Furs, this furmeet got negative attention from the larger furry community online after a photo was posted on social media from the furmeet that showed several maskless people. This occurred around the same time as meets in Poland and Florida, which resulted in all three being tarred with the same brush by one furry's tweet:

> Orlando runs a furmeet: dumb idea. Andover furs
> UK, run a furmeet: dumb idea. Poland run a furmeet:

dumb idea. Furmeets should not be during a pandemic! It only takes one carrier! And you value socialising over of risk of catching or passing to fam or immune compromised![469]

Although the Andover Furmeet had only ten attendees and adhered to the guidelines of both the bar and the country, many furries argued that even hosting smaller British furmeets was irresponsible because of the risk of contracting and spreading COVID-19 to other attendees and. by extension. their friends and families. Others still defended the meet at the time, as it occurred while the United Kingdom had more relaxed restrictions. National and local transmission data from the time indicated "an acceptable risk," and no one had symptoms before or after the furmeet.

For reference: A furmeet ran in Orlando, Florida, in June. Its organizer was later admonished for being an anti-masker who opposed local social distancing measures. Meanwhile, the Warsaw Fursuit Walk took place on September 12 and had around 300 people in attendance.

The resulting backlash and comparison to the Andover Meets led to several people who attended being harassed online. The head organiser quit as a result.[470]

Meanwhile, the online furry community remained unaffected, as furries were already well established with instant messaging groups on Telegram and Discord as well as several social media channels. As such, most furmeets used the chat groups they already had in lieu of physical meets.

However, furries are still social creatures, and the in-person interactions of both the furmeets and conventions are integral to their involvement in the furry fandom. That is not to mention the number of artists who depend on advertising and selling their work at meets and conventions losing out as much (if not more) than the people who organise them.

Fortunately, furries have also had a long history of being ahead in the world of technology, and they already had a solution on hand: running their events virtually.

VIRTUAL FURCONS

Furmeets were rather quick to go virtual, with some like London, Bristol, Leeds, and Sheffield extending their online efforts to include livestreaming through the Twitch platform or utilising the voice chat functionality in Discord to host events on the weekend of the furmeets.

Virtual conventions had their origins in SecondLife from as early as 2006, and while Japan Meeting of Furries would be the first convention in 2020 to introduce a virtual alternative in January, the fandom would not begin to see complete online replacements until March. The first was KeepCalmCon, an extension of the Canadian Furnal Equinox (and Toronto Comicon) that offered video streams and advertised local artists and dealers.

Virtual Confuzzled

On April 21, the head of events for ConFuzzled, GermanShep, sent an email to people who had planned to run events at the convention, informing them that they would be planning to host their own virtual convention during the same weekend as their cancelled convention. The email offered them a chance to submit events that would work in a digital space. After enough people were interested, ConFuzzled officially announced Virtual ConFuzzled on May 9.

Instead of meeting in a hotel, Virtual ConFuzzled met in a specially created Discord Group with events broadcasted over Twitch from May 22 to 24. Events on offer ranged from music, comedy, artwork, games, and panels, as well as a virtual dealer's den. The big plus was that everyone could attend for free, which was a huge relief considering the stressful experience people had trying to register for the physical con, along with the anxiety of getting a hotel room followed by the demands for refunds due to the pandemic. The theme for ConFuzzled 2020 (coincidentally, "A World Reborn," a post-apocalyptic theme) was moved for 2021, so the Virtual ConFuzzled did not have a proper theme.

The livestream began on Friday with the traditional opening ceremony, introduced with white text on a black background cracking jokes about how the opening ceremony would be planned,. This was followed up with a collaborative music video directed by Medosai that involved short clips of 45 furries passing smartphones to each other, each transforming into their fursuits in creative ways.

Once the introductions were made by the ConFuzzled team and the convention charity, Secret World Wildlife Rescue, ran their video detailing all their work, the virtual convention went underway. Each event was introduced by the pawpet character Frank. Some regular events returned such as the game shows Taskmaster and GamesMaster, as well as the short story competition Flash Fiction and the pub quiz. Other events included panels on the closed original furry species known as Hellkin, how to run online communities, and how to be a YouTuber, and there was also a furry-themed antique roadshow.

Closed furry species (such as Hellkin and Dutch Angel Dragons) are like original furry species (such as Sergal and Skiltaire) except the owner of said species limits how new characters can be created. Furries sometimes have to sign an agreement with the species owner and follow rules on how characters of that species are used.

Guests included the musical duo of Fox Amoore & Pepper Coyote (with Jake), who provided a livestreamed concert; furry animator Adler the Eagle, who conducted an animation seminar; and the FurScience team, who explained their sociology research into the furry fandom.

Some events were perfect for the livestreaming platform, including two art streams: one by 2019 guest of honour Gem the Squirrel and another by Medosai. The latter's final artwork of Brok the Badger proved so popular that when GermanShep suggested making it into Virtual ConFuzzled's official T-shirt design, his inbox was flooded with requests for orders.

Adler the Eagle was originally announced at the closing ceremony of ConFuzzled 2019 as the community guest of honour for 2020. Disney TV animation veteran Tad Stones was also planned to be a guest of honour, but was no longer available for the virtual convention.

Speaking of merchandise orders, the dealers' den was one of the most well-received features of the con. The dealers' den website featured numerous artists and dealers, and the website was designed to allow people to search for dealers based on what kind of artwork or products they were looking for.

The most beloved aspect of the virtual con outside of the events was the Discord channel, which featured numerous voice and text channels referencing areas around the Birmingham Hilton Metropole, including the hotel lobby, lounges, and bars such as the Corona Bar (named after the alcoholic beer, not the virus).

Many people were sad when the virtual convention ended all too soon, especially because the Discord channel, which was privately hosted, shut down and channels were locked the day after the closing ceremony. However, Virtual ConFuzzled proved to be a huge success, boasting on their front page that they had over 6,500 unique viewers to the livestream and over 20,000 page views of the Dealers Den. A total of 29 hours from the Twitch livestream were uploaded to ConFuzzled's video archive for people to watch again, and BigBlueFox broadcasted a video marathon of all his footage from prior conventions over the last twelve years.

It was several months before ConFuzzled revealed the total amount of money raised for the con's charity through auctions, T-shirt sales, and attendees who contributed part of their convention refunds. The Secret World Wildlife Fund officially received £17,785.55,[471] although the total does not include donations made directly during the convention, so it is not known how much more was raised.

Wild North: Virtual Tails

The overwhelming success of ConFuzzled inspired more conventions to follow in their footsteps. More than two weeks after its postponement announcement on 28 July, 2020, Wild North substituted the physical convention for a virtual one to run on the same scheduled weekend of September 26 and 27.[472] Wild North: Virtual Tails featured a Discord chat and Twitch livestream, promising games and many events just like those that the physical convention had planned to offer.

The livestream was hosted by Kivuli. Most of the events centered on the theme of stories, including ghost stories by Greskil, history of northern furries by Gamepopper, animal folklore by Ziegenbock, and a choose-your-own-adventure style tale by Tyde.

Not all events focused on stories, however. A professional instructor from the FederWyrm Sword fighting school, Sascha SwordDerg, provided a short instructional video on training and techniques; Ram Brissot gave his own instructional video on Fire Poi, a dance consisting of swinging tethered weights; and Miku offered her own artwork charity stream. Along with games, quizzes, and a chat with the Wild North organisers, there was a lot that the small convention had on offer. While the Birds of Prey from the Walworth Castle falconry group (a popular event from Wild North 2019) were a planned feature, , technical and scheduling issues meant they were unable to attend.

Virtual Tails concluded with a raffle and several furries contributed a sing-along of the northern folk song "The Lambton Worm." Like Virtual ConFuzzled, Wild North: Virtual Tails raised money for charity, this time directly through Twitch itself. The Newcastle Dog & Cat Shelter received a total of £417 from donations.[473] Most of the events were later uploaded onto YouTube, including the Choose Your Own Adventure video, with all available plot choices being offered as unlisted videos to allow for a unique playthrough.

Virtual Furcation and VRChat

Furcation announced its Virtual Furcation on the same day they cancelled on 25 June, 2020. The planned livestreamed weekend and Discord group took place on November 7 and 8. The originally planned theme of the "Rawring 20s" was moved to 2021, but, unlike ConFuzzled, they decided to reuse the theme from 2019.With the advent of products like the Ocullus Rift and the HTC Vive, virtual reality was booming. A new social network was created in 2014 called VRChat, which grew massively in popularity after launching on Steam in 2017. VRChat allows users to interact with each other as 3D character models and host their own servers where they can build their own 3D worlds to explore in. The productenticed furries to produce character models of their fursonas and for conventions to consider it as a fun option alongside a livestream.

Japan Meeting of Furries was the first convention to offer VRChat as an alternative. VRChat in the furry fandom soon exploded after a brand-new, and exclusively VR-based furry convention ran during the same weekend as Virtual ConFuzzled: Furality Online eXperience, or Furality for short. Other conventions quickly adopted VRChat, too, including Anthrocon and IndyFurCon. EuroFurence even used a 1:1 scale recreation of the Hotel Estrel in Berlin (named Virtualfurence) for its VRChat at EuroFurence Online in August.

Furcation decided to get involved in VRChat with the help of Sterling Gryph, who created an exclusive VRChat world based around caravans that people could hang out in. This allowed furries with the necessary technology to get closer to the physical experience of a convention without direct contact with people.[474]

Furcation's Discord group had channels named after certain caravans, and each dealer was given their own channel so attendees could talk directly with them.

Furcation is better described as a relaxed weekend furry getaway than a traditional convention, and its livestream events were more about quality than quantity. It did have some common convention events, though, such as the opening and closing ceremonies, hosted by chairman Jasper Foxx. There was also a children's TV show quiz and "My First Furry Con," which was hosted by events manager Ulfur.

Each day had a presentation of their selected dealers and an hour's lunch break. Main events took place in the afternoon, such as Shadow Raccoon hosting "Furry Fortunes," a furry twist on the game show "Family Fortunes" on Saturday afternoon, followed by an episode of the sci-fi adventure-based podcast *Cosmopunk* hosted by SaintPanic. Meanwhile, on Sunday, Cosmosnowmew gave a presentation on electronic accessories for fursuits in the morning, and in the afternoon was a roleplaying game of Trudge hosted by Frio.

Virtual Furcation also raised money through Twitch stream donations and a charity auction for their 2019 charity, the Ferne Animal Sanctuary. In total, the virtual convention raised £2,509.[475]

GOING FORWARD

As the world reached the end of 2020, there remained hope on the horizon that the pandemic will end, although perhaps not as soon as people had hoped. At the beginning of 2021, restrictions eased gradually, and vaccinations were being rolled out, and by June it was possible for all adults to get the first of two required doses. With vaccination rates being high and vaccine hesitancy being low, it was enough for some furries to feel safe.

LondonFurs returned to in-person meets on 28 August 2021, requiring attendees to provide COVID-19 test reports that showed negative as a safety precaution, and other furmeets across the country also slowly returned to in-person meets with their own mask, vaccination, and test requirements.

A few conventions did make a return to in-person events, such as Australia's FurDU, while many others remained virtual with similar formats to the previous years with livestreams, VR spaces, and Discord servers.

The British virtual conventions were kept largely the same, although with different themes to change things up. ConFuzzled brought back the video game theme by popular demand. Wild North's theme was inspired by a brief revival of Sea Shanties that started earlier in the year on the social media app TikTok. Furcation went all out with their summer pool party theme (despite taking place near the end of autumn), with their livestream staged by an outdoor swimming pool and a new VRChat room named Costa Del Furc.

The Return of Conventions

In-person conventions returned to the United Kingdom when Scotiacon took place at the Crowne Plaza Glasgow hotel from 11 to 14 February, 2022. There were 537 furries in attendance. Fursuit maker Camodile (formerly known as Blue Fox Fursuits) was guest of honour and £11,650 was raised for the Sunny Harbour Cats charity.

ConFuzzled returned to the Birmingham Hilton Metropole from 27 to 31 May with 2,079 in attendance. Adler the Eagle was once again the guest of honour, and £25,258.82 was raised for the Bumblebee Conservation Trust. The post-apocalyptic theme from 2020, A World Reborn, was reused.

Wild North came next, running from 23 to 26 September at Featherstone Castle with a theme of mythic beasts. With 45 in attendance, the staff and volunteers were slightly overwhelmed as the first evening had delays and the popular falconry event from 2019 was delayed at the last moment, but fun was had all around. The clear weather meant there was a nature walk, and the Kubb tournament sword fighting classes ran throughout the weekend led by HEMA instructor Sascha Sworderg. A trading post was available for artists, and even Tyde continued the Virtual Wild North tradition of a written Choose Your Own Adventure following the convention's mascot, Twizell. They also were able to raise £793.58 for the canine rescue charity, Stray Aid.[476]

Meanwhile, Furcation would find out how quickly the hype of in-person events would exceed their expectations. At 7 PM on 12 September, 2022, after months of preparation behind the scenes, registrations opened for its return to Sandy Glade Holiday Park from November 11 to 14. At 7:09 PM, the convention was completely sold out for the first time in its short history,[477] with 153 units being taken by over 600 people.

As incredible of an achievement as this was, many weren't happy. Exactly 1,156 people had pre-registered, arranging themselves into 309 chalet groups, and competing in a mostly first-come, first-served system (a few chalets were assigned by lottery for those needing disability access). Many complained that the website was so sluggish that when they finally reached the point of being able to

> **Charity Donations**
>
> **Virtual ConFuzzled 2:** Game On–28 to 30 May–Secret World Wildlife Rescue. £8,485
> **Wild North:** Tails of the Seven Seas–2nd–3rd October - Newcastle Cats & Dogs Shelter - £600
> **Furcation:** Pool Party–12th–14th November–The National Search and Rescue Dog Association - £1,004.88

choose their chalets, they discovered they were all taken. This was on top of bugs such as groups not appearing on the website, locking users out of the registration process. In addition, Furcation couldn't offer attending-only tickets due to Sandy Glade's insurance policy, so many people missed out.

Jasper Foxx went on camera to publicly apologise for the upset. As he explained, due to a limited IT staff working on a new registration system, they couldn't handle the huge influx of people logging in. Because of the pandemic and cost-of-living crisis across the UK, they expected fewer registrations in comparison to 2019, so the actual turnout caused Jasper Foxx and the Furcation staff to "be caught with [their] pants down."[478]

There was also a rumour that staff members hogged all the biggest and best chalets for themselves, but according to Jasper Foxx, the staff pre-registered only enough chalets to ensure that the staff could be on site while maintaining availability for as many chalets for attendees as possible.

The only UK furry convention not to return in 2022 was JFTW. That convention had been subjected to vitriol from furries before for postponing at the last moment back in 2020; and they were again the next year for being unable to refund money when the 2021 iteration was cancelled due to their suppliers holding off on refunding for longer than expected.[479]

JFTW announced on 28 October, 2021 that they wouldn't return for 2022 but would plan for 2023. The next day another statement was made by the director of welfare, who bemoaned the backlash they received and the resulting negative reputation. For the entire year, there were no more announcements or updates. As of this writing, JFTW remains on hiatus.

All of this shows us that despite the pandemic forcing furries to remain indoors for two years, in-person conventions remain alive and well for the most part. Virtual events have consequently decreased considerably, although without disappearing entirely. There have been a few furry conventions that have a concurrent virtual space such as Singapore's Little Island Furcon and Canada's Vancoufur, as well as those that are exclusively virtual.

In June 2022, Furality made headlines when its fifth iteration had 15,079 attendees and raised $22,638 for the SaveAFox Corporation, making it the largest virtual furry convention and surpassing the size of

ConFuzzled returned to the Birmingham Hilton Metropole.

the largest in-person conventions. It was a sign that one big impact of the COVID-19 pandemic on the furry fandom has been the normalization of virtual furry events.

Virtual conventions have many great benefits for attendees and organisers alike such as their accessibility and affordability. Conventions and meet-ups are always limited by the size of their venue. Virtual conventions, on the other hand, are only limited by the resilience of the host's server, and modern ones can easily handle tens of thousands of attendees. The travel requirements are reduced to zero, there are no hotel rooms to book, and furries can don a VR fursona instead of buying or making an expensive fursuit.,

This is not to mention that not every person is comfortable with the noise and crowds that the larger furry conventions can boast, even if they still pale in comparison to the anime and comic-book conventions of the world. Virtual conventions allow people to enjoy the entertainment and interact with people from the comfort of their own homes.

However, all that appeal also comes with concerns that they will replace physical conventions and meets entirely. Despite the benefits of virtual conventions, there are experiences and activities at physical conventions that do not translate well into the virtual world.

Fursuiting is not as fun when there are no people to hug and interact with. Main stage events like the PawPet Shows and concerts lack the exciting atmosphere of an actual stage surrounded by an audience. Virtual dealers' dens are essentially akin to browsing a small and curated online art portal with no way to browse and hold potential new purchases or to speak with the dealers face to face.

Traditional conventions are also largely big holidays for furries. They can travel to another part of the country or world and take in the sites and the culture in between the fun of meeting people at an exceptionally large and well-organised party.

Can virtual conventions really hold unique and personal memories like physical conventions can? Is a computer screen a substitute for a real-life experience?

Despite how much the internet has contributed to the outreach of the furry fandom, historically it has been a fandom that has thrived because of dedicated individuals who have worked to organise ways for furries to meet each other in person. Whether it be at a hotel room, house, bar, restaurant, park, camping site, or even a giant hotel hosting a convention, physical locations where people can share their creativity in person with real people are a big reason why furries adore the fandom.

The best result of the addition of virtual cons would be somewhere in the middle, where people could have the choice to go to either a physical or virtual convention or both. If people want to shoulder the expense of travelling to a physical event where they can engage with people in person, take in the atmosphere that crowds can offer, and enjoy what the surrounding scenery provides, they can do so. If people prefer to enjoy the entertainment and interaction with individuals online from the comfort of their own homes for whatever reason, they can enjoy a virtual event.

FINAL THOUGHTS

Ultimately, the acceptance and rising popularity of virtual furry events is just one of the major shifts that the furry fandom has taken. It has gone from a small and connected group of people who enjoyed animal-like characters in cartoons and comic books to accepting people who also enjoyed animals in other ways like anime, video games, mythology, and real life.

It began in hotel rooms and living rooms and later moved up to booking venues at bars, function rooms, and hotels. Fursuiting began as a form of cosplay that was incredibly rare to a luxury item that a fraction could own to becoming such a popular and recognisable aspect of the fandom that the outside world simply assumes every furry has one. There are furries who yearn for the "good old days" when the fandom was smaller and more niche, drama was less of an issue, and it was easier to get into big events if you could afford it. However, those furries forget how they had to deal with negative stereotypes from the media and fringe groups that wanted to police the fandom to extreme levels.

What will not change about the furry fandom, though, is the furries themselves. There will always be people who want to make art, run events, wear fursuits, or talk with other furries about any topic they like, even if it has nothing to do with anthropomorphic characters.

Someday—as people become more and more accepting of us and the world is less worried about plagues—furries will be much more visible in town and city squares. They might be wearing a fursuit to pose for photos, you might find them hugging as many people as they can, or they might be taking photos and answering a simple question: "What is all this about?"

The answer? "We enjoy creating anthropomorphic animal characters because it makes us happy, and we hope it makes other people happy, too."

END NOTES

1 M. Aubert et al., "Earliest Hunting Scene in Prehistoric Art," *Nature*, vol. 576, no. 7787, Art. no. 7787, Dec. 2019, doi: 10.1038/s41586-019-1806-y.

2 F. L. Coolidge and T. Wynn, *The Rise of Homo sapiens: The Evolution of Modern Thinking*. John Wiley & Sons, 2011.

3 R. David, *Religion and Magic in Ancient Egypt*. Penguin UK, 2002.

4 Philostratus and F. C. Conybeare, *The Life of Apollonius of Tyana*. London: Wm. Heinemann, 1912. Accessed: Jan. 09, 2021. [Online]. Available: http://archive.org/details/lifeofapollonius-01phil

5 J. J. Grandville, A. Second, and C. Blanc, *Les métamorphoses du jour*. Garnier frères, 1854.

6 M. Hancher, *The Tenniel illustrations to the Alice Books*. Ohio State University Press, 1985. Accessed: Jan. 09, 2021. [Online]. Available: https://web.archive.org/web/20160401201549/https:/ohiostatepress.org/index.htm?%2F-books%2Fcomplete%2520pdfs%2F-hancher%2520tenniel%2F-hancher%2520tenniel.htm

7 Kjell Knudde, "Mabel F. Taylor," lambiek.net, 1994. https://www.lambiek.net/artists/t/taylor_mabel_f.htm (accessed Jan. 09, 2021).

8 J. Taylor, *Letters to Children from Beatrix Potter*. Penguin UK, 2012.

9 Alison Prince, *Kenneth Grahame—An Innocent in the Wild Wood*. Allison & Busby Ltd, 1994. Accessed: Jan. 09, 2021. [Online]. Available: https://web.archive.org/web/20071009113210/http://www.kennethgrahamesociety.net/biography.htm

10 "The Story of Pantomime," Victoria and Albert Museum, vol. Christmas at the V&A, Dec. 03, 2016. [Online]. Available: https://www.vam.ac.uk/articles/the-story-of-pantomime

11 "Charles Lauri the Animal Impersonator," *The Sketch*, pp. 406–408, Mar. 15, 1893.

12 M. E. Swartz, *Oz before the Rainbow: L. Frank Baum's The Wonderful Wizard of Oz on Stage and Screen to 1939*. The Johns Hopkins University Press, 2000.

13 I. Curtis, "BONZO," *Furtherance*, no. 3, pp. 2–5, 1991.

14 R. Waller and K. Fletcher, "Pre-Vootie APA-zine Flyer," Feb. 29, 1976. [Online]. Available: https://www.furaffinity.net/view/19451045/

15 M. Merlino and R. O'Riley, *25 Years of Furry Conventions*. Further Confusion, San Jose Convention Center, 2015. [Convention Panel]. Available: https://archive.org/details/25YearsOfFurry-Conventions

16 F. Patten, *Watching Anime, Reading Manga: 25 Years of Essays and Reviews*. Stone Bridge Press, 2004.

17 J. Baen, Ed., "Films Program," in Iguanacon II, Phoenix, Arizona: World Science Fiction Convention, 1978, p. 18.

18 OCSFC, "Rod O'Riley and Mark Merlino on Furry Fandom," Orange Country Science Fiction Club: Past Meetings, Mar. 30, 2005. https://web.archive.org/web/20071015113244/http://members.cox.net/ocsfc/ocsf-pastmeet.htm

19 J. Strike, *Furry Nation: The True Story of America's Most Misunderstood Subculture*.

Jersey City, New Jersey: Cleis Press, 2017.

[20] R. Hansen and M. Glyer, "The Story So Far... A Brief History of British Fandom, 1931–1987," in Worldcon, Conspiracy '87, vol. 50, FILE 770, 1987, p. Appendix.

[21] T. Jones, "The History of the World Science Fiction Convention (Worldcon)," Starburst Magazine, Mar. 17, 2015. [Online]. Available: https://www.starburstmagazine.com/features/history-worldcon

[22] M. Porter, P. Kincaid, and M. Smith, "Plot," Conspiracy '87, no. 4, p. 4, Aug. 29, 1987.

[23] M. Merlino, Conspiracy '87 Furry Party. 1987. [Flyer]. Available: https://confurence.com/wp-content/uploads/2017/04/furpty3.jpg

[24] M. Merlino, "Twitter Direct Messages (to @sysable)," Jul. 23, 2018.

[25] R. Hansen, THEN: Science Fiction Fandom in the UK: 1930–1980, First. Lulu, 2015.

[26] S. Barber, "F.P.N. Bestiary #1," Furry Press Network, no. 3, Jun. 1991.

[27] G.W. Thomas, "Artists of ohe Cthulhu Mythos IV: Simon Barber," Nightscapes, Aug. 17, 1999. https://www.epberglund.com/RGttCM/nightscapes/NS11/ns11nf3.htm (accessed Aug. 07, 2022).

[28] R. O'Riley, "In-Fur-Nation," In-Fur-Nation and the ConFurence Chronicle, vol. 1, no. 1, p. 1, Nov. 01, 1991.

[29] F. Patten, "Squeeky Clean No. 5," Furry Press Network, no. 5, Dec. 1991.

[30] S. Barber, "Remembering Fred Patten," Rowrbrazzle, no. 139, Sep. 2018.

[31] F. Patten, "Patten's Europe Report," Rowrbrazzle, no. 33, pp. 26–28, Apr. 1992.

[32] Warwick, "MicroConFurence #0 (Posting for a friend)," alt.fan.furry, Nov. 02, 1992. https://groups.google.com/forum/#!msg/alt.fan.furry/_ltU-oQZFHqw/CoglaxI93PMJ

[33] D. Mitchell, T. Baverstock, and R. Deighton, "Angouleme & England," no. 33, Apr. 1992.

[34] R. Deighton, "In-Fur-Nation," In-Fur-Nation and the ConFurence Chronicle, vol. 2, no. 2, p. 2, Jul. 02, 1992.

[35] E. Vick, "Introductory Report," Rowrbrazzle, no. 33, Apr. 1992.

[36] K. Kreutzman, "Angouleme Report," Rowrbrazzle, no. 35, Oct. 1992.

[37] Mayfurr, "RE: Yateley Housecon Question," May 23, 2019.

[38] S. Davies, D. Siegal, and A. Stewart, "Voice of the Mysterons," Intersection '95, no. 4–5, Aug. 25, 1995.

[39] F. Patten, "Patten's Con-Report," Rowrbrazzle, no. 47, pp. 10–22, Jan. 1995.

[40] P. Silva, "Welcome to alt.fan.albedo," alt.fan.albedo, Oct. 30, 1990. https://groups.google.com/forum/#!topic/alt.fan.albedo/UciqwQM1wys

[41] H. Rheingold and K. Kelly, "The Dragon Ate My Homework," WIRED, Jan. 03, 1993. [Online]. Available: https://www.wired.com/1993/03/muds-2/

[42] California. The History of Furry Fandom, (Jan. 16, 1998). [Conference]. Available: https://www.youtube.com/watch?v=e5snFU0xpXI

[43] T. Smith, "The History of Furry-MUCK," May 06, 2001. https://web.archive.org/web/20010506015528/http://felis.org/FurryHistory/

[44] I. Stradling, "RE: History of UK Furries," May 24, 2019.

[45] Foxy, "RE: History of UK Furries," Sep. 21, 2019.

[46] F. Patten, "Retrospective: An Illustrated Chronology of Furry Fandom, 1966–1996," Yarf!, no. 46, Jan. 1997. [Online]. Available: http://www.flayrah.com/4117/retrospective-illustrated-chronology-furry-fandom-1966-1996

[47] D. Cugley, "EuroFurence," alt.fan.furry, Dec. 16, 1994. https://groups.google.com/forum/#!msg/alt.fan.furry/iAHQYcbnwM8/RlPG-YaBWfsJ

[48] Foxy and D. Peterson, "EuroFurence," alt.fan.furry, Dec. 17, 1992. https://groups.google.com/forum/#!msg/alt.fan.furry/iAHQYcbnwM8/-yqYhz-pyJYJ)

[49] I. Stradling, "UK Furrys! Feb 1999," UK Furry Meets—Shake a Paw!, Feb. 25, 1999. https://web.archive.org/web/19990225000315/http://www.

faradawn.demon.co.uk:80/furry/fur-con.htm

50 Candy, "Shinnenkai Masquerade Report," AAS, Feb. 10, 1999. https://web.archive.org/web/19990210073026/http://www.shef.ac.uk/~aas/uk/shinnenkai/masque/candy.html

51 Foxy, "UK anime/furry con needs your support!," alt.fan.furry, Apr. 16, 1999. https://groups.google.com/forum/#!msg/alt.fan.furry/rojt4sQG-pU8/hq5QNAsoj64J

52 Foxy, "Re: UK Furry Con thoughts," Aug. 31, 2002. [Online]. Available: https://archive.org/details/ukfurmail-inglists

53 J. Lewis, "The Bad News Is True," *Shinnenkai '99*, Oct. 01, 1999. https://web.archive.org/web/19991001234059/http://www.newmoon.ndirect.co.uk/shinnenkai/

54 J. Lewis, "UK Fandom," alt.fan.furry, Jul. 13, 1999. https://groups.google.com/forum/#!msg/alt.fan.furry/RgT-kQFx36TY/8VJkhAb4t4cJ

55 I. Stradling, "UK Furrys! Jun 2000," *Furry Meets—Shake a Paw!*, Jun. 19, 2000. https://web.archive.org/web/20000619092334/http://www.faradawn.demon.co.uk:80/furry/fur-con.htm

56 I. Stradling, "UK Furrys! 2005," *Furry Meets—Shake a Paw!*, Oct. 15, 2005. https://web.archive.org/web/20051015025239/http://www.faradawn.demon.co.uk:80/furry/fur-con.htm

57 J. Liu, "Waking Dreams," *Computer Games*, no. October 2005, pp. 58–59, Oct. 2005.

58 V. Wuttke and J. Seifert, "Gucky and the Fluffbutts," *Andromeda SF*, no. 157, pp. 77–78, 2019.

59 G. Stephens, "UK FurCon #1—Some Thanks," alt.fan.furry, Jul. 25, 1994. https://groups.google.com/forum/#!msg/alt.fan.furry/NWAFUt-T2ldw/orCz06F5vlYJ

60 Unci, "EuroFurence (or however we call it)," alt.fan.furry, Dec. 14, 1994. https://groups.google.com/forum/#!msg/alt.fan.furry/wUkc2SF-6H9c/XixsMEh59jMJ

61 'EuroFurence Archive—EF1," Eu-roFurence 1995, 1995. http://archive.eurofurence.org/EF1/

62 Unci, "UK FurCon," WikiFur, May 22, 2006. https://en.wikifur.com/wiki/Talk:FurCon_UK

63 Unci, "Ten Years of Furryness," alt.fan.furry, Nov. 30, 2003. https://groups.google.com/forum/#!msg/alt.fan.furry/Rd1nD-znKTQ/AKgchK-DGFE0J

64 D. Schiff, "GO AEROSMITH: How 'Head First' Became the First Digitally Downloadable Song 20 Years Ago Today," *VICE*, Jun. 27, 2014. Accessed: Nov. 29, 2020. [Online]. Available: https://www.vice.com/en/article/6vapxr/go-aerosmith-how-head-first-became-the-first-song-available-for-digital-download-20-years-ago-today

65 J. Dennis, "Jeremy Dennis Bio," *Alleged Literature*, Aug. 06, 2002. https://web.archive.org/web/20020806025932/http://www.alleged.org.uk/jrd/ (accessed Nov. 29, 2020).

66 D. Cugley and J. G. Constantine, "Question: FURRY FURRY ... Anyone Seen It?," alt.fan.furry, Sep. 29, 1993. https://groups.google.com/g/alt.fan.furry/c/JVeTIkqnawE/m/X_oQ0wP-MCbAJ (accessed Nov. 29, 2020).

67 D. Cugley, "Alleged Literature presents: Furry Furry #2," alt.fan.furry, May 09, 1994. https://groups.google.com/g/alt.fan.furry/c/0AA4jcHbKx-w/m/ILE_RnAFLPcJ (accessed Nov. 29, 2020).

68 I. Stradling, "Dainties #1 Progress Reports," *Dainties—Silvermane's Furry Fanzine Project*, Feb. 15, 2001. https://web.archive.org/web/20010215050516/http://www.fysh.org/~liger/Fanzine.html (accessed Dec. 08, 2020).

69 I. Stradling, "Fur Fanzine?: Dainties!," alt.fan.furry, Oct. 26, 1999. https://groups.google.com/g/alt.fan.furry/c/MiCtAZVEyqM/m/1hePG2mQw7YJ (accessed Dec. 08, 2020).

70 I. Stradling, "Dainties Issue #2," alt.fan.furry, Jun. 04, 2000. https://groups.google.com/g/alt.fan.furry/c/y-CQTqziRVg/m/Xeed3dpZz7IJ

(accessed Dec. 08, 2020).

71 I. Stradling, "Dainties #2 Progress Reports," *The Dainties Furry Fanzine Project*, Mar. 10, 2001. https://web.archive.org/web/20010429164322/http://www.fysh.org/~liger/Fanzines/Dainties2.html (accessed Dec. 08, 2020).

72 I. Stradling, "Dainties Issue #2 Available at Anthrocon," alt.fan.furry, Jul. 24, 2001. https://groups.google.com/g/alt.fan.furry/c/BsnochEN-lU4/m/5poTt10YmUwJ (accessed Dec. 08, 2020).

73 Foxy, "About Foxy," *Studio Kitsune*, Mar. 22, 2017. https://www.studiokitsune.com/pages/about.html

74 F. Patten, "The History of Furry Publishing, Part Two: Current Publishers," Dogpatch Press, Feb. 04, 2015. https://dogpatch.press/2015/02/04/the-history-of-furry-publishing-part-two-current-publishers-by-fred-patten/ (accessed Dec. 08, 2020).

75 Foxy, *Anthropomorphine*, vol. 10, 14 vols. Lazy Fox Studios, 1999.

76 M. Dudman, "AJA#2 INFO (REPOST)," alt.fan.furry, Nov. 23, 1994. https://groups.google.com/g/alt.fan.furry/c/i6B4Xh86l7k/m/uvUgKUzWVY0J (accessed Dec. 13, 2020).

77 M. Dudman, "Fur Scene Newsletter (REPOST)," alt.fan.furry, Nov. 11, 1994. https://groups.google.com/g/alt.fan.furry/c/c6zuxpbXdnY/m/jtFYofvh6YMJ (accessed Dec. 13, 2020).

78 M. Dudman, "Fur Scene #7 (AVAILABLE)," alt.fan.furry, May 24, 1996. https://groups.google.com/g/alt.fan.furry/c/GhQFS62HOfI/m/yTwWtLTTckMJ (accessed Dec. 13, 2020).

79 M. Dudman and J. Tatman, "Current Price List," Jun. 11, 1998. https://web.archive.org/web/19980611224536/http://www.lupin.demon.co.uk/PRICEL.html (accessed Dec. 13, 2020).

80 M. Dudman, Ed., *Wild Side Premiere Issue,* vol. 1, 6 vols. United Publications, 1998.

81 M. Dudman, Ed., *Wild Side*, vol. 6, 6 vols. United Publications, 1999.

82 M. Dudman, Ed., *Wild Side Volume 2*, vol. 1, 1 vols. United Publications, 2000.

83 A. Moss, "Adam's Fox Box," Apr. 27, 1999. https://web.archive.org/web/19990427044751/http://www.foxbox.org/

84 R. Desmera, "Yiff," Everything2.com, Jun. 08, 2001. https://everything2.com/title/yiff (accessed Nov. 05, 2021).

85 K. Jorgensen, "Furry Mailing Lists," alt.fan.furry, Apr. 03, 2000. https://groups.google.com/forum/#!msg/alt.fan.furry/0b_GQ9LMzWc/kfjw_bs4S38J

86 "The Rise & Rise of UK Furry," *ConFuzzled Official Conbook*, pp. 27–28, 2008.

87 D. Konig, "Oxford 1998," Wolfnose, 2000. http://wolfnose.org/fur/meets/oxford98/index.html

88 D. Majumdar, "Goth pub closes after 222 years," BBC News, London, Sep. 11, 2006. [Online]. Available: http://news.bbc.co.uk/1/hi/england/london/5328200.stm

89 Ia'Kat, "**new furry mailing list for London, UK**," alt.fan.furry, Apr. 20, 1999. https://groups.google.com/forum/#!msg/alt.fan.furry/k1ujN2hDA-Jc/kqQ7i6NzXjwJ

90 V. Crabtree, "An Intimate Exploration of the Furry Fandom," The Human Truth Foundation, 1999, [Online]. Available: http://www.humantruth.info/furry.html

91 Ia'Kat, "Comments from History of Furries in the UK—Confuzzled 2019," YouTube, May 29, 2019. https://www.youtube.com/watch?v=H_hFt3u-1oRE&lc=UgyPFJ_sYPVBSnGy-iw94AaABAg

92 A. Riggs, *Critter Costuming: Making Mascots and Fabricating Fursuits*. Ibexa Press, 2004.

93 P. O'Furr, "'Don't Dream It—Be It!' Interview with Robert Hill About Early Fursuiting and Fandom.," Dogpatch Press, Aug. 28, 2018. [Online]. Available: https://dogpatch.press/2018/08/28/interview-robert-hill/

94 J. Paxton, Pandas love the water! 2008.

[Online]. Available: http://www.furaffinity.net/view/1717568/

[95] J.-P. Flintoff, "The Fursuit of Happiness," *London Financial Times*, pp. 124–128, Oct. 20, 2001.

[96] Tae Kwon Do Tiger, "fursuitandfriends.co.uk," *Fursuit and Friends*, May 04, 2001. https://web.archive.org/web/20010504105123/http://www.lionking.org/~fursuits/

[97] Fish, "fishthecat.co.uk," *Fish the Cat*, Mar. 31, 2001. https://web.archive.org/web/20010331035235/http://fishthecat.co.uk/

[98] Makali, "Furry Bodypainting/Costuming," LondonFurs.org, May 16, 2001. https://web.archive.org/web/20010516231220/http://www.londonfurs.org:80/

[99] Marcony, "Direct Messages with Marcony on DeviantART," Oct. 28, 2020.

[100] Makali, "LondonFurs Profile List," LondonFurs, Jun. 24, 2001. https://web.archive.org/web/20010624234137/http://www.lazycat.org/londonfurs/list_users.php

[101] "HantsFurs Mailing List," Yahoo Groups, Mar. 28, 2008. https://web.archive.org/web/20080328020227/http://groups.yahoo.com/group/hantsfurs/

[102] TK Tiger, "Tae Kwon-Do Tiger, SouthPaw And Spots—The HantsFurs Group.," *Fursuit and Friends*, Jun. 24, 2001. https://web.archive.org/eb/20030207062319fw_/http://www.fursuitsandfriends.co.uk/group2.html (accessed Nov. 08, 2021).

[103] Balooo, "The First North West Furs Meet," Ursophiles, Mar. 06, 2001. https://web.archive.org/web/20010306164844/http://www.ursophiles.co.uk/meettext.htm

[104] "NorthernFurs Mailing List," Yahoo Groups, 2000. https://groups.yahoo.com/neo/groups/NorthernFurs/info

[105] Cabbit, "Finalised Meet Structure," Dec. 05, 2000. [Online]. Available: https://archive.org/details/ukfurmailinglists

[106] FurbleFox, "NorthernFurs—Change of Management," Jul. 11, 2001. [Online]. Available: https://archive.org/details/ukfurmailinglists

[107] Cabbit, "Message about Rota System, from Creator," Jan. 04, 2002. [Online]. Available: https://archive.org/details/ukfurmailinglists

[108] T. Wolfe, "Sheffield Meet Report," May 27, 2001. [Online]. Available: https://archive.org/details/ukfurmailinglists

[109] Lone Wolf, "Announcing the Midland Furs Mailing List," Jan. 26, 2001. [Online]. Available: https://archive.org/details/ukfurmailinglists

[110] Lone Wolf, "Meet this Saturday, 10th March," Mar. 07, 2001. [Online]. Available: https://archive.org/details/ukfurmailinglists

[111] Lyken Blue Paws and M. D'Israeli, "Proposal," Feb. 13, 2003. [Online]. Available: https://archive.org/details/ukfurmailinglists

[112] Blacktalon, "N.O.T.Z Website," *N.O.T.Anthro'z*, Dec. 10, 2002. https://web.archive.org/web/20021210065537/http:/www.blacktalon.co.uk:80/notz/

[113] Makali, "UKFur.org Forums," UKFur.org, Oct. 04, 2006. https://web.archive.org/web/20061004155506/http:/ukfur.org/forums/

[114] Makali, "UKFur.net," UKFur.net, Oct. 11, 2002. https://web.archive.org/web/20021011091700/http:/ukfur.net/

[115] Makali, "UKFur.net Forums," UKFur.net, May 01, 2003. https://web.archive.org/web/20030501075137/http:/ukfur.net:80/forums/

[116] SlyCat, "Furmeets.co.uk," *FurmeetsUK*, May 30, 2018. https://web.archive.org/web/20180530082501/http:/furmeets.co.uk/meets.php?old=1

[117] tseatah, "Catastrophic Failover of Critter.net," *Tseatah Critter*, Apr. 2014. https://tseatah.tumblr.com/post/82357706113/catastrophic-failover-of-critternet (accessed Jul. 16, 2021).

[118] FurbleFox, "Tynefurs Page," *NorthernFurs*, Jun. 05, 2014. https://web.archive.org/web/20140605100026/http:/northernfurs.org.uk/

index.php?option=com_os-view&id=29&Itemid=75

[119] R. Blackman and S. Guarniere, "LONDONFURS MANAGEMENT LTD," London, Certificate of Incorportation of a Private Limited Company, Apr. 2012.

[120] Branded_Bunni, "UKFur Forums," 10 Year Anniversary Celebration, Mar. 29, 2009. https://forum.ukfur.org/topic/15804-10-year-anniversary-celebration/

[121] London. LondonFurs 10th Anniversary, (25 2009).

[122] Ani Boxer, "A message from our Chairman—300th Meet Saturday 3rd November 2018," *LondonFurs*, Oct. 30, 2018. https://londonfurs.org.uk/2018/10/a-message-from-our-chairman-300th-meet/

[123] "Advertisement for ConFurence Zero," *Starburst Magazine*, vol. 11, no. 5, p. 13, Jan. 1989.

[124] Toby Williams, "Furry Cons in the UK," alt.fan.furry, Aug. 01, 2001. https://groups.google.com/forum/#!msg/alt.fan.furry/NZApEgy-ZLZo/CyqyC9peS6EJ

[125] ANTIcarrot, "Organising a Furry Con—Help Wanted," alt.fan.furry, Aug. 25, 2002. https://groups.google.com/forum/#!msg/alt.fan.furry/9vDP-qoEORc/hOxrOF91xrMJ

[126] "Minutes for the 26/09 uk_fur_con meeting," Sep. 26, 2002.

[127] "Minutes for the 16/10 uk_fur_con meeting.," Oct. 16, 2002.

[128] Marcony and UltraViolet, "BritFurCon Website," Welcome BritFurs!, Sep. 26, 2004. https://web.archive.org/web/20040926064042/http://www.britfur.co.uk/

[129] Marcony and UltraViolet, "BritFur Art and Competitions!," *BritFur 2005*, Dec. 03, 2003. https://webhttps://web.archive.org/web/20031203193839/http://www.darkfurr.co.uk/~britfur/compx.html.archive.org/web/20031203064305/http://www.darkfurr.co.uk/~britfur/locevent.html

[130] ANTIcarrot, "RE: [UK_FUR_CON] Given Up?," Feb. 09, 2004. [Online]. Available: https://archive.org/details/ukfurmailinglists

[131] ANTIcarrot, "RE: [Britfurcon] Re: Public Transportation.," Jul. 27, 2004. [Online]. Available: https://archive.org/details/ukfurmailinglists

[132] Lamar, "Quick History of BritFur," WikiFur, Jul. 14, 2013. https://en.wikifur.com/wiki/Talk:BritFur_(convention)

[133] Marcony, "Them as Forget History Are Doomed to Repeat It.," *Question*, Dec. 04, 2008. https://rb-wuk.livejournal.com/37804.html?thread=93356#t93356

[134] ANTIcarrot, "RE: [UK_FUR_CON] Call for Con Staff," Sep. 29, 2002. [Online]. Available: https://archive.org/details/ukfurmailinglists

[135] Xen, "Outrage," Dec. 22, 2002. [Online]. Available: https://archive.org/details/ukfurmailinglists

[136] Foxydragon, "Name for the Con," *Britfurcon*, Aug. 03, 2004. https://groups.yahoo.com/neo/groups/Britfurcon/conversations/topics/86

[137] chris_ince01 and Z. Tagnik`zur, "Hey, What's Happening with the Con Right Now?," Nov. 26, 2004. [Online]. Available: https://archive.org/details/ukfurmailinglists

[138] Antharro, "Time for an Update," *Britfurcon*, Feb. 15, 2005. https://groups.yahoo.com/neo/groups/Britfurcon/conversations/messages/200

[139] Tippus Tailus, "BritFur2005 Website," BritFur 2005—Fri 4 Nov 2005 to Sun 6 Nov 2005, Feb. 08, 2005. https://web.archive.org/web/20050208102128/http://www.britfur.co.uk/2005/index.html

[140] Tippus Tailus, "About BritFur2005," BritFur 2005—Fri 4 Nov 2005 to Sun 6 Nov 2005, Feb. 24, 2005. https://web.archive.org/web/20050224053634/http://www.britfur.co.uk/2005/about/index.html

[141] Rallicat, "The BritFur Convention," *Rallicat*, Jan. 18, 2005. https://rallicat.livejournal.com/97865.html

[142] Rallicat, "Thank You!," Rallicat, Jan. 20, 2005. https://rallicat.livejournal.com/98174.html

[143] Ramesses, "Final Furry Convention List 2006," alt.fan.furry, Aug. 16,

2005. https://groups.google.com/forum/#!msg/alt.fan.furry/0xar_BVRAL0/dfjmlzSyTLsJ

[144] Tippus Tailus and T. Lescott, "BRITFUR LTD," Canvey Island, Essex, Certificate of Incorporation of a Private Limited Company Company No. 05206275, Aug. 2004.

[145] S. Stepney, "Interaction: Worldcon 2005," Scottish Exhibition Centre, Glasgow, Convention Report, Dec. 2013. [Online]. Available: https://www-users.cs.york.ac.uk/susan/sf/cons/w2005.htm

[146] R. O'Riley and Rivercoon, "World Con, Glasgow," *Britfurcon*, Sep. 15, 2004. https://groups.yahoo.com/neo/groups/Britfurcon/conversations/topics/117

[147] ANTIcarrot, "[Britfurcon] Euro-furence in England," Aug. 01, 2004. [Online]. Available: https://archive.org/details/ukfurmailinglists

[148] RapidoFrog, "Direct Messages on FurAffinity," Dec. 29, 2020.

[149] Tungro, "Tungro's RBW 2006 Post," *Post Party*, Dec. 03, 2006. https://rbwuk.livejournal.com/1096.html

[150] Rallicat, "Rallicat's RBW 2006 Post," *Boat Party & Photos,* Dec. 06, 2006. https://rbwuk.livejournal.com/3844.html

[151] Greenreaper, "Red Blue & White selects 'Furs in Black' Theme," WikiFur News, Apr. 05, 2007.

[152] FoxBearance, "RBW 2007 Update," RBW Weekly Update No.1 and Just a Little Hello from Me ^_^, Jun. 12, 2007. https://rbwuk.livejournal.com/5885.html

[153] FoxBearance, "The new RBW.org.uk," RBWUK, Jul. 30, 2007. https://rbwuk.livejournal.com/7399.html

[154] F. Patten, *Furry Fandom Conventions, 1989–2015.* Jefferson, NC: McFarland, 2016.

[155] Foxbearance, "RBW 2007 Charity Auction," The RBW Charity Auction—Includes a Fatkraken Fursuit!, Nov. 19, 2007. https://ukfursuit.livejournal.com/49269.html

[156] FoxBearance, "RBW News," September RBW Update, Sep. 15, 2008. https://web.archive.org/web/20081108030435/http://www.rbw.org.uk/news.php

[157] FoxBearance, "RBW 2008 Registration Open," Its here! RBW 2008 registration is now OPEN!, Mar. 08, 2008. https://rbwuk.livejournal.com/18602.html

[158] J. Morris, "Tapewolf RBW 2008 Report," RBW 2008 (now with photos), Jun. 24, 2009. https://www.deviantart.com/tapewolf/journal/RBW-2008-now-with-photos-234563198

[159] Cheetah, "Cheetah's RBW 2008 Updates," Day Two—18:00, Dec. 01, 2008. https://cheetah-spotty.livejournal.com/90647.html

[160] B. Salter, "SouthPaw's RBW 2008 Report," RBW Review Post of Doooom (long!), Dec. 02, 2008. https://web.archive.org/web/20160913065715/https://southpaw1805.livejournal.com/59455.html

[161] Kittiah, "RBW 2009 Name," Dispelling the Myths: "Why Did You Keep the Name?," Aug. 12, 2009. https://rbwuk.livejournal.com/44846.html

[162] Kittiah, "RBW 2009 Team," Dispelling The Myths: "Why Isn't There a Chairman?," Aug. 13, 2009. https://rbwuk.livejournal.com/45240.html

[163] Kittiah, "Chairman Meows," Staff Profiles: Chairman Meows, Aug. 17, 2009. https://rbwuk.livejournal.com/45769.html

[164] A.R.F., "RBW 2009 Dealer's Den," Dealer's Den—RBW 2009—Good Vibrations, Jul. 18, 2009. https://web.archive.org/web/20090718092948/http://www.rbw.org.uk/dealers.rbw

[165] A.R.F., "RBW 2009 Venue," Venue—RBW 2009—Good Vibrations, Apr. 24, 2009. https://web.archive.org/web/20090424055844/http://www.rbw.org.uk/venue.rbw

[166] Tryst, "RBW 2009 Guests," 101 Days to Go ..., Jul. 20, 2009. https://rbwuk.livejournal.com/42914.html

[167] Kittiah, "RBW 2009 Price," Dispelling the Myths: "Why Is It So Expensive?," Aug. 21, 2009. https://rbwuk.livejournal.com/46804.html

[168] B. Salter, "LondonFur," RBW 2009—A Concerned Attendee

Writes..., Jul. 30, 2009. https://web.archive.org/web/20160914034759/http:/londonfurs.livejournal.com/95094.html

[169] Kittiah, "RBW 2009 Mistakes," Dispelling the Myths: "I Heard Last Year Was Rubbish, Is It Going to Be The Same This Year?," Aug. 14, 2009. https://rbwuk.livejournal.com/45491.html

[170] Makali, "RBW 2009 Sponsorship Upgrade," Get Upgraded for Free!, Aug. 01, 2009. https://rbwuk.livejournal.com/43585.html

[171] A.R.F., "RBW 2009 Stats," Twitter, Nov. 02, 2009. https://twitter.com/rbwcon/status/5366634728

[172] Varka, Makali, and Camrath, "RBW 2009 Post-Con Reports," RBW 2009—Post Con Reports, Videos and Photos, Nov. 01, 2009. https://forum.ukfur.org/topic/19774-rbw-2009-%E2%80%94-post-con-reports-videos-and-photos/

[173] RBW 2010 Trailer, (Feb. 28, 2010). [Online Video]. Available: https://www.youtube.com/watch?v=OtqxXsKYcj8

[174] Greenreaper, "Microsoft Matches RBW Donation to Sled Dogs," Flayrah, Dec. 19, 2010. [Online]. Available: https://www.flayrah.com/3364/microsoft-matches-rbw-donation-sled-dogs

[175] A.R.F., "RBW 2010 News," News & Announcements—RBW 2010, Mar. 15, 2010. https://web.archive.org/web/20100315122712/http://www.rbw.org.uk/news

[176] A.R.F., "RBW Announcements Mailing List," Update on RBW 2010, Feb. 02, 2011. https://forum.ukfur.org/topic/29549-the-end-of-rbw/

[177] Miyabi, "Boat Party 2011 Cancelled," Rbw Boat Party 2011, Jul. 28, 2011. https://forum.ukfur.org/topic/32786-rbw-boat-party-2011/

[178] Miyabi, "LondonFurs Summer Weekender," Lf Next Event: Londonfurs Summer Weekender—Fri 19th & Sat 20th July 2013, Feb. 03, 2013. https://forum.ukfur.org/topic/41726-lf-next-event-londonfurs-summer-weekender-%E2%80%93-fri-19th-sat-20th-july-2013/

[179] FurbleFox, "Information within Group.," Oct. 10, 2002. [Online]. Available: https://archive.org/details/ukfurmailinglists

[180] Rocky Raccoon, "Direct Messages with @RockyRaccoon on Telegram," Dec. 22, 2019.

[181] LevLion, "Direct Message with @littlelevlion on Twitter," Apr. 06, 2021.

[182] ConFuzzled UK Ltd, "ConFuzzled," About ConFuzzled, Mar. 04, 2007. https://web.archive.org/web/20070304215444/http:/www.confuzzled.org.uk/about.html

[183] ConFuzzled UK Ltd, "ConFuzzled," Welcome to ConFuzzled 2008!, Mar. 02, 2007. https://web.archive.org/web/20070302104508/http:/confuzzled.org.uk/

[184] Lofty, "Re: [MidFurs] Keep a Secret?!," Oct. 16, 2006. [Online]. Available: https://archive.org/details/ukfurmailinglists

[185] E. Brekaythi, "Entei-rah's LiveJournal," Confuzzled 2009, May 26, 2009. https://enteirah.dreamwidth.org/297400.html

[186] alexf0x, "ConFuzzled 2008," ConFuzzled 2008, Feb. 05, 2007. https://alexf0x.livejournal.com/7224.html

[187] FurbleFox, SouthPaw, and Exildd Wolf, "CONFUZZLED UK LTD," London, Certificate of Incorporation of a Private Limited Company Company No. 06185967, Mar. 2007.

[188] P. Sykes, "Wolfie Fox's Journal," ConFuzzled Staff Meeting & Registration Opening, Apr. 22, 2007. https://wolfie-fox.livejournal.com/4080.html

[189] ConFuzzled UK Ltd, "ConFuzzled," News!, May 23, 2008. https://web.archive.org/web/20070601194015/http://www.confuzzled.org.uk:80/

[190] gothwings, "Comments on Rumours Abound!," Rumours Abound!, May 08, 2007. https://confuzzledlj.livejournal.com/6352.html

[191] ConFuzzled UK Ltd, "Frequently Asked Questions," ConFuzzled 2008, Jun. 25, 2007. https://web.archive.org/web/20070625203445/http:/www.confuzzled.org.uk/content/en/Frequently+Asked+Questions

[192] FurbleFox and B. Mills, "RBW and CF Announcement," ConFuzzled 2008, Dec. 05, 2007. https://web. archive.org/web/20080314052040/ http://www.confuzzled.org.uk/content/en/RBW+And+CF+Announcement

[193] Greenreaper, "ConFuzzled sells out, as Eurofurence 14 opens its doors," WikiFur News, Jan. 10, 2008. [Online]. Available: https://www.flayrah.com/2737/confuzzled-sells-out-euro-furence-14-opens-its-doors

[194] ConFuzzled UK Ltd, "ConFuzzled 2008 Attendee List," ConFuzzled 2008—Attendee List, Jul. 09, 2008. https://web.archive.org/web/20080709045012/http://www.confuzzled.org.uk/content/en/Attendee+List

[195] Twll, "Jinxxy's Blog," A Short History of a Tall Order, Jun. 03, 2008. https://jinxxy.livejournal.com/33744.html

[196] ConFuzzled, "T-Shirt Contest," ConFuzzled 2008, Jul. 09, 2008. https://web.archive.org/web/20080709044844/http://www.confuzzled.org.uk/content/T-Shirt+-Contest

[197] K. Grey, "ConFuzzled 2008: Tori Reports," Furtean Times, Jul. 01, 2008. [Online]. Available: https://www.flayrah.com/3328/confuzzled-2008-tori-reports

[198] alexf0x, "ConFuzzled 2008," ConFuzzled 2008, Jun. 25, 2008. https://alexf0x.livejournal.com/19436.html

[199] Tungro, "ConFuzzled Convention LiveJournal," We've Hit a Milestone!, Aug. 07, 2009. https://confuzzledlj.livejournal.com/29319.html

[200] K. Grey, "ConFuzzled '09 Has Sold Out," Furtean Times, Jan. 14, 2009. [Online]. Available: https://www.flayrah.com/3238/confuzzled-09-has-sold-out

[201] K. Grey, "ConFuzzled Announces 2009 Schedule," Furtean Times, Oct. 31, 2008. [Online]. Available: https://www.flayrah.com/3197/confuzzled-announces-2009-schedule

[202] Fairlight, "Pawpet.de," LSD—Lionel Scritchie's Dormitory, Jul. 20, 2000. http://www.pawpet.de/ef6/welcome.html

[203] Utlah, Ed., "PawPet of Dreams," in ConFuzzled 2009 Official Conbook, ConFuzzled UK Ltd, 2009.

[204] FurbleFox, "UKFur Forums," ConFuzzled 2009, May 27, 2009. https://forum.ukfur.org/topic/16825-confuzzled-2009/

[205] ConFuzzled UK Ltd, "ConFuzzled 2009 Attendee List," ConFuzzled 2009—Attendee List, May 22, 2009. https://web.archive.org/web/20090522040107/http://confuzzled.org.uk:80/content/en/Attendee+List (accessed Apr. 07, 2021).

[206] Manchester. ConFuzzled 2010 Preview, (May 29, 2009). [Trailer]. Available: https://www.youtube.com/watch?v=mW4U41Vrwyg

[207] ConFuzzled UK Ltd, "October 2009," ConFuzzled Focus, vol. 2009, no. 1, Oct. 2009. [Online]. Available: https://web.archive.org/web/20100108011533/http://confuzzled.org.uk/setup/files/confuzzledfocus.pdf

[208] Tungro, "ConFuzzled Convention LiveJournal," ConFuzzled 2010 Tickets Still Available, Apr. 22, 2010. https://confuzzledlj.livejournal.com/60515.html

[209] Twll, Ed., ConFuzzled 2017 Official Conbook. ConFuzzled UK Ltd, 2017.

[210] D. Cooke, "ConFuzzled Convention LiveJournal," A Message from the Board of Directors, Nov. 26, 2009. https://confuzzledlj.livejournal.com/52920.html

[211] ConFuzzled UK Ltd, "December 2009," ConFuzzled Focus, vol. 2009, no. 3, Dec. 2009.

[212] Greenreaper, "ConFuzzled Convention LiveJournal," Latest Volcanic Ash Update (0415 UTC Thursday), May 05, 2010. https://confuzzledlj.livejournal.com/62398.html

[213] BBF TV ConFuzzled 2010 Part 2, (Jun. 21, 2010). [Documentary]. Available: https://video.bigbluefox-media.com/cont-cf2010.html

[214] K. Grey, "Tablecloth Smashes ConFuzzled Auction Record," Furtean Times, May 10, 2010. [Online].

Available: https://web.archive.org/web/20100625034928/http://www.furteantimes.com:80/r/139_tablecloth_smashes_confuzzled_auction_record

215 Greenreaper, "ConFuzzled Donates £6,200 after £2,000 Bid for Tablecloth," *Flayrah*, May 10, 2010. [Online]. Available: https://www.flayrah.com/3043/confuzzled-donates-%C2%A36200-after-%C2%A32000-bid-tablecloth

216 Matt Lion, "Update on the Hotel Takeover," ConFuzzled, Jan. 24, 2011. [Online]. Available: https://web.archive.org/web/20110325100555/http://www.confuzzled.org.uk/speakeasy/2011/01/24/update-on-the-hotel-takeover/

217 Matt Lion, "The ConFuzzled Venue Takeover," ConFuzzled, Feb. 26, 2011. [Online]. Available: https://web.archive.org/web/20110228092154/http://www.confuzzled.org.uk/speakeasy/

218 ConFuzzled UK Ltd, "ConFuzzled 2011: 400 Attendees Confirmed," Twitter, Feb. 27, 2011. https://twitter.com/cfconvention/status/41823238820597761 (accessed Jan. 11, 2023).

219 Confuzzled 2011 Closing Ceremony 1 of 2, (May 18, 2011). Accessed: Jan. 11, 2023. [Online Video]. Available: https://www.youtube.com/watch?v=xb0zGiWX6XE

220 ConFuzzled UK Ltd, "ConFuzzled 2011 Attendee List & Statistics," Statistics. https://web.archive.org/web/20190521182846/https://reg.confuzzled.org.uk/2011/

221 Nall, "Charity Update Announcement," ConFuzzled, Aug. 31, 2011. [Online]. Available: http://www.confuzzled.org.uk/premiere/2011/08/31/charity-update-announcement/

222 Matt Lion, "Welcome!," ConFuzzled: The Silver Screen, Aug. 12, 2011. [Online]. Available: http://www.confuzzled.org.uk/premiere/2011/08/12/welcome/

223 ConFuzzled UK Ltd, "CFz 2012 Sold Out," Twitter, Apr. 15, 2012. https://twitter.com/cfconvention/status/191647199384440832

224 OzKangaroo, Brok Badger—Confuzzled. 2011. [Online]. Available: https://www.furaffinity.net/view/6597111/

225 Mangusu, "Chronicles of the Mongoose Prince," Confuzzled and My Adventure in the UK: Warning Super Long Journal, May 31, 2012. https://mangusu.livejournal.com/72933.html

226 Dash Tiger, "Dash Tiger's Journal," Worst Day of My Life—Fuck You Immigration, Feb. 28, 2013. https://www.furaffinity.net/journal/4388360/

227 Twll, Ed., ConFuzzled 2013 Official Conbook. ConFuzzled UK Ltd, 2013.

228 Hinckley Island Hotel. Ode to ConFuzzled, (May 30, 2013). [Online Video]. Available: https://www.youtube.com/watch?v=e69_7KeXk-A

229 Hinckley Island Hotel. ConFuzzled 2013 Closing Ceremony, (Jun. 03, 2013). [Online Video]. Available: https://www.youtube.com/watch?v=HqjMnlFP0VE

230 Rallicat, "ConFuzzled 2013," Announcing ConFuzzled 2014, and Our New Home!, Jun. 02, 2013. http://2013.confuzzled.org.uk/2013/06/announcing-confuzzled-2014-and-our-new-home/

231 Twll, Ed., ConFuzzled 2014 Official Conbook. ConFuzzled UK Ltd, 2014.

232 TheLupineOne, "CFz 2014 Closing Ceremony," Twitter, May 26, 2014. https://twitter.com/TheLupineOne/status/470928779150643200

233 Twll, Ed., ConFuzzled 2015 Official Conbook. ConFuzzled UK Ltd, 2015.

234 CFz2015—Closing Ceremony, (2015). Accessed: Mar. 28, 2021. [Online Video]. Available: https://www.youtube.com/watch?v=NlMFqpJuNIs

235 Hinckley Island Hotel. ConFuzzled 2017 Opening Ceremony, (May 26, 2017). [Online Video]. Available: https://confuzzled.tv/watch/2017_Opening_Ceremony

236 ConFuzzled Story Animation,

(May 26, 2017). [Animation]. Available: https://www.youtube.com/watch?v=Abfgzh1FgkU&t=1s

[237] 'Volunteers Repair Gentleshaw Wildlife Centre After Animals Killed in Fire," *Midlands Today*, BBC, Staffordshire, Mar. 25, 2019. [News Report]. Available: https://www.youtube.com/watch?v=YCjnqTWj_Lw

[238] RizzoRat, "Gentleshaw Wildlife Sanctuary Visit," Twitter, Jun. 23, 2019. https://twitter.com/RizzoRattie/stat1142903310770483202

[239] MadeByMercury, "Brok v2 Public Reveal," Twitter, May 24, 2019. https://twitter.com/MadeByMercury/us/1132016692706586625

[240] Birmingham. Closing Ceremony from Confuzzled 2019, (May 28, 2019). [Online Video]. Available: https://www.youtube.com/watch?v=YCjnqTWj_Lw

[241] Ixis and I. Wolf, "Scotland to Get Its First Furry Convention," *Furtean Times*, Feb. 18, 2009. [Online]. Available: https://www.flayrah.com/3246/scotland-get-its-first-furry-convention

[242] Shining River, "ScotiaCon resets date, website," Flayrah, Jul. 19, 2010. [Online]. Available: http://www.flayrah.com/3103/scotiacon-resets-date-website

[243] ScotiaCon 2011 Official—Part 1, (2011). [Conference]. Available: https://www.youtube.com/watch?v=g8OIGKDI8Ic

[244] Equium, "Equium's Journal," ScotiaCon Episode III: The Whiskey and the Rain, Jul. 17, 2011. https://www.furaffinity.net/journal/2534778/

[245] ScotiaCon 2011 Official—Part 2, (2011). [Conference]. Available: https://www.youtube.com/watch?v=eQkIcZZsuOA

[246] Equium, "Equium's Journal," ScotiaCon Episode IV: The Very Very Long Goodbye (+ Summary), Jul. 19, 2011. https://www.furaffinity.net/journal/2534778/

[247] ScotiaCon, "ScotiaCon 2012 Website," ScotiaCon | 27th—30th July 2012, Jul. 18, 2012. https://web.archive.org/web/20120718170040/http://www.scotiacon.co.uk/

[248] Smirnoff, "The Highland Cats," Scotiacon 2012 General Thread, Aug. 07, 2012. https://forum.ukfur.org/topic/33496-scotiacon-2012-general-thread/?do=findComment&comment=1377603

[249] SilverFoxWolf, "Scotiacon 2013," Scotiacon 2013—Introducing Our Guests, Mar. 18, 2013. https://forum.ukfur.org/topic/42203-scotiacon-2013-introducing-our-guests/

[250] SilverFoxWolf, "ScotiaCon 2014," Scotiacon 2014 7th–9th November 2014, Jan. 31, 2014. https://forum.ukfur.org/topic/45148-scotiacon-2014-7th–9th-november-2014/

[251] ScotiaCon, "ScotiaCon 2015 Attendence Count," Twitter, Nov. 11, 2015. https://twitter.com/Scotiacon/status/664433147900256256

[252] ScotiaCon, "ScotiaCon 2015 Charity Total," Twitter, Nov. 11, 2015. https://twitter.com/ScotiaCon/status/665981627269558272

[253] ScotiaCon, "ScotiaCon 2016 Numbers," Twitter, Nov. 21, 2016. https://twitter.com/ScotiaCon/status/800754131946311680

[254] Scotiacon 2019 Closing Ceremony, (Nov. 17, 2019). [Online Video]. Available: https://www.youtube.com/watch?v=i7RxWX2vSnA

[255] Glasgow. Scotiacon 2021 Hotel Reveal, (Nov. 29, 2019). [Online Video]. Available: https://www.youtube.com/watch?v=8EC9W99Nq_4

[256] P. Sykes, "August 6th 2004—Furry Camping Trip," Wolfie Fox's Furmeet Photo Gallery, Sep. 24, 2004. https://web.archive.org/web/20040924105150/http://www.furnation.com/Wolfie_Fox/August_6th_2004_Furry_Camping_Trip.htm

[257] K. Wulfgar, "UKFur Community Calendar," UKFur Camp 2009, Dec. 2008. https://forum.ukfur.org/calendar/event/82-ukfur-camp-2009/

[258] K. Wulfgar, "Furstival History," History—Furstival 21st—25th July 2011, Oct. 13, 2011. https://web.archive.org/web/20101013053814/http://furstival2011.webs.com/history.htm

[259] K. Wulfgar, "UKFur Forums,"

Furstival 2011 Registration Open, May 21, 2011. https://forum.ukfur.org/topic/23895-ukfur-camp-back-by-popular-demand/

260 Jess Lyra, "South Fur Camp 2008 Gallery," SouthfurCamp, May 16, 2014. https://web.archive.org/web/20140516052421/http://southfurcamp.co.nf/gallery.php?year=2008

261 Jess Lyra, "UKFur Forums," Southfur Camp 8 19-21 June, Feb. 11, 2015. https://forum.ukfur.org/topic/47621-very-important-update-plz-readsouthfur-camp-8-19-21-june/

262 P. O'Furr, "The Furclub Survey," Dogpatch Press, vol. (Last Updated in 2018), Oct. 10, 2014. [Online]. Available: https://dogpatch.press/2014/10/10/the-furclub-survey/

263 Nicole Mazzola, "Candy Raver Subculture," Dec. 2014, Accessed: Jan. 13, 2023. [Online]. Available: https://issuu.com/nicolemazzola/docs/final_report_ravers_pdf

264 J. Foxx, "Jasper Foxie's Life," Furry Rave Is On!, May 24, 2008. https://red-fox-gt.livejournal.com/27134.html

265 C. Waters (Shirik), "UKFur Community Calendar," UK Fur Rave—Bristol, Nov. 07, 2008. https://forum.ukfur.org/calendar/event/37-uk-fur-rave-bristol/

266 J. Foxx, "UKFur Community Calendar," Ukfur Rave 3!, Feb. 27, 2009. https://forum.ukfur.org/calendar/event/56-ukfur-rave-3/

267 JasperFoxx, "Messages on Telegram," Jun. 17, 2021.

268 J. Foxx, Anthropuppy, and Ravell, "FRANTIC EUFURIA LTD," North Somerset, Certificate of Incorporation of a Private Limited Company Company Number 07720951, Jul. 2011.

269 Awkore, "Frantic Eufuria DVD," Frantic EuFuria DVD ~ Standard Mode, Dec. 12, 2010.

270 Rayne Blue, "Photos from Frantic Eufuria 8," Rayne Blue Fursuiting, Mar. 26, 2014. https://raynebluefur.tumblr.com/post/80843718020/a-couple-of-photos-taken-of-me-by-ant-a-great

271 Weremoco and Taelion, "About What the Fluff," *What the Fluff,* Mar. 25, 2016. https://web.archive.org/web/20160325210407/http://www.whatthefluff.org.uk/#!about/ct75

272 P. O'Furr, "What the Fluff Fur Dance," Dogpatch Press, Apr. 13, 2015. [Online]. Available: https://dogpatch.press/2015/04/13/what-the-fluff-fur-dance/

273 Weremoco, "What the Fluff!?," What The Fluff!? Furdance, 1st November 2014, Southampton UK, Aug. 17, 2014. https://www.furaffinity.net/journal/6034135/

274 WhatTheFluff Furdance, "WTF 5—The Spy Who Fluffed Me!," Twitter, May 23, 2016. https://twitter.com/wtffurdance/status/734852538978164736

275 WhatTheFluff Furdance, "WTF 6—The Half-Fluff Prince," Twitter, Sep. 02, 2017. https://twitter.com/wtffurdance/status/903909797338255362

276 Great Furscape 2012, (Sep. 18, 2013). Accessed: Feb. 26, 2022. [Online Video]. Available: https://www.youtube.com/watch?v=-tXMsqlUvTw

277 "The Great Furscape Official Website," Great Furscape 2013, Aug. 11, 2013. https://web.archive.org/web/20130811000906/http://greatfurscape.org.uk/index.php (accessed Feb. 26, 2022).

278 'Great Furscape Cancelled," Great Furscape 2014, Jan. 20, 2015. https://web.archive.org/web/20150120075505/http://greatfurscape.org.uk/ (accessed Feb. 26, 2022).

279 S. Hatton, P. Vaughan, and S. O'Shaughnessy, "FURVENTION," Merseyside, Certificate of Incorporation of a Private Limited Company Company No. 8844512, Jan. 2014.

280 FurVention, "FurVention Website," FurVention Convention, Oct. 14, 2014. https://web.archive.org/web/20141014195931/http://furvention.org.uk/

281 FurVention, "FurVention Guest of Honor Confirmed," Twitter, Aug. 08, 2014. https://twitter.com/FurVention/status/497770223110717440

282 FurVention, "FurVention Update," Jan. 03, 2015. https://www.facebook.com/FurVention/posts/711248455663003

283 Zippy's Vlogs #5 || Furvention 2015, (Feb. 01, 2015). [Online Video]. Available: https://www.youtube.com/watch?v=Quzgp3uAhOc

284 FurVention—Fursuit Walk—2015, (Feb. 04, 2015). [Online Video]. Available: https://www.youtube.com/watch?v=cIlaAX9-8Nw

285 FurVention, "Furvention 2 Venue & Date," Apr. 05, 2015. https://www.facebook.com/FurVention/posts/765449483576233

286 FurVention, "Furvention 2 Cancelled," Sep. 02, 2015. https://www.facebook.com/FurVention/posts/838312632956584

287 FurVention, "Coming Soon #FV2020," Twitter, Jun. 16, 2018. https://twitter.com/FurVention/at/1008105079164100610

288 Wild North 2018, (Sep. 28, 2018). [Online Video]. Available: https://www.youtube.com/watch?v=uV29C-u83Ar0

289 Z. Eisenhuf, "Wild North Facebook Page," Wild North 2019 – Post Event Newsletter, Oct. 02, 2019. https://www.facebook.com/groups/WildNorthUK/permalink/847217715675647/

290 J. Foxx, "Furcation Facebook Group," Furcation Reveal, Dec. 01, 2014. https://www.facebook.com/groups/Furcationevent/permalink/875204595863466/

291 Furcation, "Furcation FAQ," FAQs | Furcation: A new breed of furry event, Mar. 05, 2016. https://web.archive.org/web/20160305212416/http://furcation.org.uk/FAQ

292 Furcation, "Furcation Early Registration Numbers," Twitter, Feb. 12, 2015. https://twitter.com/Furcationevent/status/565871898178125825

293 B. Goldenrod, Frankie Ferret Model Sheet. 2015. [Online]. Available: https://www.furaffinity.net/view/15950908/

294 J. Foxx, "Furcation Facebook Group," Furcation Cancelled, Jun. 05, 2015. https://www.facebook.com/groups/Furcationevent/permalink/981395125244412/

295 Furcation, "Potential New Furcation Venue," Twitter, Oct. 10, 2015. https://twitter.com/Furcationevent/status/652836597457649664

296 Furcation, "Furcation 2016 Announcement," FURCATION 2016 ANNOUNCED | Furcation: A new breed of furry event, Mar. 01, 2016. https://web.archive.org/web/20160307162549/http://furcation.org.uk/

297 J. Foxx and Anthropuppy, "FURCATION LTD," Bristol, Certificate of Incorporation of a Private Limited Company Company Number 10226988, Jun. 2016.

298 Furcation, "Furcation Budget Chalet Requests," Twitter, Jul. 01, 2016. https://twitter.com/Furcationevent/status/748778085797863424

299 J. Foxx, "Furcation Facebook Group," Furcation 2016 Moving Venue, Jul. 19, 2016. https://www.facebook.com/groups/Furcationevent/permalink/1217450654972190/

300 Furcation, "Furcation 2016 Sponsor/Attendee Count," Twitter, Sep. 06, 2016. https://twitter.com/Furcationevent/status/773055353554624512

301 Furcation, "Furcation 2016 Secret World Charity Donation," Twitter, Nov. 18, 2016. https://twitter.com/Furcationevent/status/799739827021172736

302 Cueball and Cisco the Clown, "JFTW Sales Pitch," Twitter, Jul. 18, 2015. https://twitter.com/CISCO_Clown/status/622443901417353216

303 Cueball, Bristol Bigglesworth, and Tokala, "JFTW UK LTD," Bristol, Certificate of Incorporation of a Private Limited Company, Company Number 9668582, Jul. 2015.

304 JFTW, "JFTW 5 Months of Planning," Twitter, Sep. 02, 2015. https://twitter.com/jftwconvention/status/639199025523224576

305 JFTW 2016 FAQ Vlog, (Nov. 29, 2015). [Online Video]. Available: https://www.youtube.com/

watch?v=uLz0JuSlZLg

[306] JFTW, "JFTW 2016 Reaches 100 Attendees," Twitter, Dec. 31, 2015. https://twitter.com/jftwconvention/status/682504730241822721

[307] JFTW, "JFTW 2016 Fursuit Walk," Fursuit Walk, Mar. 26, 2016. https://web.archive.org/web/20160326044458/https://justfurtheweekend.org.uk/attending/fursuit-walk/

[308] A. Vance, "JustFurTheWeekend Facebook Group," Mar. 25, 2016. https://www.facebook.com/JustFurTheWeekend/posts/778515232282985

[309] JFTW, "JFTW 2017 Registration Opens," Twitter, Jul. 01, 2016. https://twitter.com/jftwconvention/status/748954340505821185

[310] JFTW, "JFTW 2017 Announced 300 Attendees," Twitter, Jan. 17, 2017. https://twitter.com/jftwconvention/status/840952700745449475

[311] Medosai and J. Foxx, Eds., Welcome to Furcation 2017! Furcation Ltd, 2017.

[312] JFTW, "JFTW 2018 Attendee Count," Twitter, Jul. 10, 2018. https://twitter.com/jftwconvention/as/1016686672874962944

[313] JFTW, "JFTW 2017 Pricing Options," Pricing—Just Fur the Weekend 2017, Nov. 11, 2016. https://web.archive.org/web/20161111001617/https://justfurtheweekend.org.uk/pricing/

[314] CosmoSnowmew, "UK Furry Convention Price Comparison Rev 3," Twitter, Aug. 27, 2017. https://twitter.com/CosmoSnowmew/status/901833675813380096

[315] T. Fox, "JFTW 2018 Attendance Only price," Twitter, Jun. 12, 2018. https://twitter.com/Timmyfox/status/1006652945650331649

[316] JFTW, "JFTW 2019 Results," Twitter, May 12, 2019. https://twitter.com/jftwconvention/stat1127639337192099841

[317] Bently Racune and J. Foxx, Eds., Furcation 2018. Furcation Ltd, 2018.

[318] Furcation, "Furcation 2018 Charity Total," Twitter, Oct. 17, 2018.

[319] XavierFox, "Furcation 2019 Auction Total," Twitter, Nov. 10, 2019. https://twitter.com/XavierFox19/us/1193632931555807233

[320] Erin, "The Fursuit Database," Shelby, Feb. 16, 2009. https://db.fursuit.me/index.php?c=viewsuit&id=1385

[321] B.H, "The Fursuit Database," Super B_H, Oct. 16, 2016. https://db.fursuit.me/index.php?c=viewsuit&id=140

[322] M. Hay, "Who Makes Those Intricate, Expensive Furry Suits?," VICE, Jul. 27, 2017. [Online]. Available: https://www.vice.com/en_us/article/7x9njz/who-makes-those-intricate-expensive-furry-suits

[323] Patrick R. Benesh-Liu, "The Animal Outside Us All: Fursuiting and the Furry Culture," Ornament, vol. 33, no. 5, 2010.

[324] FatKraken, "Fatkraken," Minami, Mar. 13, 2005. https://fatkraken.livejournal.com/17334.html

[325] FatKraken, "Cosplay Island | View Costume | Fatkraken—Link Wolf," Cosplay Island, Dec. 16, 2011. https://web.archive.org/web/20111216101501/http://cosplayisland.co.uk/costume/view/37

[326] Dasker, "Blue Fox Fursuits—Price Guide," Sep. 29, 2010. https://web.archive.org/web/20100929171256/http://www.bf-fursuits.com/PriceGuide.html

[327] Dasker, "Prices," blue-fox-fursuits, 2019. https://www.bf-fursuits.com/prices

[328] P. O'Furr, "$50,000 FURSUIT: Crypto-Fueled Bidding Smashes Auction Record at The Dealers Den," Dogpatch Press, Jun. 04, 2021. [Online]. Available: https://dogpatch.ress/2021/06/04/50000-fursuit-record-dealers-den/

[329] C. Plante, S. Reysen, S. Roberts, and K. Gerbasi, Fur Science! A Summary of Five Years of Research from the International Anthropomorphic Research Project. Waterloo, Ontario, Canada: Social Sciences and Humanities Research Council of Canada, 2017.

[330] C. Plante, S. Roberts, and K. Gerbasi,

"Summer 2020 Survey," *FurScience*, 2020. https://furscience.com/research-findings/appendix-1-previous-research/summer-2020/ (accessed Nov. 21, 2021).

331 UltraFox, The King Is Dead. 2013. [Digital]. Available: https://www.furaffinity.net/view/10011776/

332 T. Rakesh, "About Yiffstar.com," YIFFSTAR—the Yiffy Story Archive, Dec. 30, 2008. https://web.archive.org/web/20081230214839/http:/www.yiffstar.com/index.yiff?pid=16882 (accessed Jan. 21, 2021).

333 S. Silva, "Who We Are," Furry Writers' Guild, Jan. 30, 2013. https://web.archive.org/web/20130130080356/http:/www.furrywritersguild.com:80/home/who-we-are (accessed Jan. 21, 2021).

334 '2011 Cóyotl Award Winners," The Cóyotl Awards, Mar. 01, 2011. https://coyotlawards.com/2011-winners/ (accessed Jan. 21, 2021).

335 "Award Rules," The Cóyotl Awards, Dec. 17, 2020. https://coyotlawards.com/award-rules/ (accessed Jan. 21, 2021).

336 "The Ursa Major Award Winners," 2011. https://ursamajorawards.org/UMA_2012.htm (accessed Jan. 21, 2021).

337 M. F. Cross, Dog Country. Independently published, 2020.

338 Huskyteer, "Tiger Light | Pink Fox Publications," 2013. https://web.archive.org/web/20130223033416/http:/pinkfoxpublications.net:80/tiger-light/ (accessed Jan. 21, 2021).

339 Heat. Sofawolf Press, 2012.

340 ROAR, vol. 4. Bad Dog Books, 2012.

341 The Furry Future. FurPlanet Productions, 2015.

342 Gods with Fur. FurPlanet Productions, 2016.

343 Klepsydra, "About the Band," *The Donutsh*, 2012. http://donutsh.com/about.php (accessed Jan. 21, 2021).

344 Klepsydra, "Real Studio Band Goshwowboyohboy," *The Donutsh*, Oct. 28, 2009. https://the-donutsh.livejournal.com/2523.html (accessed Jan. 21, 2021).

345 Klepsydra, "We Are All Strange Jane (EP)'. Mar. 21, 2012. Accessed: Jan. 21, 2021. [Online]. Available: https://donutsh.bandcamp.com

346 FreyFox, CaveDweller, and The Colourless, "The Complete and Ultimate Raccoon Gang," Nov. 01, 2011.

347 RascallyBandit, "2018 Recap," *RascallyBandit's Journal*, Jan. 01, 2019. http://www.furaffinity.net/journal/9000426/ (accessed Jan. 21, 2021).

348 Edinburgh. THAT'S AMOORE, (Oct. 11, 2009). Accessed: Jan. 24, 2021. [Online Video]. Available: https://www.youtube.com/watch?v=Css7dDHVtGA

349 EZ Wolf, "Cast Page," Bitter Lake | Trust Is a Fickle Thing..., 2013. https://leorchn.github.io/archive/www.bitterlakethemovie.com/crew.html (accessed Jan. 24, 2021).

350 Fox Amoore, "Come Find Me—The Journey to Abbey Road," Indiegogo, 2013. http://www.indiegogo.com/projects/256698/fblk (accessed Jan. 24, 2021).

351 Come Find Me—Fox Amoore at Abbey Road Studios—A Documentary by EZwolf, (Feb. 23, 2014). Accessed: Jan. 24, 2021. [Online Video]. Available: https://www.youtube.com/watch?v=FmAyahigZVk

352 Fox Amoore, "The Dreamcatcher—The Journey Continues," Indiegogo, 2017. https://www.indiegogo.com/projects/1898516 (accessed Jan. 24, 2021).

353 Fox Amoore and J. Clark, "Hashtag, by Fox Amoore and Pepper Coyote," Fox Amoore, 2016. https://foxamoore.bandcamp.com/album/hashtag (accessed Jan. 24, 2021).

354 Making A Musical Tail, (Dec. 05, 2018). Accessed: Jan. 24, 2021. [Online Video]. Available: https://www.youtube.com/watch?v=_H1Ki39UMU

355 BLFC 2018: A Musical Tail, (May 13, 2018). Accessed: Jan. 16, 2023. [Online Video]. Available: https://www.youtube.com/watch?v=sGpmyaBH_Qo

356 Flain Falcon, Zim Skunk, and Puc, Interview with Mort L. Wombat, Episode 20. Clawcast, 2008. Accessed: Jan. 25, 2021. [Podcast]. Available: http://

www.furaffinity.net/view/1028214/

357 Mort L. Wombat, "Poll Positions," toomuchblog, Oct. 19, 2006. https://toomuchblog.livejournal.com/1115.html (accessed Jan. 25, 2021).

358 Mort L. Wombat, "Artist for Yiff! Musical," in Further Confusion 2007 Fur Your Eyes Only, Anthropomorphic Arts and Education, Inc, 2007, p. 48.

359 Edge, "Fursonality," Dec. 26, 2008. http://www.furaffinity.net/view/1829345/ (accessed Jan. 25, 2021).

360 'Events Listings for Goldsmiths Musical Theatre Showcase," TicketSource, Aug. 24, 2007. https://web.archive.org/web/20070824183337/http://www.ticketsource.co.uk/search/search-PromoterDetails.asp?promoter_id=289 (accessed Jan. 25, 2021).

361 'Yiff! & Stratford Street," The King's Head Theatre, Feb. 28, 2008. https://web.archive.org/web/20080228001242/http:/www.kingsheadtheatre.org:80/theatre-sun-mon-night-yiff.asp (accessed Jan. 25, 2021).

362 Mort L. Wombat, "Scenic," toomuchblog, Oct. 12, 2008. https://toomuchblog.livejournal.com/27670.html (accessed Jan. 25, 2021).

363 Mort L. Wombat, "timsaward's Channel," Youtube, Nov. 17, 2010. https://web.archive.org/web/20101117211947/https://www.youtube.com/user/timsaward#p/u (accessed Jan. 25, 2021).

364 D. R. Piasecki and P. O'Furr, "Furry Drama(tic Arts)—The Forgotten History of the Furry Musical, Part 1: Yiff!/," Dogpatch Press, Oct. 06, 2017. https://dogpatch.press/2017/10/06/furry-musical-yiff-furreality/ (accessed Jan. 25, 2021).

365 John Keller and Mary Lu Carnevale, "Cable Company Is Set to Plug into Internet," Wall Street Journal, New York, p. B1, Aug. 24, 1993.

366 Stuart Otterson and Axle, "BritFur. FM—British Furry Fandom Radio Station," Apr. 08, 2010. https://web.archive.org/web/20100408125036/http://britfur.fm/ (accessed Mar. 16, 2021).

367 Snack Meerkat and Ollie Pup, "WHO ARE WE," Furpile Radio, Feb. 12, 2015. https://web.archive.org/web/20150212205342/http://furpil-eradio.net/who.htm (accessed Feb. 18, 2021).

368 Snack Meerkat and Ollie Pup, "PREVIOUS SHOWS," Furpile Radio, Feb. 12, 2015. https://web.archive.org/web/20150212213436/http://furpil-eradio.net/SHOWS.htm (accessed Feb. 18, 2021).

369 Greenreaper, "Snack Raccoon Died in Breathplay Mishap, Reports Partner," Flayrah, Oct. 30, 2011. https://www.flayrah.com/3722/snack-raccoon-died-breathplay-mishap-reports-partner (accessed Feb. 23, 2022).

370 A. Grey, "The YouTube Furry War," Flayrah, Sep. 29, 2007. https://www.flayrah.com/3225/youtube-furry-war (accessed Mar. 16, 2021).

371 The Fandom EP4: Furry Youtube (Furry Documentary), (Apr. 13, 2019). Accessed: Mar. 16, 2021. [Online Video]. Available: https://www.youtube.com/watch?v=a-VaDw9xUCg

372 B. Brotman, "UNIVERSE OF THE MIND," Chicago Tribune, Sep. 02, 1991. [Online]. Available: https://www.chicagotribune.com/news/ct-xpm-1991-09-02-9103060021-story.html

373 'Confurence 8 News Report," NBC, Minnesota, 1997. [Online]. Available: https://www.youtube.com/watch?v=6h2IkMXMJXs

374 T. Fey, "SDCC FurDance reminder," alt.fan.furry, Jul. 20, 1997. https://groups.google.com/d/msg/alt.fan.furry/wrJbipm-ShE/cSv7GepniqMJ

375 E. Hohler, "I Married a Man Who Thinks He's a Wild Cat," Marie Claire, no. October 1997, pp. 28–34, Oct. 1997.

376 "Pressed Fur," PressedFur, Oct. 2002. https://web.archive.org/eb/20080725001713fw_/http://pressedfur.coolfreepages.com/press/index.html

377 'The Weasel," The Independent, Oct. 17, 1997. https://www.independent.co.uk/life-style/the-weasel-1236446.html (accessed Nov. 25, 2021).

[378] K. Meyer, Foxy, and D. Bell, "British Journalists at CF9," alt.fan.furry, Jan. 23, 1998. https://groups.google.com/d/msg/alt.fan.furry/VWjPrQiAbeA/wRnGd6MWwacJ

[379] B. Borrows, "Heavy Petting," *Loaded*, April 1998, pp. 88–92.

[380] J. Quittner, "Johnny Manhattan Meets the Furry Muckers," *WIRED*, Mar. 1994.

[381] L. Theroux, "Weekend Pass," *The Guardian*, May 8, 1999, p. 12.

[382] M. Merlino, S. Malcomson, and CannonFodder, "Debate over ConFurence and Accusations towards Merlino," Opinion: Misconceptions about the Origins of Furry Fandom, Jan. 08, 2011. http://www.flayrah.com/3377/opinion-misconceptions-about-origins-furry-fandom#comment-43966

[383] E. Kline, "Open Letter to Mark Merlino," Feb. 08, 1997. [Online]. Available: https://groups.google.com/g/alt.fan.furry/c/Jpxe_Jgm8-I/m/-sjVWvmlyYUJ

[384] UK. Eurotrash ConFurence 10 Segment, (Oct. 01, 1999). [Online Video]. Available: https://www.youtube.com/watch?v=Nh7EDdcQqdw

[385] E. Walsh, "Con Report: Mobicon Happened, and I Was There," The Mary Sue, May 30, 2015. https://www.themarysue.com/mobicon-happened/

[386] E. Morrison, "In the Beginning, There Was Fan Fiction: From the Four Gospels to Fifty Shades," *The Guardian*, Aug. 13, 2012. [Online]. Available: https://www.theguardian.com/books/2012/aug/13/fan-fiction-fifty-shades-grey

[387] B. Ashcraft and L. Plunkett, Cosplay World. Prestel Publishing, 2014.

[388] M. Merlino, "Califur Material," Dec. 02, 2022.

[389] Patch O'Furr, "A 1990's Fax to Troll Confurence Shows How Long There's Been Culture War with Furry Fandom," *Dogpatch Press*, Jul. 27, 2020. https://dogpatch.press/2020/07/27/1990s-fax-troll-confurence/ (accessed Dec. 03, 2022).

[390] L. Graf, "Public Apology—Please Read," alt.fan.furry, Feb. 23, 1997.

https://groups.google.com/g/alt.fan.furry/c/OP5luQv3RsU/m/_Ry-2fILQSo4J

[391] "There's a Persistent Rumor That Furry Fandom Was Perverted by a Bad Ad for ConFurence.," *Dogpatch Press*, Aug. 31, 2015. https://dogpatch.press/2015/08/31/rumor-ad-for-confurence/ (accessed Dec. 04, 2022).

[392] Danhan and P. Rhodes, "Debunking the Black Sheets Page," Opinion: Misconceptions about the Origins of Furry Fandom, Jan. 08, 2011. http://www.flayrah.com/3377/opinion-misconceptions-about-origins-furry-fandom#comment-43966

[393] C. Trotman, "This Sordid Little Business (The Furry Manifesto)," Dec. 23, 2003. https://web.archive.org/web/20031223070434/http://burnedfur.mv.com/manifesto.html

[394] Squeerat, "A Modest Proposal," Aug. 14, 2003. https://web.archive.org/web/20030814211812/http://burnedfur.mv.com/proposal.html

[395] P. Schorn, "Who Dealt This Mess?," Feb. 21, 2009. https://web.archive.org/web/20090221070614/http://burnedfur.mv.com/dealt.html (accessed Dec. 05, 2021).

[396] R. Guthrie, "In Defense of the Burned Furs.," alt.fan.furry, Mar. 10, 2001. https://groups.google.com/g/alt.fan.furry/c/6SlYALVFWqw/m/r6ADil9tmjgJ

[397] P. Schorn, "Got Spooge?," alt.fan.furry, Aug. 12, 2000. https://groups.google.com/g/alt.fan.furry/c/AwHPbVO4hu8/m/NpK5cpXWK8QJ

[398] A. Kennedy and R. Stohldrier, "FUR: What My Friend Has Sent to *Vanity Fair*.," alt.fan.furry, Mar. 12, 2001. https://groups.google.com/g/alt.fan.furry/c/qdivnrC3J_A

[399] E. Blumrich, "An Open Letter to *Vanity Fair*," alt.fan.furry, Feb. 22, 2001. https://groups.google.com/g/alt.fan.furry/c/3HU9Bi9yfLA/m/EsqeKZd-6h3YJ

[400] D. Exline, "[FUR]Media Trolls—Granada," alt.fan.furry, Feb. 16, 2001. https://groups.google.com/g/alt.fan.furry/c/a6zscueLnjQ/m/thCtgco-adHMJ

401 London. The Furverts, (Mar. 30, 2001).

402 J. Doolittle, "Midwest Furfest Clarification," Jan. 09, 2002. Accessed: Dec. 06, 2021. [Online]. Available: https://web.archive.org/web/20040606123202/http://pressed-fur.coolfreepages.com/comments/doolittle-letter.html

403 S. Wells, "Is Your Team's Mascot a Furvert?," *The Guardian*, Jan. 12, 2005. [Online]. Available: http://www.theguardian.com/sport/2005/jan/12/stevenwells

404 "Real Life: We're at It Like Rabbits," *The Sun*, Apr. 03, 2007. Accessed: May 16, 2021. [Online]. Available: https://web.archive.org/web/20070821220304/http://www.thesun.co.uk:80/arti/0,,11000-2007140884,00.html

405 "'Furring' Is New Sex Craze for Perverts," *The Metro*, Jun. 27, 2007. [Online]. Available: http://www.metro.co.uk/metrosexual/article.html?in_article_id=54924&in_page_id=8&expand=true#StartComments

406 A. Fox, "Super Furry Animals," *Bizarre*, no. 137, May 2008, pp. 79–83.

407 Lisa Scott, "Unleash Your Inner Sexual Beast," *Metro*, Jun. 17, 2008. [Online]. Available: https://metro.co.uk/2008/06/17/unleash-your-inner-sexual-beast-193054/

408 "Parent Death Plot Man Is Detained," *BBC News*, Jan. 07, 2010. [Online]. Available: http://news.bbc.co.uk/1/hi/england/lancashire/8446431.stm

409 "Son Plotted to Kill Parents with Internet Friend," *Metro*, Jul. 20, 2009. [Online]. Available: https://metro.co.uk/2009/07/20/son-plotted-to-kill-parents-with-internet-friend-281836/

410 D. Winterman, "Who Are the Furries?," *BBC News Magazine*, Nov. 13, 2009. [Online]. Available: http://news.bbc.co.uk/1/hi/magazine/8355287.stm

411 A.A.L.A, "Winners and Nominees," Ursa Major Awards, 2009. https://ursamajorawards.org/UMA_2009.htm

412 "10x10 Things about 10 Years of the Magazine," *BBC News*, Jul. 05, 2013. https://www.bbc.co.uk/news/magazine-23146086

413 "In 'Fursuit' of Happiness in Mexico," *BBC News*, BBC, Jul. 17, 2012. Accessed: Dec. 07, 2021. [Online]. Available: https://www.bbc.co.uk/news/av/world-latin-america-18872643

414 A. Vrydaghs, "Chat with Uncle Kage," Stumbles the Beerdragon, Sep. 11, 2006. https://omnibahumut.livejournal.com/12609.html

415 A. Hart, "Furrie Invasion: 2000 Fans Attended Eurofeurence in Berlin to Celebrate Their Love of Anthropomorphic Animals," *The Independent*, Aug. 26, 2014. Accessed: Dec. 10, 2021. [Online]. Available: https://www.independent.co.uk/arts-entertainment/films/features/furrie-invasion-2000-fans-attended-eurofeurence-in-berlin-to-celebrate-their-love-of-anthropomorphic-animals-9689926.html

416 "Adults Dress as Sexualised Bears and Cats at Eurofurence 2014," *Mail Online*, Aug. 27, 2014. Accessed: Dec. 10, 2021. [Online]. Available: https://www.dailymail.co.uk/news/article-2734854/Cats-wearing-stockings-bears-satin-corsets-2-000-adults-dress-sexualised-cuddly-toys-bizarre-festival.html

417 M. Smith, "How Left or Right-Wing Are the UK's Newspapers?," *The Times*, Mar. 06, 2017. Accessed: Dec. 10, 2021. [Online]. Available: https://www.thetimes.co.uk/article/how-left-or-right-wing-are-britain-s-newspapers-8vmlr27tm

418 "Metro UK," Media Bias/Fact Check, Sep. 28, 2021. https://mediabiasfactcheck.com/metro-uk/ (accessed Dec. 10, 2021).

419 C. Macdonald, "A Quarter of Furries Are Christian, and 4% Say the Fandom Is about Sex," *Mail Online*, Nov. 22, 2017. http://www.dailymail.co.uk/~/article-5109323/index.html (accessed Dec. 10, 2021).

420 G. du Cann, "Stunning US Navy Woman Spends Her Free Time Masquerading as a GIANT HUSKY DOG but Insists It's Not a Sexual Fetish," *The Sun*, Nov. 19, 2018. [Online].

Available: https://www.thesun.co.uk/news/7777170/stunning-us-navy-woman-spends-her-free-time-masquerading-as-a-giant-husky-dog-but-insists-its-not-a-sexual-fetish/

[421] T. Davidson, "Raunchy Couple Caught Making X-Rated Motions during Furry Costume Convention," Daily Mirror, Apr. 10, 2018. Accessed: Nov. 10, 2020. [Online]. Available: https://www.mirror.co.uk/news/us-news/raunchy-couple-caught-making-x-12335878

[422] Kino, "Direct Messages between Nikki and Pat Purcell of Daily Mirror," @KinoShepsky, Apr. 10, 2018. https://twitter.com/KinoShepsky/status/983787575575044097 (accessed Nov. 10, 2020).

[423] Kharos, "Direct Message between Raven Saunt and Kharos," @Khar0s, Apr. 09, 2019. https://twitter.com/Khar0s/us/1115564348779507712 (accessed Nov. 10, 2020).

[424] CosmoSnowmew, "If They Had Honest Intentions, Why Would They Lie about Who They're Working For?," @CosmoSnep, Apr. 10, 2019. https://twitter.com/CosmoSnep/us/1115899626819936256 (accessed Nov. 10, 2020).

[425] J. Collins, "The Daily Mail Trainee Reporter Scheme Now Open," Journo Resources, Dec. 10, 2019. https://www.journoresources.org.uk/job/daily-mail-trainee-reporters-grad-scheme/ (accessed Nov. 10, 2020).

[426] M. Hirtes, C. Destanion, and A. Chinnici, "CF Goers … BEWARE!!!," alt.fan.furry, Mar. 30, 1999. https://groups.google.com/forum/#!msg/alt.fan.furry/pWCO7q9-P-A/yQw0uh6n-wPoJ

[427] SlyCat, "Comment from SlyCat," Fursuit, Mar. 11, 2005. https://fursuit.livejournal.com/562944.htm-read=4416000#t4416000

[428] D. L. Exline, "Beasley / Ruby Wax (was: press to videotape furry con?)," alt.fan.furry, Dec. 19, 1999. https://groups.google.com/g/alt.fan.furry/c/8Vumplb_h-k (accessed Jan. 04, 2022).

[429] 'Interview with Chik'Ki," Frontal, Channel 4, London, Sep. 01, 2000.

[430] 'Furry TV," alt.lifestyle.furry, Aug. 29, 2000. https://groups.google.com/g/alt.lifestyle.furry/c/SStAIQ404P-g/m/i-CrTkTTxzMJ (accessed Mar. 05, 2022).

[431] B. Salter, "[FUR]Media Trolls—Granada," alt.fan.furry, Feb. 18, 2001. https://groups.google.com/g/alt.fan.furry/c/a6zscueLnjQ/m/gAZXg3IkbyUJ

[432] Lone Wolf, "Re: [MidFurs] Lone Wolf...," Jan. 29, 2001. [Online]. Available: https://archive.org/details/ukfurmailinglists

[433] "Big Brother's Anna Nolan Gets Her Very Own BBC Series," BBC Press Office, Press Releases, Jan. 2002. Accessed: Jan. 18, 2022. [Online]. Available: https://www.bbc.co.uk/pressoffice/pressreleases/stories/2002/01_january/16/annainwonderland.shtml

[434] D. Exline, "Article on Confurence 11," alt.fan.furry, Apr. 28, 2000. https://groups.google.com/g/alt.fan.furry/c/4DJsyqmv-uQ/m/A7KeEf-bzEJQJ

[435] R. Castro, "Bio," Rick Castro Bio, Apr. 06, 2001. https://web.archive.org/web/20010406130136/http://rickcastro.com/bio.html

[436] E. Nikolaev, "Lupin4th Visions: "Dear Mr. Castro", Something about Rick Castro...," Lupin4th Visions, Feb. 2013. https://lupin4th.blogspot.com/2013/02/dear-mr-castro-something-about-rick.html

[437] "Pressed Fur: Reader Comments: Anonymous," Jan. 06, 2002. https://web.archive.org/web/20071110214743/http://pressedfur.coolfreepages.com/comments/anonymous-sex2k.html

[438] "See Hear," See Hear, BBC, London, Dec. 18, 2004.

[439] Zenneth, "Has Anyone Had This Email?," ukFur Boards, Jan. 31, 2008. https://forum.ukfur.org/topic/8198-has-anyone-had-this-email/ (accessed Jan. 07, 2022).

[440] Aigus, "UKFur Forums," This Itv Furry's Thing...., Feb. 14, 2011. https://forum.ukfur.org/topic/29892-

this-itv-furrys-thing/

441 ITV.com, "OMG! With Peaches Geldoff," 2011. http://www.itv.com/channels/itv2/itv2shows/omgwithpeachesgeldof/

442 midori8, "Hey Everybody It's the Tyra Banks Shoooooow!," Fursuit Lounge, Aug. 20, 2009. https://fursuit-lounge.livejournal.com/590330.html

443 "Is Your Sex Life Normal?," *The Tyra Banks Show*, The CW, New York City, Sep. 16, 2009.

444 Dragoneer, "Chewfox," Dragoneer's Journal, Sep. 17, 2009. http://www.furaffinity.net/journal/945722/

445 "Meet the Furries," *OMG! With Peaches Geldof*, ITV2, Mar. 09, 2011.

446 P. Geldof, "Peaches Geldof Says TV Guest Dom Joly Is 'Embittered,'" *BBC Newsbeat*, Mar. 03, 2011. http://www.bbc.co.uk/newsbeat/article/12627743/peaches-geldof-says-tv-guest-dom-joly-is-embittered

447 "Harry Hill's TV Burp," *Harry Hill's TV Burp*, ITV, BBC Television Centre, Mar. 26, 2011.

448 "Russell Howard's Good News," *Russell Howard's Good News*, BBC Three, Riverside Studios, Dec. 13, 2012.

449 "Russell Howard's Good News," *Russell Howard's Good News*, BBC Three, Riverside Studios, May 16, 2013.

450 "Furries on Russell Howard's Good News," ukFur Boards, May 16, 2013. https://forum.ukfur.org/topic/42887-furries-on-russell-howards-good-news/

451 "Eddie Redmayne Had His Sexual Awakening During *The Lion King*," *The Graham Norton Show*, BBC, Dec. 31, 2014. Accessed: Jan. 09, 2022. [Online]. Available: https://www.youtube.com/watch?v=btUx3gb0-FE

452 "Why Do People Dress as Furries?," *World of Weird*, Channel 4, Lion Television Scotland, Nov. 02, 2016.

453 O. McAteer, "Army Soldier Lives Double Life as Furry Character Called Mark the Husky," *Metro*, Sep. 01, 2017. https://metro.co.uk/2017/09/01/army-soldier-lives-double-life-as-furry-character-called-mark-the-husky-6896204/

454 "A Pack of Furries Introduces Ea-

monn to the Fandom | This Morning," *This Morning*, ITV, Jul. 31, 2017. Accessed: Nov. 06, 2020. [Online]. Available: https://www.youtube.com/watch?v=0ftFhXBqGE0

455 The Crystal Maze, "These Guys Are Already Our Favourites #CrystalMaze," Twitter, Sep. 15, 2017. https://twitter.com/TheCrystalMaze/status/908767684707471360 (accessed Jan. 15, 2023).

456 "This Week's Crystal Maze Episode Will Go Down as One of the Classics: 'This Is the Best TV in Years,'" *Digital Spy*, Sep. 15, 2017. http://www.digitalspy.com/tv/reality-tv/a838222/the-crystal-maze-channel-4-cosplay-team/ (accessed Jan. 15, 2023).

457 D. Sillito, "Teen 'Furries' on What Their Costumes Mean to Them," *BBC News*, Leeds & West Yorkshire, 2018. Accessed: Nov. 12, 2020. [Online]. Available: https://www.bbc.com/news/av/uk-england-leeds-47585651

458 Bristol. FURRIES, (Oct. 02, 2018). Accessed: Nov. 12, 2020. [Online Video]. Available: https://www.facebook.com/tch/?v=481217832381522

459 jelly-lemon, "Hello!," ukFur Boards, Apr. 24, 2018. https://forum.ukfur.org/topic/51566-hello/ (accessed Nov. 07, 2020).

460 "Meet the Furries," *Stories*, BBC Radio 1, Jul. 20, 2018. [Online]. Available: https://vimeo.com/286510692

461 ConFuzzled, "Media Access," ConFuzzled 2018, 2018. https://2018.confuzzled.org.uk/about-us/media-access/

462 ConFuzzled, "ConFuzzled's Official Response to Meet the Furries," @cfconvention, Jul. 20, 2018. https://twitter.com/cfconvention/ta/1020283841012019200

463 'COVID-19 Pandemic Causes Furry Convention Closures and Delays Worldwide," *Flayrah*, Mar. 14, 2020. https://www.flayrah.com/7977/covid-19-pandemic-causes-furry-convention-closures-and-delays-worldwide (accessed Dec. 22, 2020).

464 RizzoRat, Crimson, and Russet, "ConFuzzled 2020?» Update: Coronavirus (COVID-19)," Mar. 15,

2020. https://2020.confuzzled.org.uk/2020/03/15/update-coronavirus-covid-19/ (accessed Dec. 22, 2020).

465 RizzoRat, Crimson, and Russet, "ConFuzzled 2020?» Update 24/03/2020: Coronavirus (COVID-19)," Mar. 24, 2020. https://2020.confuzzled.org.uk/2020/03/24/update-24-03-2020-coronavirus-covid-19/ (accessed Dec. 22, 2020).

466 Heartlilly, "Covid19," JFTW 2020, Oct. 30, 2020. https://jftw.org/covid19/ (accessed Dec. 22, 2020).

467 Furcation, "Furcation 2020 Cancellation," @Furcationevent, Jun. 25, 2020. https://twitter.com/Furcationevent/as/1276213820281651201 (accessed Dec. 22, 2020).

468 Kivuli Rider, "Wild North Postponed," Wild North Announcements, Jul. 05, 2020. https://t.me/WildNorthUD/61 (accessed Dec. 22, 2020).

469 Evil Squirrel, "Furmeets Should Not Be During a Pandemic," @Evilsquirrel123, Oct. 05, 2020. https://twitter.com/Evilsquirrel123/as/1312999664443166720 (accessed Dec. 22, 2020).

470 Weremoco, "Andover Furmeet Statement," @Weremoco, Nov. 16, 2020. https://twitter.com/Weremoco/us/1328345082982969344 (accessed Dec. 22, 2020).

471 ConFuzzled, "ConFuzzled 2020 Charity Update," @cfconvention, Sep. 02, 2020. https://twitter.com/cfconvention/us/1301130407832965121

(accessed Dec. 22, 2020).

472 Kivuli Rider, "Virtual Wild North," Wild North Announcements, Jul. 28, 2020. https://t.me/WildNorthUD/64 (accessed Dec. 22, 2020).

473 "Dog & Cat Shelter Letter to Wild North," Wild North Announcements, Oct. 17, 2020. https://t.me/WildNorthUD/89 (accessed Dec. 22, 2020).

474 Furcation, "Virtual Furcation Caravans," @Furcationevent, Oct. 10, 2020. https://twitter.com/Furcationevent/as/1314999101658890242 (accessed Dec. 22, 2020).

475 Furcation, "Virtual Furcation Amount," @Furcationevent, Nov. 10, 2020. https://twitter.com/Furcationevent/as/1326117400597557248 (accessed Dec. 22, 2020).

476 Wild North Team, "Post Meet Newsletter," Oct. 2022. https://t.me/WildNorthUD/165 (accessed Oct. 05, 2022).

477 Furcation [@Furcationevent], "Furcation 2022 Registration News," Twitter, Sep. 12, 2022. https://twitter.com/Furcationevent/us/1569405289069158400 (accessed Oct. 05, 2022).

478 Furcation 2022—Transparency and Honesty, (Sep. 12, 2022). Accessed: Oct. 05, 2022. [Online Video]. Available: https://www.youtube.com/watch?v=2MHivR6WoGk

479 Ash, "Covid19," JFTW 2020, 2021. https://jftw.org/covid19/ (accessed Oct. 05, 2022).

BIBLIOGRAPHY

Online

Ash Coyote. *The Fandom* (video), Ashes 2 Ashs Productions, https://www.youtube.com/watch?v=iv0QaTW3kEY.

Conway, Dr. Samuel (Uncle Kage). *The Olden Days: The History of Furry Fandom from One Who Lived Them* (video), https://www.youtube.com/watch?v=sS4DQcCNk8Q.

Culturally F'd. *A Brief Timeline of the Furry* (video), https://www.youtube.com/watch?v=AyGdA3rU5Yk.

Knudson, Fredrik. *Furries: Down the Rabbit Hole* (video) https://www.youtube.com/watch?v=8aF2GxWi7Ag.

Patten, Fred. *Retrospective: An Illustrated Chronology of Furry Fandom (1966–1996).* http://www.flayrah.com/4117/retrospective-illustrated-chronology-furry-fandom-1966–1996.

Prancing Skiltaire. *25 Years of Furry Conventions* (video), https://www.youtube.com/watch?v=adC7N2pcY2M.

Rhones, Perri. The Furry History Project. https://myrainbowark.com/fhp00.html.

Rivercoon. *History of the Furry Fandom (Confurence 1998)* (video), https://www.youtube.com/watch?v=e5snFU0xpXI.

Books and Periodicals

Howl, Thurston, *Furries Among Us: Essays on Furries*, Lansing, MI: Thurston Howl, 2015.

Minter, Rick. *Mascots: Football's Furry Friends.* Reading, UK: | Tempus Publishing, 2004.

Patten, Fred, *Furry Fandom Conventions: 1989–2015*, Jefferson, NC: McFarland & Co., 2016.

Riggs, Adam, *Critter Costuming*, Sunnyvale, CA: Ibexa Press, 2004.

Strike, Joe, *Furry Nation: The True Story of America's Most Misunderstood Subculture*, Jersey City, NJ: Cleis Press, 2017.

Wuttke, Volker, and Joachim Seifert. "Gucky and the Fluffbutts." *Andromeda SF Magazin*, Issue 157, 2019, pp. 73–89.

INDEX

Note: Fursona names are alphabetized by first name in cases where the furry has more than one name.

www.ingramcontent.com/pod-product-compliance
Lightning Source LLC
Chambersburg PA
CBHW060905120626
46553CB00001B/217